ACKNOWLEDGEMENTS

P9-DMW-642

Author

Susan Earle-Carlin earned a Ph.D. in Reading, Language, and Cognition from Hofstra University. She has taught at SUNY Old Westbury and Rutgers University and now teaches in the Program in Academic English/ESL at the University of California, Irvine. Her interests include addressing the needs of generation 1.5 students at the university and improving the communication skills of international teaching assistants. *Q* is her third ESL textbook.

Series Consultants

Marguerite Ann Snow holds a Ph.D. in Applied Linguistics from UCLA. She is a Professor in the Charter College of Education at California State University, Los Angeles where she teaches in the TESOL M.A. program. She has published in *TESOL Quarterly*, *Applied Linguistics*, and *The Modern Language Journal*. She has been a Fulbright scholar in Hong Kong and Cyprus. In 2006, she received the President's Distinguished Professor award at Cal State LA. In addition to working closely with ESL and mainstream public school teachers in the U.S., she has trained EFL teachers in Algeria, Argentina, Brazil, Egypt, Japan, Morocco, Pakistan, Spain, and Turkey. Her main interests are integrated content and language instruction, English for Academic Purposes, and standards for English teaching and learning.

Lawrence J. Zwier holds an M.A. in TESL from the University of Minnesota. He is currently the Associate Director for Curriculum Development at the English Language Center at Michigan State University in East Lansing. He has taught ESL/EFL in the U.S., Saudi Arabia, Malaysia, Japan, and Singapore. He is a frequent TESOL conference presenter and has published many ESL/EFL books in the areas of test-preparation, vocabulary, and reading, including *Inside Reading 2* for Oxford University Press.

Vocabulary Consultant

Cheryl Boyd Zimmerman is Associate Professor of TESOL at California State University, Fullerton. She specializes in second language vocabulary acquisition, an area in which she is widely published. She teaches graduate courses on second language acquisition, culture, vocabulary, and the fundamentals of TESOL and is a frequent invited speaker on topics related to vocabulary teaching and learning. She is the author of *Word Knowledge: A Vocabulary Teacher's Handbook* and Series Director of *Inside Reading*, both published by Oxford University Press.

REVIEWERS

We would like to acknowledge the advice of teachers from all over the world who participated in online reviews, focus groups, and editorial reviews. We relied heavily on teacher input throughout the extensive development process of the Q series, and many of the features in the series came directly from feedback we gathered from teachers in the classroom. We are grateful to all who helped.

UNITED STATES Marcarena Aguilar, North Harris College, TX; **Deborah Anholt**, Lewis and Clark College, OR; **Robert Anzelde**, Oakton Community College, IL; **Arlys Arnold**, University of Minnesota, MN; **Marcia Arthur**, Renton Technical College, WA; **Anne Bachmann**, Clackamas Community College, OR; **Ron Balsamo**, Santa Rosa Junior College, CA; **Lori Barkley**, Portland State University, OR; **Eileen Barlow**, SUNY Albany, NY; **Sue Bartch**, Cuyahoga Community College, OH; **Lora Bates**, Oakton High School, VA; **Nancy Baum**, University of Texas at Arlington, TX; **Linda Berendsen**, Oakton Community College, IL; **Jennifer Binckes Lee**, Howard Community College, MD; **Grace Bishop**, Houston Community College, TX; **Jean W. Bodman**, Union County College, NJ; **Virginia Bouchard**, George Mason University, VA; **Kimberley Briesch Sumner**, University of Southern California, CA; **Gabriela Cambiasso**, Harold Washington College, IL; **Jackie Campbell**, Capistrano Unified School District, CA; **Adele C. Camus**, George Mason University, VA; **Laura Chason**, Savannah College, GA; **Kerry Linder Catana**, Language Studies International, NY; **An Cheng**, Oklahoma State University, OK; **Carole Collins**, North Hampton Community College, PA; **Betty R. Compton**, Intercultural Communications College, HI; **Pamela Couch**, Boston University, MA; **Fernanda Crowe**, Intrax International Institute, CA; **Margo Czinski**, Washtenaw Community College, MI; **David Dahnke**, Lone Star College, TX; **Gillian M. Dale**, CA; **L. Dalgish**, Concordia College, MN; **Christopher Davis**, John Jay College, NY; **Sonia Delgadillo**, Sierra College, CA; **Marta O. Dmytrenko-Ahrabian**, Wayne State University, MI; **Javier Dominguez**, Central High School, SC; **Jo Ellen Downey-Greer**, Lansing Community College, MI; **Jennifer Duclos**, Boston University, MA; **Yvonne Duncan**, City College of San Francisco, CA; **Jennie Farnell**, University of Connecticut, CT; **Susan Fedors**, Howard Community College, MD; **Matthew Florence**, Intrax International Institute, CA; **Kathleen Flynn**, Glendale College, CA; **Eve Fonseca**, St. Louis Community College, MO; **Elizabeth Foss**, Washtenaw Community College, MI; **Duff C. Galda**, Pima Community College, AZ; **Christiane Galvani**, Houston Community College, TX; **Gretchen Gerber**, Howard Community College, MD; **Ray Gonzalez**, Montgomery College, MD; **Alyona Gorokhova**, Grossmont College, CA; **John Graney**, Santa Fe College, FL; **Kathleen Green**, Central High School, AZ; **Webb Hamilton**, De Anza College, San Jose City College, CA; **Janet Harclerode**, Santa Monica Community College, CA; **Sandra Hartmann**, Language and Culture Center, TX; **Kathy Haven**, Mission College, CA; **Adam Henricksen**, University of Maryland, MD; **Peter Hoffman**, LaGuardia Community College, NY; **Linda Holden**, College of Lake County, IL; **Jana Holt**, Lake Washington Technical College, WA; **Gail Ibele**, University of Wisconsin, WI; **Mandy Kama**, Georgetown University, Washington, DC; **Stephanie Kasuboski**, Cuyahoga Community College, OH; **Chigusa Katoku**, Mission College, CA; **Sandra Kawamura**, Sacramento City College, CA; **Gail Kellersberger**, University of Houston–Downtown, TX; **Jane Kelly**, Durham Technical Community College, NC; **Julie Park Kim**, George Mason University, VA; **Lisa Kovacs-Morgan** University of California, San Diego, CA; **Claudia Kupiec**, DePaul University, IL; **Renee La Rue**, Lone Star College-Montgomery, TX; **Janet Langon**, Glendale College, CA; **Lawrence Lawson**, Palomar College, CA; **Rachele Lawton**, The Community College of Baltimore County, MD; **Alice Lee**, Richland College, TX; **Cherie Lenz-Hackett**, University of Washington, WA; **Joy Leventhal**, Cuyahoga Community College, OH; **Candace Lynch-Thompson**, North Orange County Community College District, CA; **Thi Thi Ma**, City College of San Francisco, CA; **Denise Maduli-Williams**, City College of San Francisco, CA; **Eileen Mahoney**, Camelback High School, AZ; **Brigitte Maronde**, Harold Washington College, IL; **Keith Maurice**, University of Texas at Arlington, TX; **Nancy Mayer**, University of Missouri-St. Louis, MO; **Karen Merritt**, Glendale Union High School District, AZ; **Holly Milkowart**, Johnson County Community College, KS; **Eric Moyer**, Intrax International Institute, CA; **Gino Muzzatti**, Santa Rosa Junior College, CA; **William Nedrow**, Triton College, IL; **Eric Nelson**, University of Minnesota, MN; **Rhony Ory**, Ygnacio Valley High School, CA; **Paul Parent**, Montgomery College, MD; **Oscar Pedroso**, Miami Dade College, FL; **Robin Persiani**, Sierra College, CA; **Patricia Prenz-Belkin**, Hostos Community College, NY; **Jim Ranalli**, Iowa State University, IA; **Toni R. Randall**, Santa Monica College, CA; **Vidya Rangachari**, Mission College, CA; **Elizabeth Rasmussen**, Northern Virginia Community College, VA; **Lara Ravitch**, Truman College, IL; **Deborah Repasz**, San Jacinto College, TX; **Andrey Reznikov**, Black Hills State University, SD; **Alison Rice**, Hunter College, NY; **Jennifer Robles**, Ventura Unified School District, CA; **Priscilla Rocha**, Clark County School District, NV; **Dzidra Rodins**, DePaul University IL; **Maria Rodriguez**, Central High School, AZ; **Maria Ruiz**, Victor Valley College, CA; **Kimberly Russell,** Clark College, WA; **Irene Sakk**, Northwestern University, IL; **Shaeley Santiago**, Ames High School, IA; **Peg Sarosy**, San Francisco State University, CA; **Alice Savage**, North Harris College, TX; **Donna Schaeffer**, University of Washington, WA; **Carol Schinger**, Northern Virginia Community College, VA; **Robert Scott**, Kansas State University, KS; **Suell Scott**, Sheridan Technical Center, FL; **Shira Seaman**, Global English Academy, NY; **Richard Seltzer**, Glendale Community College, CA; **Kathy Sherak**, San Francisco State University, CA; **German Silva**, Miami Dade College, FL; **Andrea Spector**, Santa Monica Community College, CA; **Karen Stanely**, Central Piedmont Community College, NC; **Ayse Stromsdorfer**, Soldan I.S.H.S., MO; **Yilin Sun**, South Seattle Community College, WA; **Thomas Swietlik**, Intrax International Institute, IL; **Judith Tanka**, UCLA Extension–American Language Center, CA; **Priscilla Taylor**, University of Southern California, CA; **Ilene Teixeira,** Fairfax County Public Schools, VA; **Shirl H. Terrell**, Collin College, TX; **Marya Teutsch-Dwyer**, St. Cloud State University, MN; **Stephen Thergesen**, ELS Language Centers, CO; **Christine Tierney**, Houston Community College, TX; **Arlene Turini**, North Moore High School, NC; **Suzanne Van Der Valk**, Iowa State University, IA; **Nathan D. Vasarhely**, Ygnacio Valley High School, CA; **Naomi S. Verratti**, Howard Community College, MD; **Hollyahna Vettori**, Santa Rosa Junior College, CA; **Julie Vorholt**, Lewis & Clark College, OR; **Laura Walsh**, City College of San Francisco, CA; **Andrew J. Watson**, The English Bakery; **Donald Weasenforth**, Collin College, TX; **Juliane Widner**, Sheepshead Bay High School, NY; **Lynne Wilkins**, Mills College, CA; **Dolores "Lorrie" Winter**, California State University at Fullerton, CA; **Jody Yamamoto**, Kapi'olani Community College, HI; **Ellen L. Yaniv**, Boston University, MA; **Norman Yoshida**, Lewis & Clark College, OR; **Joanna Zadra**, American River College, CA; **Florence Zysman**, Santiago Canyon College, CA;

ASIA Rabiatu Abubakar, Eton Language Centre, Malaysia; **Wiwik Andreani**, Bina Nusantara University, Indonesia; **Mike Baker**, Kosei Junior High School, Japan; **Leonard Barrow**, Kanto Junior College, Japan; **Herman Bartelen**, Japan; **Siren Betty**, Fooyin University, Kaohsiung; **Thomas E. Bieri**, Nagoya College, Japan; **Natalie Brezden**, Global English House, Japan; **MK Brooks**, Mukogawa Women's University, Japan; **Truong Ngoc Buu**, The Youth Language School, Vietnam; **Charles Cabell**, Toyo University, Japan; **Fred Carruth**, Matsumoto University, Japan; **Frances Causer**, Seijo University, Japan; **Deborah Chang**, Wenzao Ursuline College of Languages, Kaohsiung; **David Chatham**, Ritsumeikan University, Japan; **Andrew Chih Hong Chen**, National Sun Yat-sen University, Kaohsiung; **Christina Chen**, Yu-Tsai Bilingual Elementary School, Taipei; **Jason Jeffree Cole**, Coto College, Japan; **Le Minh Cong**, Vungtau Tourism Vocational College, Vietnam; **Todd Cooper**, Toyama National College of Technology, Japan; **Marie Cosgrove**, Daito Bunka University, Japan; **Tony Cripps**, Ritsumeikan University, Japan; **Daniel Cussen**, Takushoku University, Japan; **Le Dan**, Ho Chi Minh City Electric Power College, Vietnam; **Simon Daykin**, Banghwa-dong Community Centre, South Korea; **Aimee Denham**, ILA, Vietnam; **Bryan Dickson**, David's English Center, Taipei; **Nathan Ducker**, Japan University, Japan; **Ian Duncan**, Simul International Corporate Training, Japan; **Nguyen Thi Kieu Dung**, Thang Long University, Vietnam; **Nguyen Thi Thuy Duong**, Vietnamese American Vocational Training College, Vietnam; **Wong Tuck Ee**, Raja Tun Azlan Science Secondary School, Malaysia; **Emilia Effendy**, International Islamic University Malaysia, Malaysia; **Robert Eva**, Kaisei Girls High School, Japan; **Jim George**, Luna International Language School, Japan; **Jurgen Germeys**, Silk Road Language Center, South Korea; **Wong Ai Gnoh**, SMJK Chung Hwa Confucian, Malaysia; **Peter Gooselink**, Hokkai High School,

WELCOME TO **Q**:Skills for Success

Q: Skills for Success is a six-level series with two strands,
Reading and Writing and *Listening and Speaking*.

READING AND WRITING

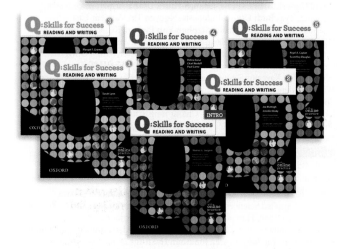

LISTENING AND SPEAKING

WITH Q ONLINE PRACTICE web+

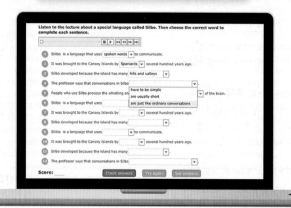

STUDENT AND TEACHER INFORMED

Q: Skills for Success is the result of an extensive development process involving thousands
of teachers and hundreds of students around the world. Their views and opinions helped
shape the content of the series. *Q* is grounded in teaching theory as well as real-world
classroom practice, making it the most learner-centered series available.

CONTENTS

Q connects critical thinking, language skills, and learning outcomes.

LANGUAGE SKILLS

Explicit skills instruction enables students to meet their academic and professional goals.

LEARNING OUTCOMES

Clearly identified **learning outcomes** focus students on the goal of their instruction.

UNIT **8**

Change

LISTENING	recognizing attitudes
VOCABULARY	phrasal verbs
GRAMMAR	gerunds and infinitives
PRONUNCIATION	consonant variations
SPEAKING	paraphrasing

LEARNING OUTCOME

Interview a classmate and report on that person's attitudes concerning change.

Unit QUESTION

How do people react to change?

PREVIEW THE UNIT

Ⓐ **Discuss these questions with your classmates.**

How many times has your family moved? Have you or your family moved for work, education, or other reasons?

List a few major changes in your life. Are you a person who welcomes new opportunities or one who avoids change?

Look at the photo. How is this an example of someone reacting to change?

Ⓑ **Discuss the Unit Question above with your classmates.**

🔊 **Listen to** *The Q Classroom*, **Track 15 on CD 3, to hear other answers.**

172 UNIT 8

173

CRITICAL THINKING

Thought-provoking **unit questions** engage students with the topic and provide a **critical thinking framework** for the unit.

 Having the learning outcome is important because it gives students and teachers a clear idea of what the point of each task/activity in the unit is.
Lawrence Lawson, Palomar College, California

PREVIEW LISTENING 2

LANGUAGE SKILLS

Two listening texts provide input on the unit question and give **exposure to academic content.**

High-Tech Nomads

You are going to hear Rudy Maxa, host of the radio show *The Savvy Traveler*, interview reporter Joel Garreau about his research on a special group of businesspeople called *high-tech nomads*.

Check (✓) the descriptions you think would apply to a high-tech nomad.

- ☐ a self-employed businessperson
- ☐ a cyberspace traveler, rather than a plane traveler
- ☐ a worker who changes offices frequently
- ☐ a computer "geek"
- ☐ an employee who can't keep one job
- ☐ a worker who has an email address but no business address
- ☐ a businessperson who works from home

CRITICAL THINKING

Students **discuss** their opinions of each listening text and **analyze** how it changes their perspective on the unit question.

WHAT DO YOU THINK?

A. Discuss the questions in a group.

1. What do the speakers seem to think of the high-tech nomads? Do you agree with them? Why or why not?

2. Do you have the type of personality required to be a high-tech nomad? Do you have any interest in that sort of lifestyle? Why or why not?

3. In what ways do you try to be "wired" to the outside world? How much has your use of high-tech devices changed your daily life?

B. Think about both Listening 1 and Listening 2 as you discuss the question.

The reports described changes in the world around us (e.g., a lack of resources; an increase in technology). What other changes in today's world can you think of that could change the way some groups of people live, work, or study?

> One of the best features is your focus on developing materials of a high "interest level."
> *Troy Hammond, Tokyo Gakugei University, International Secondary School, Japan*

Explicit skills instruction prepares students for academic success.

LANGUAGE SKILLS

Explicit instruction and practice in listening, speaking, grammar, pronunciation, and vocabulary skills **help students achieve language proficiency.**

LEARNING OUTCOMES

Practice activities allow students to **master the skills** before they are evaluated at the end of the unit.

Listening Skill | **Listening for pros and cons** web⁺

Speakers can compare and contrast options by listing the **pros and cons**, or benefits and drawbacks. They may signal their intentions with phrases such as these.

There are some advantages and disadvantages . . .
Let's compare . . .
We'll examine both sides of . . .

When you can predict that a speech, lecture, or program will compare pros and cons, you can divide your paper into a T-chart and note information in the appropriate column.

Small restaurants

Pros	Cons
nice atmosphere	more expensive
owner greets you by name	less variety

Speakers often use transitions to show that they are going to present contrasting information. It is important to note the points being made about each of the sides discussed. Speakers may follow one of these patterns.

- Pros of A. Transition, cons of A.
- Pros of A. Transition, cons of B.
- Cons of A. Transition, pros of B.

Listen for organizational cues such as these:

on (the) one hand . . . on the other hand   however
on the other side   yet
in contrast   though
but

Listen to the organizational cues in these examples.

CD 4
Track 16

A large law firm may have many lawyers that specialize in different areas. **However,** smaller firms often hire lawyers who have better training.

On the one hand, Craigslist probably has happier employees because it is small. **On the other hand,** it may lose employees who prefer to work for a bigger company.

| Listening and Speaking

Speaking Skill | **Discussing preferences and alternatives** web⁺

In a meeting or a planning session, discussion often involves expressing preferences and offering alternatives. Additionally, you might need to investigate people's past preferences to help make choices about future actions.

Here are some common expressions for talking about preferences and alternatives.

To talk about past preferences	To talk about current preferences
prefer + noun or noun phrase **Students preferred the expedition** to China.	*preference + is +* infinitive **My preference is to attend** a science fair.
choose + infinitive **Students chose to visit** indigenous people.	*would rather (not)* + verb **I'd rather do** something that helps society.
first/second choice + be **My first choice was** to visit a nature reserve.	*If it were up to me, . . .* **If it were up to me,** we'd do an ecological study.
had hoped + infinitive **I had hoped to spend** the summer volunteering in Africa.	*I like . . . more than . . .* **I like** studying in my dorm **more than** in the lab.
	I'd like + verb **I'd like to explore** the idea of working abroad.

A. With a partner, take turns asking and answering these questions about the Listening texts. Use expressions for preferences and choices in your answers. Pay attention to your intonation in any choice questions.

1. Does Linda Stuart prefer the volunteering or the tourist side of voluntourism?

   A: *Does Linda Stuart prefer the volunteering or the tourist side of voluntourism?*
   B: *Stuart would rather be a volunteer than a tourist.*

2. Does Stuart's organization choose to take large or small groups of travelers?

3. If it were up to the speaker from Cambridge, would the science fair there have many more participants?

4. What does the professor at UC Santa Barbara hope to show the young students, especially girls?

70   UNIT 3 | Where can work, education, and fun overlap?

 The tasks are simple, accessible, user-friendly, and very useful.
Jessica March, American University of Sharjah, U.A.E.

Q Online Practice provides all new content for additional practice in an easy-to-use online workbook. Every student book includes a *Q Online Practice access code card*. Use the access code to register for your *Q Online Practice* account at www.Qonlinepractice.com.

Vocabulary Skill   Phrasal verbs

Phrasal verbs, made up of a verb followed by a **particle**, are a common type of collocation. The particle (usually a preposition or an adverb) following the verb changes the meaning. For example, *take on* does not have the same meaning as *take* or *take over*. Phrasal verbs are listed separately in learners' dictionaries and are marked with a symbol.

> ˌtake sth/sb↔ˈon **1** to decide to do something; to
> agree to be responsible for something or someone: *I can't*
> *take on any extra work.* ◆ *We're not taking on any new clients at*
> *present.* **2** (of a bus, plane, or ship) to allow someone or
> something to enter: *The bus stopped to take on more*
> *passengers.* ◆ *The ship took on more fuel at Freetown.*

Some phrasal verbs take an object. A phrasal verb is **separable** if the object can be placed between the verb and the particle (*take* something *on*) as well as after it (*take on* something).

All dictionary entries are taken from the *Oxford Advanced American Dictionary for learners of English*.

A **research-based vocabulary program** focuses students on the words they need to know academically and professionally, using skill strategies based on the same research as the Oxford dictionaries.

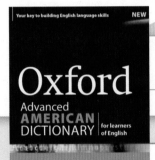

All dictionary entries are taken from the *Oxford Advanced American Dictionary for learners of English*.

The *Oxford Advanced American Dictionary for learners of English* was developed with English learners in mind, and provides extra learning tools for pronunciation, verb types, basic grammar structures, and more.

The Oxford 3000™
The Oxford 3000 encompasses **the 3000 most important words to learn in English.** It is based on a comprehensive analysis of the Oxford English Corpus, a two-billion word collection of English text, and on extensive research with both language and pedagogical experts.

The Academic Word List AWL
The Academic Word List was created by Averil Coxhead and contains **570 words that are commonly used in academic English,** such as in textbooks or articles across a wide range of academic subject areas. These words are a great place to start if you are studying English for academic purposes.

Clear learning outcomes focus students on the goals of instruction.

Unit Assignment | **Narrate a personal experience**

 In this section, you will narrate an experience involving language loss or an inability to communicate. As you prepare your narrative, think about the Unit Question, "How does language affect who we are?" and refer to the Self-Assessment checklist on page 50.

For alternative unit assignments, see the *Q: Skills for Success Teacher's Handbook.*

CONSIDER THE IDEAS

A. Maxine Hong Kingston, a Chinese-American writer, was born in the United States, but her parents spoke only Chinese at home. In her autobiographical novel, *The Woman Warrior*, she describes her discomfort speaking English after years of silence in American school and narrates a painful experience in Chinese school. Read this excerpt.

Check (✓) the skills you learned. If you need more work on a skill, refer to the page(s) in parentheses.

LISTENING	○	I can listen for pros and cons. (p. 231)
VOCABULARY	○	I can use connotations. (p. 237)
GRAMMAR	○	I can use parallel structure. (p. 239)
PRONUNCIATION	○	I can speak with word stress patterns. (p. 241)
SPEAKING	○	I can develop interview skills. (p. 243)
LEARNING OUTCOME	○	I can role-play interviews for a job or a school and be prepared to answer a question that is creative or unusual.

 Students can check their learning . . . and they can focus on the essential points when they study.

Suh Yoomi, Seoul, South Korea

For the student

- **Easy-to-use:** a simple interface allows students to focus on enhancing their speaking and listening skills, not learning a new software program
- **Flexible:** for use anywhere there's an Internet connection
- **Access code card:** a *Q Online Practice* access code is included with this book—use the access code to register for *Q Online Practice* at www.Qonlinepractice.com

For the teacher

- **Simple yet powerful:** automatically grades student exercises and tracks progress
- **Straightforward:** online management system to review, print, or export reports
- **Flexible:** for use in the classroom or easily assigned as homework
- **Access code card:** contact your sales rep for your *Q Online Practice* teacher's access code

Teacher Resources

Q Teacher's Handbook gives strategic support through:

- specific teaching notes for each activity
- ideas for ensuring student participation
- multilevel strategies and expansion activities
- the answer key
- special sections on 21st century skills and critical thinking
- a **Testing Program CD-ROM** with a customizable test for each unit

For additional resources visit the *Q: Skills for Success* companion website at www.oup.com/elt/teacher/Qskillsforsuccess

Q Class Audio includes:

- listening texts
- pronunciation presentations and exercises
- *The Q Classroom*

It's an interesting, engaging series which provides plenty of materials that are easy to use in class, as well as instructionally promising.

Donald Weasenforth, Collin College, Texas

UNIT	LISTENING	SPEAKING	VOCABULARY
1 New Media **How do people get the news today?** **LISTENING 1: Citizen Journalism** An Online Interview (Journalism) **LISTENING 2: Pod-Ready: Podcasting for the Developing World** A Podcast (Cultural Anthropology)	• Listen for the relationships between main ideas and details • Listen for specific vowel sounds • Predict content • Listen for main ideas • Listen for details	• Use note cards • Converse about advantages and disadvantages • Convey numerical information • Conduct a survey • Take notes to prepare for a presentation or group discussion	• Using the dictionary • Assess your prior knowledge of vocabulary
2 Language **How does language affect who we are?** **LISTENING 1: My Stroke of Insight: A Brain Scientist's Personal Journey** A Radio Interview (Neuroscience) **LISTENING 2: The Story of My Life** An Autobiography (Cognitive Science)	• Understand inferences • Listen for events in a chronology • Predict content • Listen for main ideas • Listen for details	• Use figurative language • Practice using word stress to emphasize ideas • Imply ideas instead of stating them directly • Narrate a story • Take notes to prepare for a presentation or group discussion	• Negative prefixes • Assess your prior knowledge of vocabulary
3 Work and Fun **Where can work, education, and fun overlap?** **LISTENING 1: Voluntourism** An Online Interview (Travel and Tourism) **LISTENING 2: Science Fairs and Nature Reserves** Academic Reports (Environmental Science)	• Listen for examples • Relate examples to main ideas • Formulate pre-listening questions about a topic • Predict content • Listen for main ideas • Listen for details	• Discuss preferences and alternatives • Use intonation to express choices and alternatives • Plan a persuasive presentation • Convince listeners to opt for one choice among many • Take notes to prepare for a presentation or group discussion	• Compound words • Assess your prior knowledge of vocabulary

GRAMMAR	PRONUNCIATION	CRITICAL THINKING	UNIT OUTCOME
• Participial adjectives	• Vowel variation with *a* and *o*	• Identify people/items that fit a definition • Interpret survey data • Assess your prior knowledge of content • Relate personal experiences to listening topics • Integrate information from multiple sources	• Develop and administer a survey focused on media preferences, analyze the results, and report your findings.
• Passive voice	• Emphatic word stress	• Contrast good and bad aspects of a situation • Experiment with brain stimuli • Assess your prior knowledge of content • Relate personal experiences to listening topics • Integrate information from multiple sources	• Develop a narrative incorporating figurative language that chronologically details an incident of language loss or an inability to communicate.
• Comparative structures	• Intonation with choices	• Identify personal preferences • Categorize activities • Assess your prior knowledge of content • Relate personal experiences to listening topics • Integrate information from multiple sources	• Plan and present a school vacation in a way that will persuade your classmates to select it for their spring break alternative trip.

UNIT	LISTENING	SPEAKING	VOCABULARY
4 **Deception** ② **How can the eyes deceive the mind?** **LISTENING 1:** Wild Survivors A Television Documentary (Zoology) **LISTENING 2:** Magic and the Mind A Radio Interview (Psychology)	• Recognize appositives that explain • Listen to identify word roots and suffixes • Predict content • Listen for main ideas • Listen for details	• Ask for and give clarification of information • Narrate incidents in your life • Explain reasons for opinions • Use relative clauses in a presentation • Take notes to prepare for a presentation or group discussion	• Word forms and suffixes • Assess your prior knowledge of vocabulary
5 **Global Cooperation** ② **What does it mean to be a global citizen?** **LISTENING 1:** The Campaign to Humanize the Coffee Trade A Radio Report (Business) **LISTENING 2:** The UN Global Compact A Report (Economics)	• Organize notes with a T-chart • Listen for problems and solutions • Listen for numbers • Predict content • Listen for main ideas • Listen for details	• Cite sources • Use numbers in presentations • Practice stress and intonation patterns in quoting directly from sources • Take notes to prepare for a presentation or group discussion	• Collocations • Assess your prior knowledge of vocabulary
6 **Personal Space** ② **How do you make a space your own?** **LISTENING 1:** Environmental Psychology A University Lecture (Psychology) **LISTENING 2:** What Your Stuff Says About You A Radio Interview (Social Psychology)	• Recognize organizational cues • Understand the overall structure of a passage • Predict content • Listen for main ideas • Listen for details	• Give advice • Practice conversational skills in an advice-giving situation • Take notes to prepare for a presentation or group discussion	• Words with multiple meanings • Assess your prior knowledge of vocabulary
7 **Alternative Thinking** ② **Where do new ideas come from?** **LISTENING 1:** Alternative Ideas in Medicine Radio Reports (Public Health) **LISTENING 2:** Boulder Bike-to-School Program Goes International A Radio Interview (Recreation and Fitness)	• Use a table to organize note-taking • Distinguish between facts and opinions • Predict content • Listen for main ideas • Listen for details	• Use formal and informal language • Practice persuading listeners to accept a new idea • Take notes to prepare for a presentation or group discussion	• Idioms and informal expressions • Assess your prior knowledge of vocabulary

GRAMMAR	PRONUNCIATION	CRITICAL THINKING	UNIT OUTCOME
• Relative clauses	• Stress shifts with suffixes	• Infer ideas from pictures • Speculate about a speaker's attitudes • Assess your prior knowledge of content • Relate personal experiences to listening topics • Integrate information from multiple sources	• Deliver a presentation that describes and gives examples of how optical illusions are used and discusses implications of their use.
• Reported speech	• Linking with final consonants	• Draw conclusions from pictures • Associate problems with solutions • Assess your prior knowledge of content • Relate personal experiences to listening topics • Integrate information from multiple sources	• Identify and report on aspects of a global problem.
• Conditionals	• Stress, intonation, and pauses to indicate thought groups	• Evaluate generalizations about groups of people • Draw conclusions from data • Assess your prior knowledge of content • Relate personal experiences to listening topics • Integrate information from multiple sources	• Role-play a talk show focused on identifying and solving conflicts centered on issues of personal space.
• Noun clauses	• Reduced sounds in conditional modals—affirmative and negative	• Identify personal thought processes • Evaluate the factual basis of ideas • Assess your prior knowledge of content • Relate personal experiences to listening topics • Integrate information from multiple sources	• Develop a marketing presentation designed to sell a new invention or idea.

UNIT	LISTENING	SPEAKING	VOCABULARY
8 **Change** **How do people react to change?** **LISTENING 1:** The Reindeer People A Radio Documentary (Cultural Anthropology) **LISTENING 2:** High-Tech Nomads A Radio Interview (Business)	• Recognize attitudes • Recognize meaning conveyed by intonation patterns • Predict content • Listen for main ideas • Listen for details	• Paraphrase • Speak about future plans and conditions • Conduct an interview • Take notes to prepare for a presentation or group discussion	• Phrasal verbs • Assess your prior knowledge of vocabulary
9 **Energy** **Where should the world's energy come from?** **LISTENING 1:** Nuclear Energy: Is It the Solution? A City Council Meeting (Public Policy) **LISTENING 2:** Tapping the Energy of the Tides A News Report (Engineering)	• Listen for cause and effect • Listen to associate ideas with different speakers • Predict content • Listen for main ideas • Listen for details	• Debate opinions • Converse informally about social issues • Take notes to prepare for a presentation or group discussion	• Greek and Latin word roots • Assess your prior knowledge of vocabulary
10 **Size and Scale** **Is bigger always better?** **LISTENING 1:** Small Is the New Big A Book Chapter (Business Management) **LISTENING 2:** Sizing Up Colleges: One Size Does Not Fit All A Podcast (Education)	• Listen for pros and cons • Listen for a speaker's attitudes • Listen for word stress and determine its impact on meaning • Predict content • Listen for main ideas • Listen for details	• Develop interview skills • Develop skills for answering interview questions • Take notes to prepare for a presentation or group discussion	• Connotations • Assess your prior knowledge of vocabulary

GRAMMAR	PRONUNCIATION	CRITICAL THINKING	UNIT OUTCOME
• Gerunds and infinitives	• Consonant variations	• Infer a speaker's attitudes • Hypothesize reasons why someone's attitudes changed • Assess your prior knowledge of content • Relate personal experiences to listening topics • Integrate information from multiple sources	• Interview a classmate and report on that person's attitudes concerning change.
• Adverb clauses	• Sentence rhythm	• Evaluate the feasibility of solutions to a problem • Assess your prior knowledge of content • Relate personal experiences to listening topics • Integrate information from multiple sources	• Participate in a class debate in which you support opinions concerning the future of energy.
• Parallel structure	• Word stress patterns	• Sort items into groups • Assess the usefulness of pieces of information • Assess your prior knowledge of content • Relate personal experiences to listening topics • Integrate information from multiple sources	• Role-play interviews for a job or a school and be prepared to answer a question that is creative or unusual.

UNIT 1

New Media

LISTENING ●	identifying main ideas
VOCABULARY ●	using the dictionary
GRAMMAR ●	participial adjectives
PRONUNCIATION ●	vowel variation with *a* and *o*
SPEAKING ●	using note cards

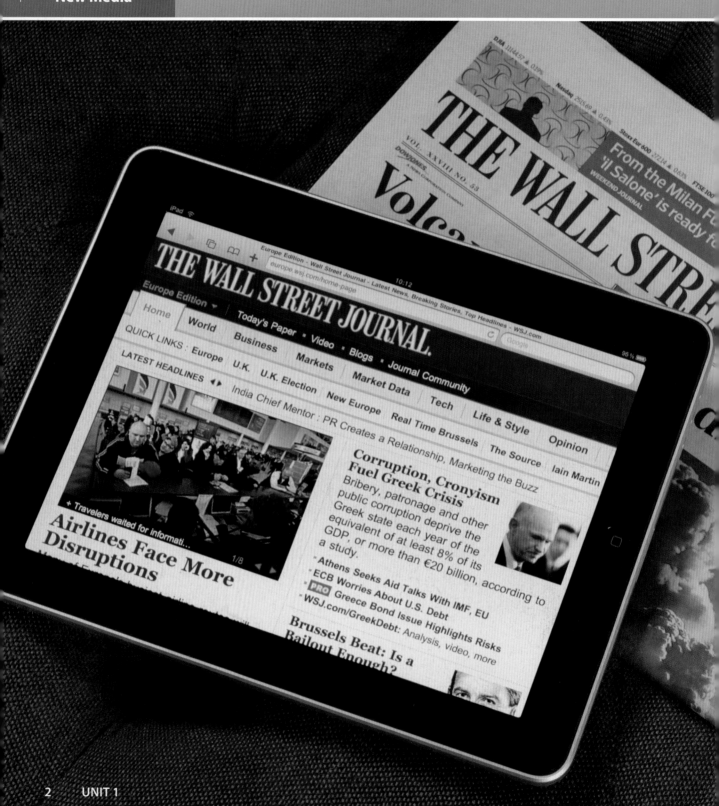

Unit QUESTION

How do people get the news today?

PREVIEW THE UNIT

A Discuss these questions with your classmates.

Which form of media do you turn to when you want to get the latest news? Why?

How do you judge if the information from the news is correct?

Look at the photo. What new media have appeared in the last 50 years? What changes have they caused?

B Discuss the Unit Question above with your classmates.

Listen to *The Q Classroom*, Track 2 on CD 1, to hear other answers.

C Complete the survey about news sources.

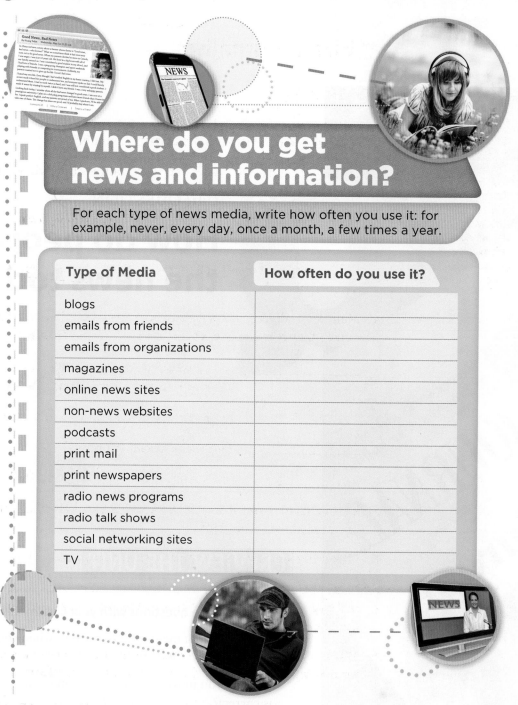

Where do you get news and information?

For each type of news media, write how often you use it: for example, never, every day, once a month, a few times a year.

Type of Media	How often do you use it?
blogs	
emails from friends	
emails from organizations	
magazines	
online news sites	
non-news websites	
podcasts	
print mail	
print newspapers	
radio news programs	
radio talk shows	
social networking sites	
TV	

D Work in groups. Share your responses to the survey. Ask and answer follow-up questions.

A: I check one blog every day. Some others I check once a week, or when they post updates.

B: Which blog do you check every day? What's it about?

LISTENING 1 | Citizen Journalism

VOCABULARY

Here are some words from Listening 1. Read each set of sentences. Then write each bold word next to the correct definition.

Tip for Success

Figuring out the part of speech (such as verb, noun, adjective, and adverb) can help you guess the meanings of unfamiliar words.

1. My parents don't like to check the news online. Their **viewpoint** is that online news is too subjective and is less reliable.

2. The **foundation** for any good news report is a strong desire to uncover and deliver the truth.

3. Ted is doing a lot of **networking** with fellow journalists because he wants to find a new job.

4. Many blogs don't seem to have a **unique** opinion about stories or events; in fact, they're sometimes copied directly from other places!

    a. _foundation_ (n.) an underlying principle, an idea, or a fact that supports something further *defn*

    b. _viewpoint_ (n.) a way of thinking about a subject; an opinion

    c. _unique_ (adj.) very special or unusual

    d. _networking_ (n.) a system of trying to meet and talk to people

5. The events were **unfolding** so quickly that the photographer was unable to capture them all on film.

6. That statement was not **accidental**. He meant to say it.

7. That reporter has a **bias** in favor of one presidential candidate, but she still writes fair and balanced reports that give equal attention to all of the candidates.

8. When reporters are held **accountable** and know there are consequences for making mistakes, they check the facts more carefully.

    e. _accidental_ (adj.) happening by chance; not planned

    f. _unfolding_ (v.) happening at the moment; taking place

    g. _accountable_ (adj.) responsible for decisions or actions

    h. _bias_ (n.) a strong feeling for or against something

9. The person who supplied the information wanted to remain **anonymous**, so we will never know who it was.

10. Don't hide the truth. Be **upfront** and explain exactly what happened.

11. My friends aren't a reliable **source** of information. They don't check facts before they repeat a rumor; they believe everything they hear!

12. My favorite **technique** for staying up to date with the news topics that I'm interested in is to subscribe to several blogs about those issues. They send updates to my email whenever there is fresh news.

i. _anonymous_ _(adj.)_ with a name that is not known or made public

j. _technique_ _(n.)_ a way of doing something, using special skills

k. _upfront_ _(adj.)_ not trying to hide what you think or do; honest

l. _source_ _(n.)_ a person or document that provides information

PREVIEW LISTENING 1

Citizen Journalism

You are going to listen to an interview with Robin Hamman from the website cybersoc.com. The topic is citizen journalism and the way members of the public help collect and report the news.

Check (✓) the activities you have participated in. Then listen to see if you fit Hamman's description of a citizen journalist.

☐ Written articles for a school or local newspaper

☐ Posted blog entries and responded to comments and opinions online

☐ Posted something about the news on a social networking site

☐ Uploaded photos to the Internet of people or events that seem important

☐ Posted a video to a site such as YouTube

LISTEN FOR MAIN IDEAS

CD 1
Track 3

Read the questions posed by the host of the interview. Then listen to the interview and circle the answer that best represents Hamman's response.

1. **Host:** "And I, uh, I began by asking him to define what *citizen journalism* is."

   a. Citizen journalism is news reported by someone with or without journalistic experience who is interested in the story.

   b. Citizen journalism is news reported by newspaper journalists that includes personal viewpoints and opinions of ordinary citizens.

2. **Host:** "You've been, you've been sort of involved in watching citizen media and social networking sites for a long time. How have they changed over the years?"

   a. The quality of citizen media reports has been going down steadily over the years.

   b. It is easier for people to participate in citizen media now because of easy access to technology.

3. **Host:** "Are there times where citizen journalism has really sort of taken to the forefront of, of news gathering?"

   a. The "accidental" journalist is the most common example: someone who happens to be at the scene of a news event and can report on it more quickly.

   b. Reports or news by a nonprofessional reporter can be more accurate and less biased than those by journalists.

4. **Host:** "It seems that one of the criticisms of citizen journalism is, uh, that they're not as accountable. . . . [B]logs haven't been around long enough, some of them are anonymous—how are they dealing with that concern?"

   a. This concern has caused citizen journalists to be more open and honest about who they are and what their biases are than traditional journalists.

   b. Citizen journalists who are serious about reporting the news often go on to become more educated and get journalism degrees.

5. **Host:** "What's the next step in the evolution of, of journalism and citizen journalism?"

   a. In another decade, almost all journalists will be citizen journalists.

   b. Traditional journalists will use techniques started by citizen journalists.

LISTEN FOR DETAILS

CD 1
Track 4

Listen again. Circle the word or phrase that best completes each sentence.

1. Hamman says that good journalists should check facts _____.

   a. when there is a good reason to doubt the truthfulness of something

   b. just once, but with a reliable source

   c. two or three times

2. Hamman says that some citizen journalists _____.

   a. begin by just sharing something interesting with their friends

   b. are trying to become famous through Internet exposure

   c. are motivated by money they hope to earn

3. The accidental citizen journalist who used the Internet to share information on the plane sinking into the Hudson River posted a _____.
   a. blog entry
   b. news article
   c. photograph

4. According to Hamman, when reporting the news, newspaper journalists _____.
   a. should never express their own points of view
   b. can include their own opinions and let their readers decide
   c. should cover only stories that they believe in

5. In the future, Hamman thinks we might see _____.
   a. more mainstream journalists who pick up on the techniques of citizen journalists
   b. a decline in ordinary citizen journalism as people start to lose interest in it
   c. more rules and regulations to govern the content of blogs

6. Hamman points out that journalists are using blogging, Facebook, and Twitter to reach out to _____.
   a. new audiences and advertisers
   b. new sources of information and different points of view
   c. new audiences and sources of information

Q WHAT DO YOU THINK?

Discuss the questions in a group.

1. Do you think citizen journalism could be more effective than traditional or mainstream journalism? If so, in what circumstances? —less bias

2. If fewer young people read newspapers and watch TV news these days, what can mainstream news organizations do to attract them?

3. Do you think citizen journalism would be equally popular in every country? Why or why not?

Main ideas are often stated directly. A speaker may give the main idea first and then add supporting details, or he or she might give the details first and then state the main idea. Sometimes, however, the main idea is *not* stated directly. The speaker will provide only examples, arguments, or other types of supporting information, and the listener must draw conclusions from this supporting information.

Here are some tips to help you identify main ideas when you listen to an interview, lecture, or report.

- Consider the title. The title should give you the topic and often will give you an overall idea of what the interview, lecture, or report will be about. It may also give you the bias of the speaker.

  Blogs: A great way to share your ideas

- Listen closely to questions that a reporter or speaker asks. The questions will often lead you to the main idea of all or part of the piece.

  "What's the next step in the evolution of, of journalism and citizen journalism?"

- Main ideas are sometimes stated first and then followed by supporting details. They are sometimes announced by phrases such as these, but not always.

  Today I'm going to talk about . . .

  Let's look at three ways that . . .

  A major reason for . . . is that . . .

- Main ideas can also be stated last. Summary words and phrases show that a conclusion is being drawn from supporting information.

  So, that means . . .

  Therefore, we can see that . . .

  All of this points to . . .

  These are techniques that . . .

  This is the reason that . . .

A main idea statement is too broad if it is vague (unclear) or goes beyond what the speaker is trying to say. It is too narrow if it doesn't fully cover what the speaker is saying about the topic or if it sounds like a specific example.

Topic: Local News

Main Idea That Is Too Broad: TV news is not for everybody.

Main Idea That Is Too Narrow: Local reporters provide the best small-town news.

Good Main Idea: People in small towns want local news.

Tip for Success

A **topic** is what the speaker is talking about. The **main ideas** give a general idea of what the speaker wants to communicate to the listener. The **details** support each main idea.

Tip Critical Thinking

Activities A through C ask you to **apply** the information about identifying main ideas. When you apply something, you take a concept and put it into use. In this case you are demonstrating your understanding of the difference between main ideas and details and applying your knowledge.

A. Work with a partner. Look at these topics from Listening 1. Circle the best main idea statement for each topic and discuss why the others are too broad or too narrow.

1. The main idea of the program "Citizen Journalism" is:
   a. Citizen journalism is a new trend that allows people to share news stories.
   b. Some of the new ways people share stories are by blogging and posting messages on Facebook.
   c. It's interesting that people can write their own news stories today.

2. The main idea the speaker presents about the influence of citizen media on mainstream journalists is:
   a. Mainstream journalists should stick to what they do best.
   b. Mainstream journalists can learn new techniques and develop a more open style of reporting.
   c. Mainstream journalists might benefit from using Facebook and Twitter.

B. Work with a partner. Look at these sentences from the beginning of Listening 1. Write *M* by the main idea and *D* by the details. Then put the sentences in the order you would say them.

D 1. But they're people who become interested in a story or an idea, and they go out and they start reporting on it and telling the world about it.

D 2. Other times it's full of opinion and, and personal viewpoints that haven't been checked, that may or may not have any kind of foundation in truth.

D 3. Sometimes they'll do that in the same way as, as one would hope journalists do, which is you know, gather the facts, make sure everything has been checked two or three times, and then run the story.

M 4. Citizen media is ordinary people.

CD 1
Track 5

C. Listen to these details from Listening 1. Match the details with the main ideas they support (*a*, *b*, *c*, or *d*). Then listen again and check your answers.

1. a   a. So, he wasn't trying to become a journalist . . .

2. b   b. So, people are used to kind of the basic tools of home computing.

3. d c. So I think that's one change that we're going to see where citizen journalism and blogging is actually going to affect the, the future of journalism.

4. c

    d. They do have a bias, they do have an opinion.

LISTENING 2 | Pod-Ready: Podcasting for the Developing World

VOCABULARY

Here are some words from Listening 2. Read the sentences. Circle the answer that best matches the meaning of each bold word.

1. New media technology is one of the key **components** of the government's plan to improve communication.
   a. mistakes
   b. parts
   c. businesses

2. The numerous **on-demand** TV and radio shows available nowadays let you watch or listen to your favorite shows whenever you want.
   a. biased
   b. popular
   c. immediate

3. Listening to the news on the radio or on a podcast is a **liberating** experience for adults who can't read.
   a. unnecessary
   b. troubling
   c. freeing

4. The podcast on food and diet was so **compelling** that soon more than 30,000 people were downloading and listening to it each day.
   a. unclear
   b. interesting
   c. common

5. In many parts of the world, radio is still a popular **medium** for getting news and information to people.
   a. a way to communicate
   b. an audio program
   c. a small machine

6. There was a **finite** amount of money, and when it was gone, the project had to be canceled.
   a. limited
   b. sufficient
   c. necessary

Tip for Success

Even though *news* looks like a plural noun, it is singular. (The *news is* shocking). Even though *media* looks like a singular noun, it is plural; the singular form is *medium*. (The *media are* kind).

7. The plan to provide computers and Internet access to the rural town was not **feasible** due to limits on electricity.
   a. interesting
   b. well-known
   c. possible to do

8. Planning the two-day trip to the small village in Zimbabwe, Africa, required solving many **logistical** problems, such as finding reliable transportation and buying food for the trip. *examples*
   a. sensible
   b. educational
   c. organizational

9. The United Nations Children's Fund (UNICEF) has several **initiatives** that aim to protect and help children all over the world.
   a. offices where people work
   b. plans for achieving a purpose
   c. employees who work for an organization

10. It is easy for media companies to **transmit** ideas and information to the public via the Internet.
    a. look for or find
    b. send or broadcast
    c. see or read

11. It is difficult to deliver newspapers to people who live in **isolated** areas.
    a. far away; cut off from others
    b. large and crowded
    c. expensive and developed

12. Cell phones and MP3 players are examples of **devices** that are easy to carry and can store audio files.
    a. tools
    b. lies
    c. methods

PREVIEW LISTENING 2

Pod-Ready: Podcasting for the Developing World

You are going to listen to a podcast adapted from Scidev.Net, the website for the Science and Development Network, based in the United Kingdom. It examines both the popularity and the usefulness of podcasts.

Check (✓) the difficulties you think people in developing countries might have in getting news and information. Add your own ideas if you can.

☐ limited electricity   ☐ too much rain

☐ old equipment   ☐ limited education

☐ high cost   ☐ poor Internet access

☐ _____   ☐ _____

[handwritten: podcast = digital audio files that are automatically downloaded from internet]

LISTEN FOR MAIN IDEAS

CD 1
Track 6

Listen to the podcast. Circle the correct answer.

[handwritten: Vocab before listening!]
[handwritten: uptake (N) - the process by which something is taken into a system]
[handwritten: agriculture (N) - practice of farming]
[handwritten: initiative - (N) - a new plan for dealing with a problem or achieving a particular purpose]
[handwritten: cultivation - (N) use of land for growing crops]
[handwritten: trundle (V) to move or roll somewhere slowly & noisily. eg. The tractor trundled along the farm]

1. Why are podcasts important to developing countries?
   a. They can provide a way for more people to get more information and different kinds of information.
   b. They are easier for people to understand than traditional forms of communication.
   c. They are more common there now than traditional forms of communication.

   [handwritten: tuk tuk - mobile broadcast unit]

2. Why is radio less effective than podcasts?
   a. People in developing countries feel that radio is old-fashioned and that developed countries prefer podcasts.
   b. Radio needs a more reliable power source.
   c. Radio has less flexibility and is more expensive than podcasts.

   [handwritten: telephone > newspaper]

3. What conclusion did McChesney draw from noticing that Peruvian people preferred the telephone to the computer?
   a. The people preferred to communicate and receive information through audio.
   b. More education and training would be needed before people could use computers well.
   c. Computers didn't provide access to the kind of information people wanted.

   [handwritten: rural poor, feasab..., How..., local people asked]

[handwritten: ICT How can... succeed in dif. countries; on-demand listen control when to listen communicate, complex ideas, links to traditional radio]

4. What is important about the e-tuk tuk in Sri Lanka?

   a. It provides a totally new way for people to stay connected with local, national, and international news.

   b. It uses modern technology to communicate in a traditional style.

   c. It proves that this kind of system can be used anywhere in the world.

5. What does David Benning believe about the future of podcasts in developing countries?

   a. The technology will remain limited because of basic access problems such as a poor electric power supply and the lack of special machines and parts.

   b. The technology will adapt to the special conditions and needs of developing countries.

   c. Developing countries will someday enjoy the same type of information and communication technology (ICT) as the developed world, but it may take another 10 or 15 years.

an e-tuk tuk

LISTEN FOR DETAILS

 CD 1 Track 7

Read the statements. Then listen again. Write *T* (true) or *F* (false) according to what the speakers say. Then correct the false statements with a partner.

Access to information

F 1. ICT stands for International Communication Technology.

F 2. Podcasts started in about 1994.

T 3. It is more expensive to broadcast by radio than by podcasting.

T 4. Local people in developing countries asked to be taught how to make podcasts.

_F_ 5. Podcasting is popular because it is a one-way medium.

_F_ 6. You need a license in order to create a podcast.

_F_ 7. Most people in the Cajamarca region of Peru make a living through manufacturing.

_T_ 8. Practical Action set up solar-powered computers in the Cajamarca region.

_T_ 9. The residents of the Cajamarca region had Internet access for two hours a day.

_T_ 10. The residents of the Cajamarca region want information that will help support their livelihoods.

_F_ 11. The biggest barrier for podcasting to overcome is to find cheaper digital audio players.

_T_ 12. In Zimbabwe, Practical Action is researching how to use podcasts to educate girls while they work.

Q WHAT DO YOU THINK?

A. Discuss the questions in a group.

1. Why do you think radios and telephones are the preferred devices for communication in many developing countries?

2. Do you agree or disagree that podcasts could become the solution to providing education in remote or isolated places?

3. What do you think is the biggest obstacle to overcome in order to help people get the news in developing countries? What is the best solution?

B. Think about both Listening 1 and Listening 2 as you discuss the questions.

1. What do you think influences people most in choosing a media format?

2. What changes do you predict we will see in the way people create and receive news and information over the next 50 years?

A **learner's dictionary** gives you more than just the definition and pronunciation of words. It also gives important information about each word that will help you use it correctly. You may find synonyms, antonyms, common expressions, and grammatical information.

The entry for *mainstream* shown below gives information about:

- **parts of speech:** It can be a singular noun, an adjective, and a verb.
- **meanings:** The most common meaning or use is listed first.
- **usage:** There are often notes, such as, for the adjective form, [*usually before noun*].
- **examples:** There are often example sentences, such as *Vegetarianism has been mainstreamed.*

> **main·stream** /ˈmeɪnstrim/ *noun, adj., verb*
> • *noun* **the mainstream** [sing.] the ideas and opinions that are thought to be normal because they are shared by most people; the people whose ideas and opinions are most accepted: *His radical views place him outside the mainstream of American politics.* ▶ **main·stream** *adj.* [usually before noun]: *mainstream education*
> • *verb* **1 ~ sth** to make a particular idea or opinion accepted by most people: *Vegetarianism has been mainstreamed.*
> **2 ~ sb** to include children with mental or physical problems in ordinary school classes

The labels and abbreviations may not be the same in every dictionary. Check the front or back pages of the dictionary for a guide. Here are some common abbreviations.

adj.	adjective	**n.**	noun	**sth**	something
adv.	adverb	**pl.**	plural	**T**	transitive verb (verb followed by noun)
BrE	British English	**pt**	past tense	**U**	uncountable (another term for *noncount*)
C	countable noun	**sb**	somebody	**US**	American English
I	intransitive verb (verb not followed by noun)	**sing.**	singular	**v.**	verb

All dictionary entries are from the *Oxford Advanced American Dictionary for learners of English* © Oxford University Press 2011.

A. Work with a partner. Use a dictionary to find answers to these questions.

1. Which of these words is *not* both a noun and a verb: *network, inform, hurdle*?

   _____

2. What is the negative or opposite form of *finite*? _____

3. What preposition is used with *isolate*? _____

4. What are two synonyms of *upfront*? _____

5. What is the noun form of *feasible*? _____

   Is it a countable or an uncountable noun? _____

6. What two adjectives are shown as commonly used with the noun *component*?

   _____

B. Circle the correct word or phrase to complete each sentence. Look up the <u>underlined</u> words and phrase in a dictionary to check your answers.

1. Reporters are <u>accountable</u> (to / for) their readers and so they should check their facts carefully.

2. His blogs were outside (the <u>mainstream</u> / the <u>mainstreams</u>) of news media.

3. The story <u>compelled</u> him (to take / from taking) action.

4. To be left to your own (<u>devices</u> / <u>device</u>) means to be left alone without being told what to do.

5. <u>On demand</u> is a(n) (verb phrase / idiom).

6. <u>Prospect</u> is a(n) (uncountable / countable) noun when it means *possibility that something will happen.*

Reporters should check their facts.

Grammar   Participial adjectives

Often it is possible to create an adjective from a verb by using the present or past participle form of the verb.

Present participial adjectives

The **present participle** is the *-ing* form of a verb. A present participial adjective is used to describe:

- an ongoing state

You can get **breaking** news on the Internet. (The news is happening now.)

- the cause of a feeling or emotion

The students thought that TV news was **boring**. (TV news causes the feeling.)

Past participial adjectives

The **past participle** is the verb form used in perfect and passive sentences. The form is usually verb + *-ed*, but there are also several irregular verbs, such as *written* and *spoken*. A past participial adjective is used to describe:

- a completed state

Ben's iPod is **broken**; he has to borrow his friend's. (The iPod does not work.)

- the person or thing that feels or has the quality of the adjective

The students are **bored**. They don't have patience with TV news. (Students feel bored.)

Note: Past participial adjectives can only be formed from verbs that take an object (transitive verbs).

Note: You can form both present and past participial adjectives from some verbs. Use your dictionary if you are not sure.

In **developed** countries, there are many sources of news.
In **developing** countries, it can be difficult to get the news.

The past participial adjective *developed* refers to countries that are already advanced economically, while *developing* refers to those that are still developing their economies.

A. Read the sentences and circle the correct participial adjective.

1. The most (interesting / interested) news stories make the front page.

2. The editor told Louisa that her article was very well (writing / written).

3. Online weather websites have up-to-date information on (approaching / approached) storms.

4. The (downloading / downloaded) podcasts can be transferred to any audio device.

5. The bloggers who publish the most (compelling / compelled) stories become famous.

6. An (illustrated / illustrating) story is easier for young readers to understand.

B. Work with a partner. Write a short conversation about new media. One partner talks about its advantages, and one partner talks about its disadvantages. Use at least three present and three past participial adjectives in the conversation. Create adjectives from the verbs in the box, or choose your own. Practice your conversation and then present it to the class.

bore	develop	frustrate	surprise
compel	excite	interest	tire

A: *What are you listening to?*
B: *It's a really exciting podcast about the election. Want to hear it?*
A: *No, thanks. I'm not very interested.*
B: *Don't you think the election is interesting?*
A: *I do, but podcasts are so boring. I'd rather read the newspaper.*

There are only five letters that represent vowels (*a, e, i, o, u*), but there are 15 vowel sounds. They may sound similar, but failure to produce them correctly or distinguish between them can lead to misunderstanding. As an example, the letter *a* can be pronounced as /æ/ in *hat*, /ɑ/ in *father*, or /eɪ/ in *relate*.

Vowel sounds change with slight variations in your mouth (the shape of your lips and the positions of your tongue and jaw). Pay attention to how your mouth changes as you make these sounds one after another:

- /eɪ/ Your tongue should be in the front and middle of your mouth with your jaw slightly open and your lips spread.
- /æ/ Your tongue moves lower, your jaw opens a little wider, and your lips spread more.
- /ɑ/ Your tongue is lowest in your mouth as your jaw opens widest and your lips open wide as if you are yawning.
- /oʊ/ Your tongue shifts back in your mouth as your jaw starts to close and your lips are rounded.

A common rule is that when *a* and *o* are the only vowels in a one-syllable word, *a* is often pronounced /æ/ as in *hat* and *o* is pronounced /ɑ/ as in *not*. However, when a final *-e* is added, they are usually pronounced as /eɪ/ and /oʊ/ as in *hate* and *note*.

CD 1
Track 8

Listen and repeat the examples in the chart. Pay attention to the way your mouth changes.

/eɪ/	/æ/	/ɑ/	/oʊ/
stake	stack	stock	stroke
late	land	lot	lone
made	mad	mod	mode
plane	plan	plod	explode
rate	rat	rot	remote

It is also important to remember that all vowels in an unstressed syllable can be reduced to the schwa /ə/ sound. The first unstressed syllables in *about* and *concede* are pronounced as /ə/.

A. Work with a partner. Read the paragraphs about the ideas in Listening 1 and Listening 2 out loud. Pay special attention to the underlined parts of the bold words.

Track 8

1. Robin Hamman works for Headshift, which is an **agency** that advises **organizations** and governments on **blogging** and other **aspects** of **social** media. He **states** that often citizen journalists are **common** people who work **alone** and just **happen** to have **access** at the **moment** a story breaks. There are many **examples** of such **accidental** journalists who then **create documents** on their computers and **upload** them to a website. He thinks journalists with a bias should be **honest**, but **also** need to **watch** out to make sure their opinions **don't** affect the coverage of the story.

2. Ben McChesney works for **Practical** Action, a charity group that **hopes** to bring **technology** to poor rural areas so farmers can produce **podcasts**. What **makes** podcasting more **attractive** than **radio** is its **low** cost. On one **project** in Peru, McChesney realized the **telephone** was more **popular** than the computer. People preferred audio to text for some **information**. His group is working **on** new ways to **promote** education through podcasts.

CD 1
Track 9 *Track 8*

B. Listen to the excerpts from Activity A and check your pronunciation. Then write each bold word from Activity A in the correct place in the chart according to the pronunciation of the underlined syllable. Compare your chart with a partner.

/eɪ/	/æ/	/ɑ/	/oʊ/
agency	-aspects	-blogging	-social
organizations	-happens	-common	-alone
states	-access	-documents	-moment
create	-examples	-honest	-upload
makes	-accidental	-watch	-also
radio	-practical	-technology	-don't
information	-attract	-podcasts	-hopes
	alone	-project	-low
		-popular	-telephone
		-on	-promote

C. Work with a partner. Ask and answer the questions.

1. What are some advantages of blogging?

2. What are some advantages of self-produced podcasts?

3. What do blogs and podcasts have in common?

It is important to be organized when you give presentations. Note cards are a simple way to make sure you say everything you want to say, in the correct order. Note cards act as reminders; they should not be a complete transcript of your talk!

Here are some tips for preparing effective note cards.

- Use index cards. Plan to use one or two cards per minute of speaking.
- Write key words from the main ideas you plan to speak about in big, clear letters on one side.
- List examples or details (using numbers or bullets) on the other side.
- Don't write complete sentences.
- Make your words large enough to see easily.
- Number your cards in case they fall out of order.

Here are some tips for speaking with note cards.

- Practice a few times in front of a mirror or a friend before you speak to a group.
- Try to look at your cards less and less each time you speak.
- Remember not to speak too fast or read your note cards.
- Look at your audience most of the time; only look at each note card briefly as necessary.

Here is an example of one student's note card, front and back.

> **((Tip) for Success**
>
> PowerPoint slides are like note cards, but your audience can see them, too. Turn your key words into headings and make a bulleted list on each slide to help you and your audience stay focused through a speech.

1

podcast definition

- *digital audio file*
- *downloaded from the Internet to computer*
- *can be put on MP3 player*
- *iPods*

Here is what the student might say from this note card during a speech.

Many of you probably already know what a podcast is. But just to be clear and accurate, a podcast is a digital audio file that is downloaded from the Internet onto your computer. Then, you can transfer it to an mp3 player, like an iPod. In fact, the word *podcast* comes from the brand name iPod.

A. Choose three of the topics below. Write each topic on the back of a note card. Then complete your note cards with your own ideas. (If you do not have note cards, do the work in your notebook.)

my media preferences	podcasting: pros or cons
different types of media	popularity of social networking sites
where to go for online news	types of "citizen media"
how to write a blog	problems with today's media

There are many ways to get the news today.

B. Work with a partner. Present a 1–2 minute talk each on one aspect of new media. Use your note cards as necessary. When you have both finished, change partners and repeat the exercise. Did you use your note cards less the second time?

In this section, you will survey people about their media preferences. As you prepare your survey and discuss the results, think about the Unit Question, "How do people get the news today?" and refer to the Self-Assessment checklist on page 26.

For alternative unit assignments, see the *Q: Skills for Success Teacher's Handbook.*

CONSIDER THE IDEAS

Work in a group. Look at the photo. Then discuss the questions below.

1. How are the man and woman in this photo accessing news and information?

2. What types of media do you think your classmates use to get news and information? Do you think they are similar to the man in the photo or the woman?

PREPARE AND SPEAK

A. **GATHER IDEAS** **Work in a group. Complete the tasks below to create and conduct a survey about news habits in your classroom or community.**

1. Brainstorm a list of *Yes / No* questions about where, how, and how often people get their news.

2. Practice asking your questions to your group members and brainstorm possible follow-up questions together.

3. Each group member should choose 6–8 questions. You do *not* all need to choose the same ones! Then create a chart like the one below to write questions and record responses.

Question	Yes	No	Further Information
Do you ever listen to the news on Internet radio?	☐	☑	already listens to news on car radio while driving to school
Are blogs more useful than books for keeping up with the news?	☑	☐	information is more current

4. Each group member should survey ten people outside of class if possible (if necessary, you can speak to classmates). You will need to complete one survey form for each person you interview or create a chart large enough to record the information from ten people.

B. **ORGANIZE IDEAS** Follow these steps to analyze the information from your survey. (Note that the small sample size of ten people means that your "statistics" are not accurate for a general population! You are practicing with the language of reporting surveys.)

1. Tally your answers; that is, how many people answered each question *yes* or *no*? Circle any interesting extra information that you might want to use in your talk.

2. Write the percentages of *yes* answers and *no* answers on your chart. For example, if four people said they listen to the news on Internet radio, then write the figure 40%.

3. Decide which questions gave you the most interesting or important information. You may choose to speak about only a few questions, or you could speak about all of them.

4. Prepare note cards for your presentation.

C. **SPEAK** Present the results of your survey to your group or the whole class. Remember to summarize detailed information with main ideas. Start with an overall main idea for your group report. Each speaker should use note cards, but only as a guide. Refer to the Self-Assessment checklist below before you begin.

CHECK AND REFLECT

A. **CHECK** Think about the Unit Assignment as you complete the Self-Assessment checklist.

Yes	No	SELF-ASSESSMENT
☐	☐	I was able to speak fluently about the topic.
☐	☐	My group or class understood me.
☐	☐	I used both main ideas and details.
☐	☐	I used participial adjectives correctly.
☐	☐	I used vocabulary from the unit to express my ideas.
☐	☐	I pronounced vowels correctly.
☐	☐	I used note cards to communicate more effectively.

B. **REFLECT** Discuss these questions with a partner.

What is something new you learned in this unit?

Look back at the Unit Question. Is your answer different now than when you started this unit? If yes, how is it different? Why?

Track Your Success

Circle the words and phrase you learned in this unit.

Nouns
bias AWL
component 🔑 AWL
device 🔑 AWL
foundation 🔑 AWL
initiative 🔑 AWL
medium 🔑 AWL
networking AWL
source 🔑 AWL
technique 🔑 AWL
viewpoint

Verbs
transmit AWL
unfold

Adjectives
accidental 🔑
accountable
anonymous
compelling
feasible
finite AWL
isolated AWL

liberating AWL
logistical
unique 🔑 AWL
upfront

Phrase
on demand (idiom)

🔑 Oxford 3000™ words
AWL Academic Word List
For more information on the Oxford 3000™ and the AWL, see page xi.

Check (✓) the skills you learned. If you need more work on a skill, refer to the page(s) in parentheses.

LISTENING ●	I can identify main ideas. (p. 9)
VOCABULARY ●	I can understand a dictionary entry. (p. 16)
GRAMMAR ●	I can understand and use participial adjectives. (p. 18)
PRONUNCIATION ●	I can correctly pronounce the vowels *a* and *o*. (p. 20)
SPEAKING ●	I can use note cards effectively when I speak. (p. 22)
LEARNING OUTCOME ●	I can develop and administer a survey focused on media preferences, analyze the results, and report my findings.

UNIT 2

Language

LISTENING	●	making inferences
VOCABULARY	●	negative prefixes
GRAMMAR	●	passive voice
PRONUNCIATION	●	emphatic word stress
SPEAKING	●	using figurative language

LEARNING OUTCOME ●

Develop a narrative incorporating figurative language that chronologically details an incident of language loss or an inability to communicate.

Unit QUESTION

How does language affect who we are?

PREVIEW THE UNIT

A Discuss these questions with your classmates.

What difficulties might an English speaker visiting your home country have while trying to communicate?

Do people who know two languages have different thoughts in each language or just different words for them?

Look at the photo. How are the people communicating? What are other forms of non-standard communication?

B Discuss the Unit Question above with your classmates.

Listen to *The Q Classroom*, **Track 10 on CD 1**, to hear other answers.

C Work with a partner. Read the following situations and discuss them. Then choose one and role-play it for the class.

Have you ever experienced one of these difficulties in communicating?

1. Two friends see each other across a large, crowded, noisy restaurant. They try to communicate different issues, such as the time (one person is late), where to sit, and whether or not to leave.

2. A tourist who doesn't speak the language is lost in a big city. He or she tries to get directions from a local resident to get to a specific location (such as a hospital, a train station, a restaurant, or a museum).

3. A patient in a doctor's office tries to explain to the doctor how he or she woke up with a terrible headache and weak muscles and now is unable to speak.

Tip Critical Thinking

In Activity D, you will **give examples** of the different kinds of causes and effects. Giving examples shows you understand concepts.

D With your partner, use this mind map to brainstorm causes and effects of communication difficulties such as those in Activity C or another situation. Then discuss the questions below using your mind map.

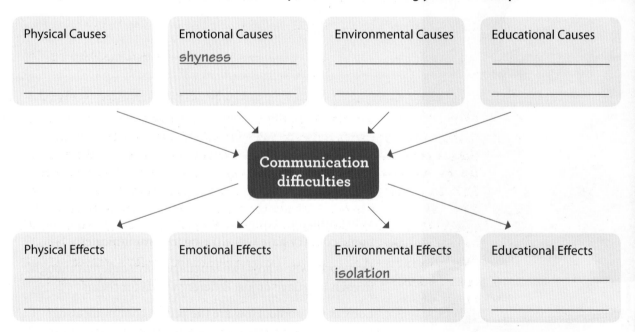

Physical Causes
_____
_____

Emotional Causes
shyness
_____

Environmental Causes
_____
_____

Educational Causes
_____
_____

Communication difficulties

Physical Effects
_____
_____

Emotional Effects
_____
_____

Environmental Effects
isolation
_____

Educational Effects
_____
_____

1. What do you think are the most common causes?

2. What are the most harmful effects?

LISTENING 1 | # My Stroke of Insight: A Brain Scientist's Personal Journey

VOCABULARY

Here are some words from Listening 1. Read the paragraphs. Then write each bold word next to the correct definition.

The brain is one of the most **fascinating** organs in the human body, partly because it is such a mystery. It is studied by doctors called neurologists and neuroanatomists, who hope to gain an **insight** into the way the brain works. The **structure** of the brain is important: it is divided into two equal sections called hemispheres. One part, the cerebral cortex, coordinates what we think and feel with what we see and our **perceptions** of the outside world. Each part of the brain has a specific **function**, and if injured, it may become unable to perform this role.

1. _____ (*n.*) awareness; how things are noticed by the senses

2. _____ (*n.*) an understanding of what something is like

3. _____ (*adj.*) extremely interesting

4. _____ (*n.*) the purpose of someone or something

5. _____ (*n.*) the way in which the parts of something are arranged or organized

A stroke occurs when blood flow to part of the brain is cut off due to a hemorrhage (heavy bleeding); this can result in an inability to speak or move. Stroke victims sometimes lose **consciousness** and later have no memory of what has happened. They may not be aware of **external** events or things around them. The line between what is real and unreal may become unclear, and the inability to understand this **boundary** may cause confusion. However, some patients experience the opposite feeling of **tranquil** euphoria, a sense of calm when they are disconnected from the real world. For all stroke victims, **recovery** depends on the seriousness of the stroke, but with a lot of physical and speech therapy, patients can **regain** their ability to walk and communicate. Although the **overall** survival rate for stroke victims is not bad, on the whole, 40 percent have some resulting disability.

6. _____ (*v.*) get back something you no longer have, especially an ability or quality

7. _____ (*n.*) the state of being aware of something

8. _____ *(n.)* the process of becoming well again after an illness or an injury

9. _____ *(adj.)* quiet; peaceful

10. _____ *(adj.)* happening or coming from outside a place or your situation

11. _____ *(adj.)* general; considering everything

12. _____ *(n.)* a real or imaginary border; a dividing line

PREVIEW LISTENING 1

| My Stroke of Insight: A Brain Scientist's Personal Journey

Dr. Jill Bolte Taylor

You are going to listen to a radio interview. Dr. Jill Bolte Taylor is a neuroanatomist who had a stroke and later wrote a book titled *My Stroke of Insight: A Brain Scientist's Story*. She describes the effects of her stroke in her book and in this interview with David Inge of radio station WILL from the University of Illinois.

How do you think Dr. Taylor's ability to think and communicate was affected when she had a stroke? Check (✓) your prediction.

☐ She could think using language, but could not speak.

☐ She could not think or speak using language.

LISTEN FOR MAIN IDEAS

 CD 1
Track 11

A. Read the key phrases in the chart that indicate main ideas. Listen to the interview and take notes to explain the ideas.

 **Tip** for Success

Anticipating key words or phrases about a topic, and then taking notes about them when you listen, will help you understand and remember the details.

Introduction

Key Phrases	Notes
1. The right hemisphere and the big picture	
2. The left hemisphere and language	

Call-in Show

Key Phrases	Notes
3. Memories and a sense of identity	
4. Stroke victims and English speakers in a foreign country	

B. Use your notes to write the main ideas that Taylor explains to her listeners. Compare your sentences with a partner.

Introduction

1. The right hemisphere and the big picture

   _____

   _____

2. The left hemisphere and language

   _____

   _____

Call-in Show

3. Memories and a sense of identity

   _____

   _____

4. Stroke victims and English speakers in a foreign country

   _____

   _____

LISTEN FOR DETAILS

CD 1
Track 12

Listen again. Circle the answer that best completes each statement.

Introduction

1. When Jill Bolte Taylor had her stroke in 1996, she was working at (Harvard / Indiana) University.

2. Dr. Taylor describes her feeling during her stroke as one of (peace and tranquility / panic and fear).

3. The two halves of the brain process information in (similar / different) ways.

4. The right hemisphere of the brain is concerned with (overall perception / details).

5. The right and left hemispheres (have to / don't have to) work together for people to have a normal perspective.

6. When Dr. Taylor had a stroke, she lost the (right / left) hemisphere of her brain.

Call-in Show

7. The behavioral psychologists mentioned by the caller believed that language could be lost only if a person (remained conscious / lost consciousness).

8. Dr. Taylor lost her perception of (past and present / past and future).

9. According to Taylor, a tourist who doesn't speak the language will have (less / greater) awareness of other communicative signals, such as people's voices and facial expressions.

10. When Dr. Taylor lost the basic human ability to use language, she (no longer saw herself / still saw herself) as a human being.

WHAT DO YOU THINK?

Discuss the questions in a group.

1. Do you think you focus more on "the big picture" and general ideas or details? Would you say that you are more "right-brained" or "left-brained," according to the ideas in the Listening?

2. Which effect of a stroke would upset you more, the loss of the ability to speak or the loss of your past memories? Why?

3. Describe your overall perception of one of the pictures, which will engage the right hemisphere of your brain (the side that looks at the big picture). Describe the details of the other picture, which will engage the left hemisphere of your brain (the side that looks at details).

Picture A

Picture B

Listening Skill | Making inferences

Speakers do not always state their ideas or opinions directly. They may give facts or examples and expect the listener to draw a logical conclusion, or *make an inference*. It is important, however, to make sure you don't make inferences that were not suggested by the information!

If you are not sure what someone is implying, here are some phrases to check your understanding.

> So, do you mean that . . . ?
> So, are you saying that . . . ?
> So, would you say that . . . ?

CD 1
Track 13

A. Listen to the excerpts from Listening 1. Circle the best inference for each one.

1. a. People have no idea how the brain works.
   b. People don't understand the exact functions of the different parts of the brain.

2. a. A normal, healthy person uses both hemispheres.
   b. Different people prefer to use different hemispheres of the brain.

3. a. Dr. Taylor found an advantage in the results of her stroke.
   b. Dr. Taylor was very upset at losing some of her brain's abilities.

4. a. Dr. Taylor feels that foreign tourists function somewhat as if they were brain-damaged.

  b. Dr. Taylor feels that foreign tourists make up for the lack of language skills by increasing other communicative abilities.

B. Choose two of the situations below or use your own ideas. Write some sentences that imply the ideas—but do not state them directly!

Your concerns about learning English

Your communication difficulties with grandparents

Your thoughts on teenage slang and text abbreviations

Your feelings about your language classes

Your fears about a miscommunication with a best friend

Your idea: _____

Your idea: _____

C. Work with a partner. Take turns reading the sentences about your situation. Can your partner infer what you are trying to say?

LISTENING 2 | The Story of My Life

VOCABULARY

Here are some words from Listening 2. Read the sentences. Circle the answer that best matches the meaning of each bold word.

1. Children learn to speak by **imitating** words and trying to sound like adults.

   a. copying   b. ignoring

2. When we were trying to use our hands to communicate without language, we found that the way we **gesticulated** did not always get the message across.

   a. made signs with our hands   b. complained loudly

3. There were many **incidents** that showed the child's frustration with learning the language, even though she never said anything directly.

   a. results   b. examples

4. The experience was so **intense** that it caused the woman to cry.
   a. powerful   b. unexpected

5. If you feel your language skills are **adequate** for that job, then you should apply!
   a. good enough   b. not good enough

6. Those who are bilingual **invariably** get jobs more easily and are grateful to their parents for making them learn a second language.
   a. almost never   b. almost always

7. These passionate **outbursts** helped the little boy get his way because no one could ignore the noise he made.
   a. sudden strong expressions   b. songs
      of emotion

8. Without **tangible** evidence to support their theory, the researchers didn't feel confident publishing their study.
   a. popular; widely accepted   b. clearly seen to exist;
                                      able to be touched

9. The answer to the mystery was not **revealed** until the last few pages of the book.
   a. explained; shown   b. hidden

10. If that annoying sound **persists**, I will have to complain to the neighbors. I can't sleep!
    a. gets louder   b. continues

11. Because the stroke victim had lost some of her vision, she could only make out **fragments** of the picture and had to connect the pieces in her mind.
    a. small portions; bits   b. soft colors

12. There was no strong **sentiment** visible in the actor's face, no feeling of anger or sorrow.
    a. damaged area   b. emotion

Annie Sullivan and
Helen Keller

PREVIEW LISTENING 2

The Story of My Life

You are going to listen to an excerpt from an audiobook of Hellen Keller's autobiography, *The Story of My Life*. Helen Keller (1880–1968) lost her sight and her hearing from an illness when she was 19 months old. She learned to communicate through hard work with her teacher, Annie Sullivan.

In what ways do you predict a child who lost her sight and hearing at such a young age would try to communicate? Write your ideas.

_____

_____

_____

_____

LISTEN FOR MAIN IDEAS

 CD 1
Track 14

Read the descriptions of Helen Keller's emotions during each period of her life. Then listen to the audiobook excerpt. Write the letter of the description under the event on the timeline on page 39. Compare your answers with a partner.

a. Helen could make finger signs to spell many words but became <u>impatient</u> because she didn't understand how the actions connected with the words.

b. Helen used her hands, touched every object, and felt <u>protected</u> by her mother who understood her crude signs to communicate.

c. Helen's desire to communicate grew so strong that she was often <u>angry</u> and had passionate outbursts.

d. Helen grew <u>confident</u> as she explored with her hands and learned the names and uses for objects.

e. Helen understood what was going on about her and could imitate actions, but she felt <u>different</u> from others.

f. Helen touched people's lips and imitated their movements but became <u>frustrated</u> when it did not produce any result.

g. Helen felt <u>free and hopeful</u> once the mystery of language was revealed to her, and she was <u>eager</u> to learn.

Helen Keller's Life

2. Her early childhood (ages 2–4) ____

4. The weeks before her teacher came (age 6) ____

6. Several weeks after her teacher came ____

____

1. The first months after her illness

____

3. Her later childhood (ages 4–5)

____

5. The days after her teacher came

____

7. The summer of 1887

LISTEN FOR DETAILS

  CD 1 Track 15

Read the lists of examples and descriptions from the audiobook excerpt. Then listen again. Match the examples with the descriptions.

Tip for Success

Over time, the meaning of a word can change. The word *dumb*, for example, means "unable to speak," but today the meaning "unintelligent" is more common. Check up-to-date dictionaries and ask your teacher if you are confused about a word.

a. touching with her hands

b. a doll

c. pushing someone to tell her to go

d. her teacher

e. the strength of the sun

f. water

g. her mother

h. breaking the doll

i. touching someone's lips and trying to move her own

j. knowing which clothes meant she was going out

____ 1. an example of Helen's simple "crude signs" to communicate

____ 2. the person to whom Helen owed "all that was bright and good in my long night"

____ 3. Helen's saying "She brought me my hat, and I knew I was going out" is an example of Helen's understanding of what was going on about her

____ 4. the way Helen tried to learn to speak that left her "so angry at times that [she] kicked and screamed until [she] was exhausted"

_____ 5. the person "who had come to reveal all things to me, and, more than all things else, to love me"

_____ 6. the way Helen knew that the "sweet southern spring" season had begun

_____ 7. the gift that "the little blind children at the Perkins Institution had sent"

_____ 8. the "living word" that "awakened [her] soul" and made Helen finally realize what language was

_____ 9. the action that Helen said made her feel satisfied and showed she knew "neither sorrow nor regret"

_____ 10. the way Helen explored her world in order to "learn the name of every object"

WHAT DO YOU THINK?

A. Discuss the questions in a group.

1. In the modern world, do you think it is better for a child like Helen Keller to have a private tutor at home or learn in a school setting?

2. Helen Keller felt lost and empty without language. She was angry and even violent at times when she couldn't communicate. What are some emotions that are hard to put into words, and how do different people express them?

3. What message do you think Helen Keller wants readers to get from her descriptions of her childhood before and after she met her teacher?

B. Think about both Listening 1 and Listening 2 as you discuss the questions.

1. If Helen Keller and Jill Bolte Taylor could meet, what do you think they would talk about?

2. What mental attitudes did Helen Keller and Jill Bolte Taylor have in common? In what ways were their attitudes different?

Knowledge of prefixes helps you expand your vocabulary. Here are prefixes that are added to adjectives to give an opposite or negative meaning.

il-	**il**legal
im-	**im**possible
in-	**in**capable
ir-	**ir**regular
un-	**un**thinkable

With *il-*, *im-*, and *ir-*, there are patterns, but also exceptions.

Use *il-* for words that begin with *l*.	**il**legal, **il**logical (but **un**lawful)
Use *im-* for words that begin with *p*, *m*, and *b*.	**im**possible, **im**measurable (but **un**popular)
Use *ir-* for words that begin with *r*.	**ir**relevant, **ir**regular (but **un**reliable)

The prefix *dis-* is the form that is most often used to form the negative of verbs, though *un-* is also used.

   disagree   **dis**obey   **dis**qualify   **dis**like   **un**do   **un**tie

Both *dis-* and *un-* are also used for participial adjectives.

   dissatisfied   **dis**appointing   **un**decided   **un**ending

Tip for Success

Although we rarely stress prefixes, we put strong secondary stress on a prefix that means *not* so it is easy for a listener to understand the negative meaning (un<u>im</u>PORtant, <u>dys</u>FUNCtional).

A. Write the correct negative prefix on the line in front of the adjectives.

1. Dr. Taylor said that she was able to enjoy the experience of being

   ____connected from the left hemisphere of her brain.

2. Dr. Taylor told the caller she wasn't ____conscious even though she had had a stroke.

3. The caller was surprised that the neuroanatomist could get help in spite of her ____regular style of communicating.

4. A stroke victim who wasn't a doctor like Taylor was could have been ____aware of what was happening.

5. Helen Keller's parents might have thought that a teacher without direct experience with blindness would have been more ____sensitive about Helen's condition.

6. Helen Keller was ____patient with her teacher's attempts to teach her the difference between *mug* and *water*.

B. Write sentences to describe Helen Keller and Jill Bolte Taylor. Use one of these adjectives in a negative form in each sentence. Compare sentences with a partner.

adequate	conscious	perfect	tangible
capable	connected	possible	usual
comfortable	measurable	satisfied	visible

Helen Keller's earliest attempts to communicate were inadequate.

1. _____

_____

2. _____

_____

3. _____

_____

4. _____

_____

from the movie *The Miracle Worker*

SPEAKING

Grammar | Passive voice

1. The **passive voice** is used to put the emphasis on the object of the verb instead of the subject.

For example, imagine we want to talk about why Jill Bolte Taylor lost her language ability: because of the effects of a stroke on her brain. The most important part of the sentence is *her brain* and not a *stroke*. Therefore, instead of the active sentence *A stroke damaged Taylor's brain* we would say:

☐ Taylor's brain **was damaged** by a stroke.

2. The passive voice is used when the subject of the sentence isn't known.

☐ This audiobook **was recorded** in 2007.

If we don't know (and don't care) who recorded the audiobook, it sounds awkward to say *Somebody recorded this audio book in 2007*. The important element of the sentence is *this audiobook*, so it sounds better at the beginning of the sentence.

3. The passive voice is only used with **transitive verbs** (verbs that take an object).

☐ ✓ Helen Keller **was taught** a new way to speak.
☐ ✗ Dr. Taylor's stroke was happened in the morning.

4. In passive sentences, the verb tense is indicated in the verb *be*. Modal verbs can also be made passive.

Past perfect passive	Past passive	Present perfect passive
had been found	was lost	has been studied
Present passive	**Future passive**	**Modal passive**
is taken	will be given	may be revealed could be gained

The active voice is more common than the passive voice. Overusing the passive voice can make your speaking sound flat, impersonal, or too formal. This is why some word-processing grammar checks underline passive sentences. However, there are times when the passive voice is more appropriate and should be used.

 Tip for Success

Remember that not all sentences with a form of *be* + a participle are passive! *This article was written by Helen Keller* is passive. *I was tired after a long, difficult day* is not passive. It is the simple past of the verb *be* + an adjective.

A. Read these sentences from Helen Keller's story. Write *P* if the underlined verb is passive and *A* if it is active.

_____ 1. I felt my teacher sweep the fragments to one side of the hearth, and I had a sense of satisfaction that the cause of my discomfort <u>was removed</u>.

_____ 2. She brought me my hat, and I knew I <u>was going out</u> into the warm sunshine.

_____ 3. This thought, if a wordless sensation <u>may be called</u> a thought, made me hop and skip with pleasure.

_____ 4. Someone <u>was drawing</u> water, and my teacher placed my hand under the spout.

_____ 5. As the cool stream gushed over one hand she <u>spelled</u> into the other the word *water*, first slowly, then rapidly.

_____ 6. I stood still; my whole attention <u>was fixed</u> upon the motions of her fingers.

_____ 7. Suddenly I felt a misty consciousness as of something that <u>had been forgotten</u>—a thrill of returning thought; and somehow the mystery of language was revealed to me.

_____ 8. I knew then that "w-a-t-e-r" meant the wonderful cool something that <u>was flowing</u> over my hand.

B. Work with a partner. Discuss whether the passive or the active version of the sentence sounds more natural. (Sometimes one is clearly better; sometimes both can sound all right, although the emphasis is different.)

1. a. I forgot my textbook.
   b. My textbook was forgotten by me.

2. a. Some scientists made many significant advances in the field of neuroscience in the last century.
   b. Many significant advances in the field of neuroscience were made in the last century.

3. a. Louis Braille invented a system of writing for the blind known as Braille.
   b. Braille, a system of writing for the blind, was invented by Louis Braille.

4. a. Someone added Braille signs to places such as elevators and restrooms.
   b. Braille signs have been added to places such as elevators and restrooms.

5. a. Today, some blind children may attend regular public schools.
   b. Today, regular public schools may be attended by some blind children.

6. a. Helen Keller's story inspired me.
   b. I was inspired by Helen Keller's story.

Pronunciation | Emphatic word stress

Speakers engage their audiences by emphasizing key words in three main ways.

1. Saying key words more loudly
2. Making the vowels in the key syllables longer
3. Using a higher pitch for stressed words

Key words in sentences are usually content words (nouns, verbs, adjectives, and adverbs).

We also stress words that provide new information or information that contrasts with or corrects previous information. New or particularly important information often comes at the end of a clause or sentence.

CD 1 Track 16

Listen and practice the examples.

> She's a SCIENTIST. (noun)
> She was COMPLETELY CONSCIOUS. (adverb + adjective)
> He was RESPONSIBLE. (adjective)
> She ISOLATED herself. (verb)

Any word (pronouns, auxiliaries, prepositions) can be stressed, however, when the speaker wants to emphasize a particular point. Notice which words indicate corrective or contrasting information.

CD 1 Track 16

Listen and practice the examples.

> A: She's a SCIENTIST?   B: No, she's a DENTIST.
> A: Are you afraid of oral reports?   B: YES! I NEVER take speaking classes.
> A: Can Gary speak MANDARIN?   B: HE can't, but LISA can.

When you emphasize key words, a strong rhythm develops and key words stand out clearly to listeners. Knowing how stress and intonation work will help you with both speaking fluency and listening comprehension.

CD 1
Track 17

A. Jill Bolte Taylor is a strong and dynamic speaker. Listen to her describe the morning of her stroke. Circle the key words you hear emphasized; then compare transcripts with a partner and discuss the ways the speaker uses stress to help tell her story.

Then I would have this wave of clarity that would bring me and reattach me back to normal reality, and I could pursue my plan, and my—the only plan that I had in my head was to call work and that somebody at work would get me help. Um, but it—it took, uh, over 45 minutes for me to figure out what number to dial and how to dial and by the time, um, I got the information I could not see uh the, the phone number on my business card. I couldn't pick the numbers out from the background pixels, cause all I could see were pixels. Uh, and it's a you know, it's a, big drama. By the time my colleague, I'm very fortunate he was at his desk. I spoke. I said "Woo Woo Woo Woo Er" I had no, no language and when he spoke to me he sounded "Woo Woo Wer." He sounded like a golden retriever. So, uh, but he did recognize that it was I and that I needed help and then eventually he did get me help.

B. In a group, take turns adding some expressive details to these sentence starters, stressing key words so your listeners understand what information is important or contrastive.

1. We use our right brains to . . . , and our left brains to . . . .

2. Many ESL learners have difficulty . . . , but I . . . .

3. When I had to stand up in front of the class to give a speech, ...

4. I'll never forget the day when (name of a person) asked me . . . .

5. When I went to visit my relatives in . . . , I couldn't . . . .

6. Taylor's experience made me think about . . . .

7. My worst experience trying to speak English was when . . . .

Speaking Skill | **Using figurative language** web⁺

One way to make your speaking more interesting is to use *similes* and *metaphors*. These devices create images that help listeners experience the intensity of something you are describing.

A **simile** is a way of describing something by comparing it to another thing. Similes include the word *like* or *as*.

> Learning English is **like** climbing a mountain.
> Her skin was as soft **as** silk.

Some similes become so common in a language that they become idioms.

> as pretty as a picture   as gentle as a lamb
> as sharp as a tack   roar like a lion

A **metaphor** describes something as if it were something else. Here, *words* are being compared to *swords that cut through the silence*.

> His **words** were swords that cut through the silence.

Metaphors can be quite indirect. Here, *his heart* is being described as if it were something that could actually *break*, such as glass.

> His **heart** was broken.

A. Match the parts of the phrases to form common similes in English.

____ 1. You are as light as

____ 2. That horse can run like

____ 3. When I lost my diamond ring, I cried like

____ 4. You are as busy as

____ 5. His words cut me like

____ 6. Please be as quiet as

____ 7. The children were as good as

____ 8. My sister can swim like

a. a baby

b. a bee

c. a feather

d. a fish

e. a knife

f. a mouse

g. gold

h. the wind

B. Work with a partner. Explain what the underlined metaphors from Listening 1 and Listening 2 mean. What is the literal meaning of the words?

1. These are all the memories associated with who I had been, and when that person went <u>offline</u>, which is the best way for me to explain it, I lost all of her likes and dislikes.

2. You wake up one day and you're in <u>the heart</u> of China.

3. That <u>living</u> word awakened my soul.

4. There were barriers still, it is true, but barriers that could in time be <u>swept</u> away.

5. . . . words that were to make the world <u>blossom</u> for me.

C. Work with a partner. Describe one of the items or situations below in a short paragraph. Use your imagination and be colorful! Use similes and metaphors. Then read your description to the class.

My room is a disaster area. It looks like a tornado blew through, scattering my papers like leaves in an autumn wind. If you can wade through the piles of clothes near my bed, . . .

1. Your room or home
2. Your friend or someone you know
3. Learning a new language
4. Speaking in front of the class
5. Being a tourist in a foreign country
6. Listening to music

| Unit Assignment | Narrate a personal experience |

 In this section, you will narrate an experience involving language loss or an inability to communicate. As you prepare your narrative, think about the Unit Question, "How does language affect who we are?" and refer to the Self-Assessment checklist on page 50.

For alternative unit assignments, see the *Q: Skills for Success Teacher's Handbook*.

CONSIDER THE IDEAS

A. Maxine Hong Kingston, a Chinese-American writer, was born in the United States, but her parents spoke only Chinese at home. In her autobiographical novel, *The Woman Warrior*, she describes her discomfort speaking English after years of silence in American school and narrates a painful experience in Chinese school. Read this excerpt.

When I went to kindergarten and had to speak English for the first time, I became silent. A dumbness—a shame—still cracks my voice in two, even when I want to say "hello" casually, or ask an easy question in front of the check-out counter, or ask directions of a bus driver. I stand frozen, or I hold up the line with the complete, grammatical sentence that comes squeaking out at impossible length. "What did you say?" says the cab driver, or "Speak up," so I have to perform again, only weaker the second time. A telephone call makes my throat bleed and takes up that day's courage. . . .

Not all of the children who were silent at American school found voice at Chinese school. One new teacher said each of us had to get up and recite in front of the class, who was to listen. My sister and I had memorized the lesson perfectly. We said it to each other at home, one chanting, one listening. The teacher called on my sister to recite first. It was the first time a teacher had called on the second-born to go first. My sister was scared. She glanced at me and looked away; I looked down at my desk. I hoped that she could do it because if she could, then I wouldn't have to. She opened her mouth and a voice came out that wasn't a whisper, but it wasn't a proper voice either. I hoped that she would not cry, fear breaking up her voice like twigs underfoot. She sounded as if she were trying to sing though weeping and strangling. She did not pause or stop to end the embarrassment. She kept going until she said the last word, and then she sat down. When it was my turn, the same voice came out, a crippled animal running on broken legs. You could hear splinters in my voice, bones rubbing jagged against one another. I was loud, though. I was glad I didn't whisper.

B. Discuss these questions with a group.

1. How did Hong Kingston's communication difficulties affect her identity?

2. In what ways can you relate to Hong Kingston's story about language and silence?

3. Discuss the similes and metaphors she uses. Which ones affected you the most?

PREPARE AND SPEAK

A. GATHER IDEAS Work in a group. Follow these steps to gather ideas.

1. Brainstorm examples of stories about language-related difficulties that you can use as models or inspiration for your narrative.

2. Talk about the stories you have listened to and read in this unit and the examples your classmates have shared. What makes these stories compelling?

3. When you have chosen an idea, briefly describe it to your group. Ask your group where they think your story should begin and end. Should you use a humorous or a serious tone?

B. **ORGANIZE IDEAS** **Follow these steps to prepare your narrative.**

1. Use a time line like the one on page 39 to organize the main events and/ or emotional states in your story. Choose your starting and ending points. Make sure the emotions and events between are in chronological order.

2. Work with a partner. Practice narrating your stories to each other. Use your skills to make your story come alive.

   - metaphors and similes
   - positive and negative descriptive adjectives
   - emphasis on key words when speaking
   - hand gestures, body movements, and eye contact
   - an expressive tone of voice

C. **SPEAK** **Narrate your experience in groups or for the whole class. As you listen to your classmates, write down similes and metaphors that you especially liked. At the end of the activity, share these with the whole class. Refer to the Self-Assessment checklist below before you begin.**

CHECK AND REFLECT

A. **CHECK** **Think about the Unit Assignment as you complete the Self-Assessment checklist.**

SELF-ASSESSMENT		
Yes	No	
☐	☐	I was able to speak fluently about the topic.
☐	☐	My group and class understood me.
☐	☐	I used the correct negative prefixes for adjectives.
☐	☐	I used the active voice and the passive voice appropriately.
☐	☐	I used similes and metaphors to make my language more interesting.
☐	☐	I emphasized words in the correct places to express my meaning.

B. **REFLECT** **Discuss these questions with a partner.**

What is something new you learned in this unit?

 Look back at the Unit Question. Is your answer different now than when you started this unit? If yes, how is it different? Why?

Circle the words you learned in this unit.

Nouns
boundary
consciousness
fragment
function 🔑 AWL
incident
insight AWL
outburst
perception AWL
recovery 🔑 AWL
sentiment
structure 🔑 AWL

Verbs
gesticulate
imitate
persist AWL
regain
reveal 🔑 AWL

Adjectives
adequate 🔑 AWL
external AWL
fascinating
intense 🔑 AWL
invisible AWL

overall 🔑 AWL
tangible
tranquil

Adverbs
invariably AWL

🔑 Oxford 3000™ words
AWL Academic Word List

Check (✓) the skills you learned. If you need more work on a skill, refer to the page(s) in parentheses.

LISTENING	⚪	I can make inferences. (p. 35)
VOCABULARY	⚪	I can use negative prefixes. (p. 41)
GRAMMAR	⚪	I can use the passive voice. (p. 43)
PRONUNCIATION	⚪	I can use emphatic word stress. (p. 45)
SPEAKING	⚪	I can use figurative language. (p. 47)
LEARNING OUTCOME	⚪	I can develop a narrative incorporating figurative language that chronologically details an incident of language loss or an inability to communicate.

UNIT 3

Work and Fun

LISTENING ● listening for examples
VOCABULARY ● compound words
GRAMMAR ● comparative structures
PRONUNCIATION ● intonation with choices
SPEAKING ● discussing preferences and alternatives

Plan and present a school vacation in a way that will persuade your classmates to select it for their spring break alternative trip.

Unit QUESTION

Where can work, education, and fun overlap?

PREVIEW THE UNIT

Ⓐ Discuss these questions with your classmates.

What are some of the factors that you consider when planning a vacation?

Can you describe a time when work or school was fun?

Look at the photo. Do you think the man is doing work or having fun? Why?

Ⓑ Discuss the Unit Question above with your classmates.

Listen to *The Q Classroom*, Track 18 on CD 1, to hear other answers.

C Write the goals in the appropriate part of the Venn diagram. If you think a goal can suit education and work, write it in the center area where the circles overlap.

appreciate cultures	have fun	meet new people
~~discover new ideas~~	help society	pass tests
~~earn money~~	interact with others	play sports
~~get good grades~~	keep to a schedule	solve problems
get promoted	learn a language	think critically

Tip) Critical Thinking

In Activity C, you will complete a Venn diagram. **Diagramming** the relationships between ideas is one way of analyzing information.

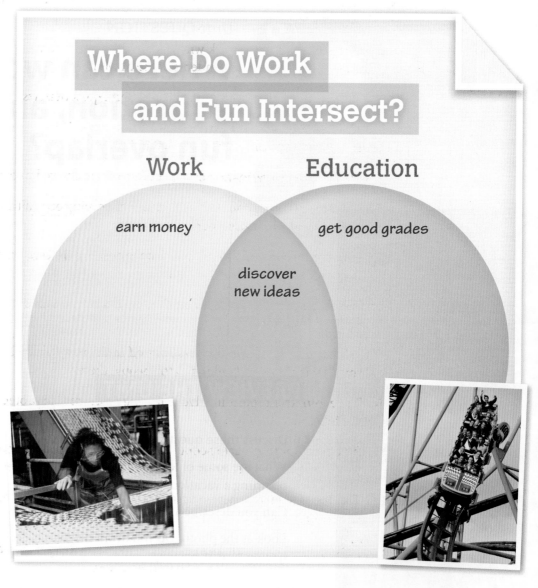

Where Do Work and Fun Intersect?

Work   Education

earn money   get good grades

discover new ideas

D In a group, compare your Venn diagrams. What does your diagram say about your attitudes toward education and work? Do you think work can be educational? Do you think education can be work?

LISTENING 1 | Voluntourism

VOCABULARY

Here are some words and phrases from Listening 1. Read the sentences. Then write each bold word or phrase next to the correct definition.

1. The senior citizens from Canada went on a cross-cultural **expedition** to explore Peru.

2. The group wanted to work with the **indigenous**, or native, people of Guatemala who are descendents of the Mayans.

3. The ads for cheap airfare, great weather, and quiet beaches were **enticing**.

4. This position calls for a wide **range** of work experience because it's a high-level position with a lot of responsibilities.

5. We will have to **validate** our visas before we are allowed in that country.

6. By learning more about the importance of keeping our culture, we work toward the **preservation** of our traditions.

7. Parents who want their children to be exposed to **diverse** groups travel to many different countries.

8. The **demographics** from the study show that 10 percent of the people there cannot read.

9. When I travel, I like to **immerse myself in** the new culture by eating at small restaurants and talking to the people there.

10. The **ecological** project involved planting more trees to protect the hillsides.

11. It's important to educate people about global issues. Seeing how other people live helps **raise awareness** of the need to protect other cultures.

12. The desire to learn a new language **prompted** me to go abroad to study for the first time.

a. _preserve_ (n.) the act of keeping something in its original state or in good condition

b. _validate_ (v.) to state officially that something is useful and of an acceptable standard

c. _immerse myself in_ (v.) to become completely involved in (something)

d. diverse _____ (adj.) very different from each other

e. expedition _____ (n.) an organized journey with a particular purpose

f. prompt _____ (v.) to make (somebody) decide to do (something)

g. demographics (n.) data relating to populations and groups of people

h. entice _____ (adj.) very attractive and interesting

i. range _____ (n.) a variety of things or experiences of a
particular type

j. indigenous _____ (adj.) belonging to a particular place, rather than
coming to it from someplace else; native

_____) to increase knowledge of or interest in (something)

_____ dj.) connected to the relation of plants and other
living creatures to each other and to their
environment

IG 1

You are going to listen to an interview titled "Voluntourism" from
the Amateur Traveler website. Linda Stuart talks with show host
Chris Christensen about the nonprofit organization Global Citizens
Network (GCN).

If a *volunteer* is someone who does work without pay, and *tourism* is
the business of travel, what do you think *voluntourism* is? Write your
own definition.

LISTEN FOR MAIN IDEAS

CD 1
Track 19
Listen to the interview and answer the questions. Compare answers with
a partner.

1. According to Stuart, what is the overall purpose of Global Citizens Network?

Tip for Success

Remember that in abbreviations such as GCN and UN, each letter is pronounced separately, with stress on the final letter. In acronyms, letters are pronounced together as a word, such as TOEFL and UNICEF.

2. Some people might believe that volunteer vacations are just for wealthy people, young men, or bilingual people. What would Stuart say in response?

- Women make up most of volunteers, average age is 30-35, people go to meet people + learn new lang.

3. What effects do volunteer vacations have on both the travelers and the countries they visit?

Travelers get to contribute to society while experiencing new cultures 'Countries get aid in completing projects, education + special programs.

LISTEN FOR DETAILS

CD 1
Track 20

Fill in this Web page for Global Citizens Network with the information you remember. Then listen again and complete it. Compare your answers with a partner.

gcn

Serving the volunteer tourist for over __16__ years.
                                      1

Essential information:

Average age range __30__ to __55__   Average group size __4__ to __12__
                  2   3   6   7

Trip length __1__ to __3__ weeks   Fees range from $__900__ to $__2400__.
            4   5   8   9

Some of our projects include:

working on __Construction__ of a health center
            10

teaching __English__,
          11

helping indigenous groups preserve their __culture__.
                                          12

Volunteers get to:

practice __new language__, try new __foods__, learn weaving and other new skills.
          13   14

We have programs around the world in urban and __rural__ areas in
                                                 15

Mexico, Ecuador, __Africa__, and __Asia__. canada
                  16   17
                                        (or Peru, Guatemala, Tanzania, Nepal, Thailand)

WHAT DO YOU THINK?

Discuss the questions in a group.

Slide #9.

✗ 1. Linda Stuart says that one of the benefits of voluntourism is that it's an "eye-opening experience" and it helps people see that it's "not us versus them, but it's us all together." What does she mean by that? Do you agree?

2. In what ways has this interview been successful or unsuccessful in motivating you to take a volunteer vacation?

✗ 3. Think of a place in the world that could benefit from the contributions of volunteer tourists. What kind of work could people do there? How could it be fun?

Listening Skill | **Listening for examples**

In an interview, a lecture, or a report, a speaker often provides examples so the listener can understand key concepts better. Active listeners can use different strategies to notice examples.

- Listen for phrases that introduce examples: *for example, take for instance, for instance, as an example, let me give you an example, including,* and *such as.*
- Notice rising intonation that signals items in a list. A speaker who is listing examples will use rising intonation for each item in a list except for the last one. The rising intonation works like a comma to let the listener know the speaker is not finished.

 CD 1
Track 21

Listen to this example. Notice how the speaker identifies the main point and then lists examples. Pay attention to the speaker's rising intonation.

> There is a wide range of opportunities. Others include individual placement; some are in rural areas versus urban areas; others may be more of a tutoring or English teaching placements. . .

One way to take notes involving examples or other details is to write the main point on the left and examples on the right.

Main point	Examples
	individual placement
Range of volunteer opportunities	rural vs. urban
	tutoring or English teaching

A. Listen to the excerpts. Complete the chart with two examples of each main point.

Main point	Examples
1. Small-scale development projects	
2. Motivating reasons	
3. Countries GCN works in	

B. Take turns asking and answering questions with a partner about the Amateur Traveler interview.

1. What are some reasons people do voluntourism?

2. What types of people take these trips?

3. What kinds of projects do GCN volunteers work on?

4. What countries does GCN operate in?

LISTENING 2 | Science Fairs and Nature Reserves

VOCABULARY

Here are some words from Listening 2. Read the sentences. Circle the answer that best matches the meaning of each bold word.

1. The **outreach** programs bring science to rural areas so children there have equal opportunities to learn about chemistry and physics.
   a. the activity of providing a service to underprivileged people in a community
   b. designed to be not only educational but also entertaining and motivating

2. The **atmosphere** in the classroom was so energized and motivating that students didn't mind working very hard.
   a. a mood or feeling in a particular location
   b. the mixture of gases that surrounds the Earth

3. If it is a hands-on, **interactive** show, students are motivated to participate in the demonstrations.

    a. involving several performers at the same time

    b. involving both performers and audience members

4. When we visit a science **exhibit** related to elasticity, we expect to see a demonstration on how an object can stretch and bend.

    a. a written report

    b. a show or display

5. We need to choose a new **site** for that research project because the current building is too far away from our labs.

    a. a place or location

    b. a plan or idea

6. Because of the old building's historical value, the city decided to **restore** it and bring it back to life.

    a. repair; return to its original condition

    b. replace with something better

7. Schools that are famous for research such as Oxford University and the University of California **pioneer** ideas and often discover ways to cure diseases and solve problems.

    a. travel to new areas

    b. be the first to do or try something

8. The **coordinator** of the program was responsible for bringing workers together while developing that project.

    a. a person who manages

    b. a person who investigates or inspects

9. With all of the **resources** available in the library, students can find enough information for their reports.

    a. raw materials such as wood or metal

    b. things that can be used to help achieve a goal

10. The **collaboration** between environmental organizations and governments is extremely important for the success of ecological programs.

    a. the act of working together

    b. the act of working independently or separately

11. When the result of an experiment has an **impact** on science, it influences scientific ideas and may change our perspectives.

    a. a collision or accident with somebody or something

    b. a powerful effect of something on something else

12. Since we are new to the campus, we need to **familiarize** ourselves with the labs before we do any experiments.
   a. get acquainted with conditions
   b. begin a close relationship with somebody

(handwritten notes: vocab before listening; staid (N) - not interesting; squelch (V) - to make a wet, sucking sound; innovative (adj) - intro new ideas for doing something; microorganism (N) - small living thing seen w/ microscope; docent (N) - person who shows tourists a/round museum or other places; county (N) - area in US that has its own gov't; anatomy (N) - scientific study of structure of human or animal bodies; generate (V) - to produce or create something; botany - (N) scientific study of plants & their structure; K through 12 - kindergarten; grade 13)

PREVIEW LISTENING 2

Science Fairs and Nature Reserves

The Sedgwick Reserve

You are going to listen to two reports from universities, "The Cambridge Science Festival," about a science fair in England, and "The Sedgwick Reserve," about protected lands in California. They present different experiences that have been developed to engage students in science.

In your notebook, write five information questions (questions using *wh-* words) about things you would like to know about these programs.

LISTEN FOR MAIN IDEAS

CD 1
Track 23

A. Listen to the university reports. Use this T-chart and the T-chart on page 62 to take notes about the goals and outcomes of each science event as you listen.

Science Festival

Goals	Outcomes

a science fair

Sedgwick Reserve

Goals	Outcomes

B. Use your notes from the T-charts in Activity A to answer these questions.

1. The science festival at Cambridge and the nature programs at the Sedgwick Reserve have two specific goals for students beyond just making science fun. What are they?

   ① To relate to the real world

   ② To make more students interested in becoming scientist

2. What are three or four of the ways mentioned by the speakers that help their programs accomplish these goals?

   ① experiments are fun but also serious

   ② cause kids to think about science in everyday life

   ③ break barriers between scientist, researchest

   ④ students realize they can become scientist

3. What does *public outreach* mean, and why is it important to these universities?

   means bridging gap between the university & public.

LISTEN FOR DETAILS

Place these details about the science programs in the correct circles in the Venn diagram. (You can use the letters to save space.) If a detail describes both programs, write it in the overlapping area. Then listen again and correct any information.

a. botany and biology	g. open to the public
b. in school buildings	h. week-long event
c. students from all grades	i. over 45,000 visitors
d. geology and engineering	j. praised by teachers
e. inspires interest in science	k. year-long experience
f. interactive activities	

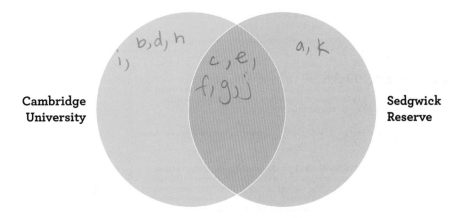

Cambridge University

i, b, d, h

c, e, f, g, j

a, k

Sedgwick Reserve

WHAT DO YOU THINK?

A. Discuss the questions in a group.

1. Which of the two science programs would you most enjoy participating in? Why?

2. What should teachers be more concerned about: whether students are interested and excited about what they need to learn or whether they are learning as much information as possible about the subject?

B. Think about both Listening 1 and Listening 2 as you discuss the question.

How might going abroad to study or testing video games for a software company be considered areas where work, education, and fun overlap? Can you think of other examples?

Compounds are made up of two or more words, usually a combination of nouns, adjectives, and verbs. The most common compounds are nouns (*nature reserve*), but there are also compound adjectives (*short-term*) and verbs (*underline*).

Over time, compounds tend to become written as single words (*classroom*). Sometimes the words are hyphenated (*short-term*), and sometimes the words remain separate (*high school*) although they are considered one-word units.

Compound words are listed as separate entries in the dictionary. Since there are no strict rules for how compounds are written, it is important to check a dictionary to see if a compound is written as one word, as two words, or with a hyphen.

---

class·room /ˈklæsrum; -rʊm/ *noun*
a room where a class of children or students is taught: *classroom activities* ◆ *the use of computers in the classroom*

ˈhigh school *noun* [C, U]
a school for young people between the ages of 14 and 18
⊃ collocations at EDUCATION ⊃ see also JUNIOR HIGH SCHOOL, SENIOR HIGH SCHOOL

ˌshort-ˈterm *adj.* **1** [usually before noun] lasting a short time; designed only for a short period of time in the future: *a short-term loan* ◆ *to find work on a short-term contract* ◆ *short-term plans* ◆ *a short-term solution to the problem* ◆ *His short-term memory* (= the ability to remember things that happened a short time ago) *is failing.* ⊃ compare LONG-TERM **2** [only before noun] (of a place) where you only stay for a short time: *a short-term parking garage* ◆ *short-term patients* (= who only stay in a hospital for a short time)

Compounds are content words, so they are stressed in a sentence. Within the compound itself, there is usually a strong stress on the first word and a lighter stress on the second (*WOODlands, HOMEwork*). If the first word has more than one syllable, the stress is the same as it is in the word by itself (*DAta, DAtabase*).

All dictionary entries are from the *Oxford Advanced American Dictionary for learners of English* © Oxford University Press 2011.

A. Write the words in the right column on the correct lines.

1. computer _____   boomer

2. baby _____   reach

3. eye _____   cultural

4. out _____   ground

5. net _____   sight

6. grass _____   opening

7. senior _____   game

8. cross _____   lands

9. over _____   citizen

10. testing _____   working

B. Work with a partner. Take turns reading the compound words in Activity A aloud. Listen for your partner's stress on the first word. Check a dictionary to find out if the compounds are written as one word (with or without a hyphen) or two.

C. Complete these sentences with compounds from Activity A.

1. Realizing how much fun science can be is a(n)

   _____ experience for many teenagers.

2. Students walked through the _____ while they

   were at the Sedgwick Reserve.

3. GCN specializes in _____ for those who want to

   meet indigenous groups while traveling.

4. A small community is often the _____ for new

   ideas that later spread to larger cities if they are successful.

5. The _____ center on campus provides a place for

   students from diverse communities to meet.

6. An American born right after World War II, between 1946 and 1964,

   is called a(n) _____.

SPEAKING

When discussing similarities and differences, comparative structures can be used with various word forms.

Word form	Comparison	Negative comparison	Intensified comparison	Comparison of equality
Adjective	clearer than more enticing than	less aware	much clearer than much less aware than	as enticing as
Adverb	faster than more slowly than	less slowly than	much faster than much more/less slowly than	as fast as as slowly as
Noun	more exhibits than more time than	fewer exhibits than less time than	many more/fewer exhibits than much less time than	as many exhibits as as much time as
Verb	travels more than	travels less than	travels much more/less than	travels as much as

Tip for Success

Even native speakers sometimes get confused when using pronouns with comparisons. Is it correct to say *Jane is taller than me* or *Jane is taller than I*? To find the answer, complete the sentence in your head: *Jane is taller than I am.* Therefore, the correct comparison is *Jane is taller than I.*

Remember when making comparisons that you must compare parallel elements.

✓ The trip to China had more stops than the trip to India.
      noun phrase   noun phrase

✗ The trip to China had more stops than India.
      noun phrase   noun

Repetition of elements in a comparison can be avoided in two ways:

1. Using a synonym of the element compared

   The Cambridge science demonstrations covered more fields than **the Stanford exhibits**.

2. Using pronouns (*this, that, these, those, the one, the ones, mine, yours, his, hers, ours, theirs, other,* and *others*)

   The meals we ate in Thailand were better than **those in England**.

A. Circle the correct answers to complete these comparative sentences. Avoid repetition in the comparative.

1. My father has traveled less than (I / me).

2. I don't like these travel options as much as (them / those).

3. The Cambridge program is shorter than the (Sedgwick one / Sedgwick program).

4. Jose's science project is more interactive than (Tim / Tim's).

5. The flight to Dubai was twice as long as (the flight to Frankfurt / Frankfurt).

6. Volunteer vacations usually cost less money than (regular trips / regular vacations).

7. Your method for solving that problem takes more time than (me / my way).

8. An expedition to China is more enticing than (England / a term in England).

Tip for Success

When making a comparison, make sure to stress the comparative words and phrases. *PHY-sics is MORE IN-ter-est-ing than CHEM-is-try.*

B. Work with a partner. Take turns reading the sentences below and then restating the comparison using a comparative structure from the Grammar Box.

1. The trip to Peru costs $5,000. The trip to Bolivia costs $5,000.

   A: *The trip to Peru costs $5,000 and the trip to Bolivia costs $5,000.*
   B: *The trip to Peru costs as much as the trip to Bolivia.*

2. A science fair sounds good. A nature expedition sounds exciting.

3. The bus trip is ten hours long. The train ride is five hours long.

4. The grasslands stretch for 50 miles. The woodlands cover 25 miles.

5. GCN needs 50 volunteers. Earthwatch needs 50 volunteers.

6. The wagon moves slowly, at five miles per hour. The tractor moves slowly, at ten miles per hour.

Choice Statemen...

When a list of cho... ...ts on the stressed syllable of each ch... ...ds with a rise-fall intonation that si... ...xample.

CD 1 Track 25

☐ With GCN, we can take an exp... ..., or Argentina.

If the last item ends in a stressed syllable, glide up and down on that word. Listen to this example.

CD 1 Track 25

☐ They need to find out if that institute is in China or Japan.

Choice Questions

Questions that offer the listener two or more possible choices (or answers) have rising intonation starting with the stressed syllable in the first choice, a drop in pitch on *or*, and a rise and then a low fall (or a glide up and down) on the last choice. Listen to these examples.

CD 1 Track 25

Did they visit Cambodia, Vietnam, or Thailand?

Is it a science fair or a science camp?

If the choice question is an information question, the *wh-* clause ends with rise-fall intonation. The pitch rises on each choice, falls on *or*, and ends with a rise-fall or a glide-fall on the last choice. Listen to these examples.

CD 1 Track 25

What did they build in Mexico, schools or houses?

Where are the exhibits, in the school, at the beach, or in the park?

CD 1
Track 26

A. Work with a partner. Mark the intonation in these sentences and take turns reading them. Then listen and check your answers. Correct any sentences whose stress you didn't mark correctly.

Tip for Success

Remember, the answer to a choice question is not *Yes* or *No*; the answer should be one of the choices.

1. Who paid for the travel expenses, the students or the school?

2. Would you choose to initiate a new project or work on an old one?

3. I'm not sure if I prefer Cambridge, Oxford, Harvard, or Stanford.

4. Which adjective is best: *compelling, liberating,* or *enticing*?

5. You have your choice of staying in a tent, a home, or a hotel.

6. Can everyone go on a volunteer vacation, including children, teens, and adults?

B. Complete the questions. Give two choices for three of the questions and more than two choices for three of the questions. Then ask and answer the questions with a partner. Pay attention to your intonation patterns.

1. Where would you like to travel, _____

   _____ ?

2. What kind of ethnic food would you like to try, *spicy or mild* _____

   _____ ?

3. How long does it take to fly to Egypt, _____

   _____ ?

4. Which activities are both fun and educational, *excursions in*

   nature or trips to historical sites ?

5. What kind of outdoor places do you like to explore, _____

   _____ ?

6. Who is the best coordinator for a trip to _____, _____

   _____ ?

In a meeting or a planning session, discussion often involves expressing preferences and offering alternatives. Additionally, you might need to investigate people's past preferences to help make choices about future actions.

Here are some common expressions for talking about preferences and alternatives.

To talk about past preferences	To talk about current preferences
prefer + noun or noun phrase Students **preferred** the expedition to China.	*preference* + *is* + infinitive **My preference is to attend** a science fair.
choose + infinitive Students **chose to visit** indigenous people.	*would rather (not)* + verb I**'d rather do** something that helps society.
first/second choice + *be* My **first choice was** to visit a nature reserve.	*If it were up to me,* . . . **If it were up to me,** we'd do an ecological study.
had hoped + infinitive I **had hoped to spend** the summer volunteering in Africa.	*I like . . . more than . . .* **I like** studying in my dorm **more than** in the lab.
	I'd like + verb **I'd like to explore** the idea of working abroad.

A. With a partner, take turns asking and answering these questions about the Listening texts. Use expressions for preferences and choices in your answers. Pay attention to your intonation in any choice questions.

1. Does Linda Stuart prefer the volunteering or the tourist side of voluntourism?

   A: Does Linda Stuart prefer the volunteering or the tourist side of voluntourism?
   B: Stuart would rather be a volunteer than a tourist.

2. Does Stuart's organization choose to take large or small groups of travelers?

3. If it were up to the speaker from Cambridge, would the science fair there have many more participants?

4. What does the professor at UC Santa Barbara hope to show the young students, especially girls?

5. Do you think the students in the Kids in Nature program would rather learn about plants in the classroom or at the nature reserve?

6. Do you think the children who go to the science fair will choose to become scientists and study at Cambridge?

7. Could you tell if the director's preference would be to have more visitors to the reserve?

B. Work in groups of three. Create a short role-play to present to the class. Student A is a travel agent. Students B and C want to take a trip. Student A asks B and C about their travel preferences—destination, length of trip, activities, etc. Use as many different structures as you can.

A: Would you prefer to take a relaxing vacation or go on a learning expedition?

B: My preference is a relaxing vacation.

C: Hmm. I'd like to explore the possibility of an expedition to Africa!

Unit Assignment | Plan and present a school trip

 In this section, you will work with a group to plan a fun and meaningful vacation that you will try to convince your classmates to join. As you prepare your presentation, think about the Unit Question, "Where can work, education, and fun overlap?" and refer to the Self-Assessment checklist on page 74.

For alternative unit assignments, see the *Q: Skills for Success Teacher's Handbook*.

CONSIDER THE IDEAS

A. Read these two end-of-program evaluations from two people who went on a school trip to Baja, California, to study the marine and desert environments.

1.

The trip started out great. I really liked the scenery. Unfortunately, I hurt my back the second day when we spent the whole day setting up tents and digging trenches. I would have preferred more help from the teachers with that work. Then I got a bad sunburn from looking for research specimens in the desert all day, and that evening I got more mosquito bites than I have ever gotten in my life before. Next time, I would prefer to camp somewhere without mosquitoes.

I thought the project was interesting, certainly more interesting than regular classroom study, but we weren't able to collect as many specimens as we needed for our research, so we couldn't finish our project. That was pretty disappointing. Oh, and the food was worse than the school cafeteria's.

2.

This school trip was better than any other school trip I have ever taken. We worked hard (maybe harder than I have ever worked before!), saw some amazing sights, and learned a lot. I prefer this kind of hands-on learning to just reading textbooks. I think I learn better when I actually do something myself.

The only thing I didn't like about the trip was some of the other students. I think they just didn't want to be there. I'd rather do this kind of expedition with people who are as motivated as I am. Maybe you should charge more money for the trip, and then only people who really want to be there will come.

B. Compare the two experiences of hands-on vacations revealed here. What did the two participants like and not like?

C. Which do you think plays a bigger role in how much someone enjoys a trip such as this one: the person's attitude or what he or she actually experiences on the trip?

PREPARE AND SPEAK

A. GATHER IDEAS An organization has requested your help in planning a five-day alternative vacation for students over spring break. They want the vacation to be meaningful and educational, but also fun. The organization has received funding for a large group, so money does not have to be considered.

1. In a group, brainstorm trip ideas by asking one another questions. Find out preferences and make comparisons. Make notes of your ideas.

   Would you prefer to work on a science project or do volunteer work?
   Which type of trip do you think would be more fun?

2. Look at your list of ideas and choose one trip to present to the class.

B. **ORGANIZE IDEAS** Follow these steps to prepare your presentation.

1. As a group, complete the chart below with details about your trip.

Alternative Spring Break	
Plan	
Location	
Purpose of program	
Opportunities for fun, learning, work	
Benefits	
Travel details	

2. Choose one person in the group to present each different part of the trip plan. One person should add a summary comment about why the class should vote for your trip.

C. **SPEAK** Practice your parts of the presentation individually and then together as a group. Then present your alternative spring-break plan as a group to the class. Refer to the Self-Assessment checklist on page 74 before you begin.

D. After you listen to all of the class presentations, vote on which trip to take. You can vote for your own trip, but you don't have to. Your teacher may call on volunteers to explain why they chose the trip they did.

I thought the trip to Antarctica was more exotic than any of the others.

CHECK AND REFLECT

A. **CHECK** Think about the Unit Assignment as you complete the Self-Assessment checklist.

Yes	No	SELF-ASSESSMENT
☐	☐	I was able to speak fluently about the topic.
☐	☐	My group and the class understood me.
☐	☐	I used comparative structures correctly.
☐	☐	I used vocabulary from the unit to express my ideas.
☐	☐	I used correct intonation to question and list choices.
☐	☐	I discussed preferences and alternatives.

B. **REFLECT** Discuss these questions with a partner.

What is something new you learned in this unit?

 Look back at the Unit Question. Is your answer different now than when you started this unit? If yes, how is it different? Why?

Circle the words and phrases you learned in this unit.

Nouns
atmosphere 🔑
baby boomer
collaboration
concept 🔑 AWL
coordinator AWL
database
demographics
exhibit 🔑 AWL
expedition
grasslands
high school 🔑
homework 🔑
impact 🔑 AWL
nature reserve
network 🔑 AWL

outreach
oversight
preservation
range 🔑 AWL
resource 🔑 AWL
site 🔑 AWL
testing ground
woodlands

Verbs
familiarize
pioneer
prompt 🔑
restore 🔑 AWL
underline
validate AWL

Adjectives
cross-cultural
diverse AWL
ecological
enticing
eye-opening
hands-on
indigenous
interactive AWL
short-term

Phrases
immerse oneself in
raise awareness

🔑 Oxford 3000™ words
AWL Academic Word List

Check (✓) the skills you learned. If you need more work on a skill, refer to the page(s) in parentheses.

LISTENING	●	I can listen for examples. (p. 58)
VOCABULARY	●	I can use compound words. (p. 64)
GRAMMAR	●	I can use comparative structures. (p. 66)
PRONUNCIATION	●	I can use intonation with choices. (p. 68)
SPEAKING	●	I can discuss preferences and alternatives. (p. 70)
LEARNING OUTCOME	●	I can plan and present a school vacation in a way that will persuade my classmates to select it for their spring break alternative trip.

LISTENING	●	recognizing appositives that explain
VOCABULARY	●	word forms and suffixes
GRAMMAR	●	relative clauses
PRONUNCIATION	●	stress shifts with suffixes
SPEAKING	●	clarifying information

Unit QUESTION

How can the eyes deceive the mind?

PREVIEW THE UNIT

A **Discuss these questions with your classmates.**

Have your eyes ever "played tricks" on you, causing you
to see something that wasn't there or not see something
that was?

Look at the photo. This photo is of a real city that has been
made to look like a toy city. Can you think of other things
that are not what they seem?

B **Discuss the Unit Question above with your classmates.**

◔)) Listen to *The Q Classroom*, Track 2 on CD 2, to hear other answers.

C Look at these examples of visual deception by animals. With a partner, discuss their purpose.

Arctic fox

Eastern screech-owl

Brimstone butterfly

D Look at these examples of visual deception that people use. Check (✓) the ones that you have tried yourself. Can you think of other examples?

☐ a costume

☐ a mask

☐ dark glasses

☐ a wig

☐ hair coloring

☐ high-heeled or elevated shoes

☐ make-up

☐ plastic surgery

☐ tight or restrictive clothing

☐ whitened teeth

E In a group, discuss these questions.

1. In what ways are the examples of animal deception similar to those that people use? In what ways are they different?

2. Look at the examples of human deception in Activity D. What are some reasons that people use them?

3. Give an example of one type of deception in Activity D that you have used yourself. Why did you use it? Do you think that other people were truly deceived? Why or why not?

LISTENING 1 | Wild Survivors

VOCABULARY

Here are some words from Listening 1. Read the paragraphs. Then write each bold word next to the correct definition.

Animals and plants are in a constant battle for **survival** as they compete for limited resources against other living things. Those animals and species that can **adapt** to the challenges of their environment will survive. Those that are not capable of adapting will not live. Different animals use different ways of coping in their environment. For example, animals that are **predators** learn how to hunt in ways that allow them to surprise their **prey**. The prey, in turn, sometimes use **camouflage**, such as changing color to protect themselves.

1. _____ (n.) an animal that kills and eats other animals

2. _____ (n.) the way in which an animal's color or shape matches its surroundings and makes it difficult to see

3. _____ (n.) the state of continuing to exist

4. _____ (n.) an animal that is hunted, killed, and eaten by another

5. _____ (v.) to change in order to be more suitable for a new situation

In addition to using color for camouflage, some animals naturally **resemble** the shape of a rock or a leaf, so they can hide very well in their environment. Some birds can **mimic** other birds and so defend their nests from predators by copying the song of a stronger or more dangerous bird. Disguises like these allow many animals to **mature**, safe from predators until they are old enough to defend themselves.

6. _____ (v.) to copy the behavior of someone or something

7. _____ (v.) to be or look like something or someone else

8. _____ (v.) to become fully grown or developed

There's an almost **infinite** variety of living things on the planet, so scientists are constantly discovering new examples of animals using these tricks to survive. Some are **obvious**, and some are harder to see. However, what is clear is that **virtually** every species has developed a clever and **elaborate** system to protect itself and ensure its survival.

9. _____ *(adj.)* complicated; done or planned carefully

10. _____ *(adv.)* almost or nearly

11. _____ *(adj.)* easily seen or understood; clear

12. _____ *(adj.)* without end or limits

PREVIEW LISTENING 1

Wild Survivors

You are going to listen to an excerpt from a documentary television show, *Wild Survivors*, that explores some ways in which animals use a certain type of deception, camouflage, in order to survive.

Work with a partner. How do you think these animals use camouflage? What type of environment or background are they trying to match?

caterpillar

flounder

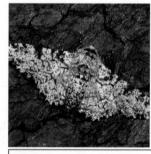
moth

 Tip for Success

Taking notes in a graphic organizer such as a table or chart can help you collect and organize information as you listen to a lecture.

praying mantis

ptarmigan

snake

LISTEN FOR MAIN IDEAS

CD 2
Track 3

Listen to the documentary. As you listen, complete the chart on how animals use camouflage.

Animal	Type of camouflage	How it works
1. Ptarmigan		• Matches the color of its environment; also keeps it warm • Only protection for young ones
2.	Body color, shape, and movement	• Changes depending on what it eats • Looks like flowers in spring or like twigs in summer • Keeps it safe from birds
3. Praying mantis		
4.	Body color	
5.		

LISTEN FOR DETAILS

CD 2
Track 4

Listen again. Circle the answer that best completes each statement.

1. The ptarmigan lives in Europe and (North America / Asia).

2. In the winter, the ptarmigan grows long white feathers on its (feet / back).

3. Camouflage is the (best / only) defense for the ptarmigan in the Pacific Northwest.

4. The moth lays its eggs (between two leaves / under leaves).

5. The caterpillars mimic the (movement / scent) of the oak tree flowers.

6. The caterpillars use camouflage to avoid being eaten by (rats / birds).

7. The praying mantis's body can look just like a (predator / flower).

8. The (lizard / spider) is prey for the desert snake.

9. When it hides, only the (tail / eyes) of the flounder can be seen.

10. Animals pass on successful appearances and (behaviors / intelligence) to future generations.

 WHAT DO YOU THINK?

Discuss the questions in a group.

1. Listening 1 mainly describes how animals use camouflage to hide from predators. In what ways do you think predators can use camouflage to their advantage?

2. In what ways can people camouflage themselves to blend in with their environment (for example, a group of other people)? What are some advantages to looking like other people? What are some disadvantages?

3. For what reasons might a person want to stand out in his or her environment, or look different from other people?

| Listening Skill | Recognizing appositives that explain | |

An **appositive** is a phrase that gives additional information in a sentence. Grammatically, an appositive is extra; you could remove it and still have a complete sentence. Functionally, an appositive often serves to provide a definition or explanation of the word or idea just before. Scientific or specialized terms are commonly defined by appositives with *or*.

In writing, appositives are set off by commas. In speaking, appositives are marked by intonation. Listen to these sentences and note the intonation of the appositives.

CD 2
Track 5

The chameleon, *a type of lizard*, changes its skin color to match its background.

The animal most famous for its ability to camouflage itself is the chameleon, *a type of lizard*.

Chameleons are oviparous, *or egg-laying*, animals.

Listen to these excerpts from *Wild Survivors*. Match the appositives with the words or ideas they explain. There are three extra appositives.

CD 2
Track 6

____ 1. conditions that change

____ 2. ptarmigan

____ 3. camouflage

____ 4. summer outfit

____ 5. Caribbean flounder

a. a bird about the size of a pigeon that lives in Europe and North America

b. a fish whose flat body is the color of the ocean floor

c. a bird that preys on moths

d. speckled grey and brown feathers

e. a sea creature from the Atlantic Ocean

f. availability of food and water, temperatures, the presence of predators both animal and human

g. a disguise that helps the ptarmigan hide from predators by matching the color of its environment

h. rocks, moss, and wildflowers

LISTENING 2 | Magic and the Mind

VOCABULARY

Here are some words and phrases from Listening 2. Read the sentences. Circle the answer that best matches the meaning of each bold word or phrase.

Tip for Success

When learning new words, make a note of the prepositions that go with them. For example, you *notice a link <u>between</u> two events* and *manipulate someone <u>into</u> doing something*.

1. Teachers must be aware of children's level of emotional maturity as well as their **cognitive** abilities in order to select appropriate material for classroom use.
    a. mental
    b. physical

2. You thought you saw the car hit the bus. However, that was just your **perception**. In reality, the accident was the fault of the bus.
    a. what you believe based on what you think you noticed
    b. what you think based on what others say

3. I don't believe in the **supernatural**. I'm sure there's a scientific explanation for what happened.
    a. magical events, forces, or powers
    b. caused by plants or animals

4. After watching a new trick, magicians cannot really **utilize** it in a show until they practice it many times.
   a. learn
   b. use

5. The magician was able to **manipulate** the audience volunteers into choosing the cards he wanted them to without their even realizing it.
   a. threaten or force someone to take a particular action
   b. control or influence someone in a skillful way

6. Scientists will sometimes study a **phenomenon** in nature to learn how animals use deception.
   a. an action that can be imitated by humans
   b. an event that is sometimes not clearly understood

7. Do you think there is a **link** between the study you read and the experiment you are planning to do?
   a. space; separation
   b. connection

8. A good magician knows how to **tap into** the audience's desire to be entertained.
   a. access a power or attitude that already exists
   b. stop or prevent something from happening

9. People traveling in deserts sometimes think they see a pool of water in the distance that isn't really there. This is an **illusion** created by the intense heat.
   a. a visual trick
   b. a strong wish

10. It's dangerous to use a cell phone while driving because it can **distract** you, and you might not notice other cars or people in the road.
    a. remind; help you recall information
    b. take your attention away from something

11. You can't really say that one painting is definitely better than another because opinions about art are very **subjective**.
    a. personally biased
    b. carefully researched

12. I've watched that magician's trick about a dozen times, but I just can't **work out** how he does it.
    a. believe
    b. solve

PREVIEW LISTENING 2

Magic and the Mind

Scientists are studying magic shows to see what magicians can teach them about perception. You are going to listen to an interview with Dr. Gustav Kuhn, a research fellow at Durham University in England. Marco Werman talks with Dr. Kuhn about "The Science of Magic" for PRI Radio's program *The World*.

Check (✓) the topics you think will be discussed in the interview.

☐ psychology   ☐ intelligence

☐ biology   ☐ optical illusions

☐ visual perception   ☐ camouflage

☐ supernatural powers

LISTEN FOR MAIN IDEAS

CD 2
Track 7

Dr. Kuhn talks about three techniques that magicians use. Listen to the interview and take notes about each technique. Then explain them in your own words to a partner.

Tip for Success

Discourse markers help speakers gain time to think and allow listeners to show they are following a discussion, acknowledge an idea, or hedge while thinking of a response. Some common discourse markers in Listening 2 are *right*, *so*, *uh*, *I mean*, and *well*.

1. misdirection

_____

_____

_____

2. illusions

_____

_____

_____

3. forcing

_____

_____

_____

LISTEN FOR DETAILS

Read these questions. Then listen again. Circle the correct answers.

1. Why are scientists in Britain and Canada interested in magic?
   a. They believe they could help magicians be more effective with their tricks.
   b. They think they can learn more about perception from magicians.
   c. They want to make science more entertaining.

2. What is Dr. Kuhn's profession?
   a. a magician
   b. a psychologist
   c. a psychologist and a magician

3. What does Dr. Kuhn say about the age of magic as an art form?
   a. It is quite old.
   b. It is relatively recent.
   c. Some forms are old, but the best tricks are modern ones.

4. What does Dr. Kuhn mean by the "science of magic"?
   a. explaining the history of magic
   b. using science to explain magic to an audience
   c. discovering scientific explanations for why magic tricks work

5. What does Dr. Kuhn say about misdirection?
   a. Scientists use it more often than magicians.
   b. Magicians have been aware of it longer than scientists have.
   c. Scientists are not interested in misdirection.

6. What word or phrase would Dr. Kuhn *not* use to describe perception?
   a. easily manipulated
   b. scientific
   c. subjective

7. How does Dr. Kuhn feel about keeping magician's secrets and techniques?

    a. As a magician, he is against sharing secrets and techniques with scientists.

    b. Even when people know the techniques, they can still be fooled by magicians.

    c. The study of the science of magic is not really concerned with the secrets and techniques.

8. Which statement summarizes Dr. Kuhn's ideas about perception?

    a. People cannot perceive events that haven't taken place.

    b. People's perceptions are based on what they actually see.

    c. People can be prevented from perceiving certain things.

WHAT DO YOU THINK?

A. Discuss the questions in a group.

1. How would Dr. Kuhn respond to the question "How can the eyes deceive the mind?"

2. Do you think Dr. Kuhn the psychologist is more interested in learning how magic works, or is Dr. Kuhn the magician more interested in understanding how psychology works? Explain your reasons.

 **Critical Thinking**

The questions in Activity B ask you to **extend** the information you have learned to apply to a new situation.

B. Think about both Listening 1 and Listening 2 as you discuss the questions.

1. In what ways do the ideas of misdirection and the expectations of the audience in a magic trick apply to camouflage and mimicry in nature?

2. How do people sometimes use deception for entertainment, to avoid unpleasant situations, or to cover up mistakes?

A **suffix** is a group of letters at the end of a word. A suffix can show the part of speech of a word. For example, *-ary* often signals an adjective, and *-tion* indicates a noun. Sometimes when you add a suffix, there are spelling changes to the original word root. For example, when you add a suffix to a word ending in silent *-e*, you usually delete the *-e*.

Children **imagine** all sorts of wonderful stories.
verb

He believed in lots of **imaginary** creatures.
adjective

He had a very vivid **imagination**.
noun

Learning related forms of words helps build your vocabulary. When you learn one new word, you can also learn its related forms. It can also help you understand unfamiliar words. When you see a word that is related to a word you know, you can sometimes guess its meaning.

Here are some common suffixes that indicate nouns, verbs, adjectives, and adverbs.

Suffixes that show . . .			
Nouns	**Verbs**	**Adjectives**	**Adverbs**
-ance/ence	-ate	-able/ible	-ly
-tion	-ify	-al/ical	-ward
-ee	-ize	-ary/ory	
-er/or		-ent/ant	
-ian		-ese	
-ism		-ful	
-(i)ty		-ive	
-ment		-less	
-ology		-ous	

A. Work with a partner. Complete the chart with correct word forms. Sometimes there is more than one noun or adjective form. Write *X* if there is no related word form. Check a dictionary to make sure your word forms are correct.

	Noun	Verb	Adjective	Adverb
1.	imagination	imagine	imaginative	imaginatively
2.	adaptation			
3.		deceive		
4.	decoration			
5.		differ		
6.				individually
7.			mature	
8.			predatory	
9.			technical	

B. Choose the correct word forms from the chart in Activity A to complete these sentences. Use the context and the position of the word in the sentence to help you.

1. Since some children have a more vivid _____ than an adult, they are more likely to believe in a magician's magic instead of trying to figure out the trick.

2. When a _____ is hunting for food, it stays quiet and tries to blend in with the background.

3. Magicians can _____ an audience by distracting attention away from their hands.

4. Please distribute one card to each _____ in the audience.

5. Animal species that are least _____ to changes may not survive for many more generations.

6. As we _____, we often lose our belief in magic and imaginary creatures.

Grammar | **Relative clauses**

Relative clauses identify, define, or comment on the noun, noun phrase, or pronoun they follow. They can make your sentences more varied, interesting, and informative.

You can think of a sentence with a relative clause as a combination of two sentences.

The magician walked onto the stage. + He was wearing a tall hat.

relative clause

The magician, **who was wearing a tall hat**, walked onto the stage.

noun   relative
           pronoun

Relative clauses usually begin with a relative pronoun: *who, whom, whose, that, when, where,* or *which*. The relative pronoun refers to the same person or thing as the noun or noun clause being modified. So in the example above, "who" refers to "the magician."

Relative clauses are dependent clauses. They must connect to a main clause. They cannot stand alone as sentences.

Relative clauses can be either **subject relative clauses** or **object relative clauses**.

Relative pronoun	Use	Example
who who(m)	subject/object pronoun for people (Informally, many people use "who" instead of "whom.")	The psychologist **who was a practicing magician** was Dr. Kuhn. The scientist **whom I read about** was a cognitive psychologist.
whose	possessive pronoun for people, animals, or things	The bird **whose feathers I found** was a ptarmigan.
that	subject/object pronoun for people, animals, or things	The paper **that I read** was too difficult to understand.
which	subject/object pronoun for things; can refer to a previous clause	Dr. Kuhn said that the art of magic is very old, **which surprised me**.

Subject relative clauses

In subject relative clauses, the relative pronoun takes the place of the subject of the clause. It is followed by a verb. The verb agrees with the noun that the clause modifies.

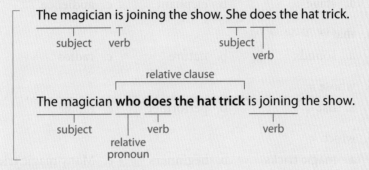

Object relative clauses

In object relative clauses, the relative pronoun takes the place of the object of the clause. It is followed by a subject and a verb. The verb agrees with the subject.

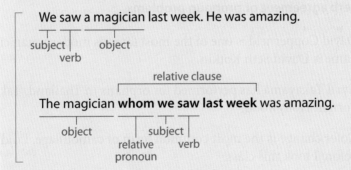

You can omit the relative pronoun in object relative clauses. This is common in everyday speech.

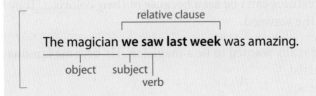

A. Listen to the sentences. For each one, circle the noun or pronoun that the relative clause modifies.

1. that =
   a. boxes   b. knives   c. magic show

2. whom =
   a. France   b. we   c. magician

3. that =
   a. stage   b. elephant   c. audience

4. that =
   a. sounds   b. nature   c. radios

5. whose =
   a. hat   b. performer   c. rabbit

6. which =
   a. magic tricks   b. beginners   c. Many magic tricks are actually
                                           easy for a beginner to learn

B. In your notebook, combine the sentences with a relative clause. Then take turns reading the sentences aloud with a partner. Listen for subject-verb agreement or pronoun problems.

1. David Copperfield is one of the most famous modern magicians. His real name is David Seth Kotkin.

2. Cyril Takayama has performed for orphans in Thailand. Takayama was born in Hollywood.

3. Color change is the most common form of camouflage. I didn't know that before I took this class.

4. Stage illusions are performed for large audiences. Stage illusions often use exotic animals such as tigers.

5. Some creatures can't be seen because of their coloring. They hide in the sand or the seaweed.

6. Houdini really wanted to be a magician. He became famous as an escape artist.

Changing a word to a different form by adding a suffix can sometimes cause the primary word stress to change. Although deciding where to stress words of more than one syllable can be difficult, there are a few rules you can follow. When in doubt, always check a dictionary.

CD 2
Track 10

Listen to the examples in the chart below.

Rules	Suffixes	Examples
1. Put the primary stress on these suffixes.	*-ee, -ese, -ier*	re-TIRE / re-tir-**EE** CHI-na / Chi-N**ESE** cash / ca-**SHIER**
2. Keep the same syllable stress as the base word.	*-al, -ment, -ness, -ous, -or, -y, -ism, -ly*	pro-FE-ssion / pro-FE-ssion-**al** e-QUIP / e-QUIP-**ment** e-FFECT-ive / e-FFECT-ive-**ness** sub-JECT-ive / sub-JECT-ive-**ly**
3. Put the primary stress on the syllable just before these suffixes.	*-ial, -ian, -ion, -ic(s), -ical, -ient, -ious, -ify, -itive, -ity, -graphy, -logy, -ual*	MA-**gic** / ma-GI-**cian** psy-CHO-**lo-gy** / psy-cho-LO-**gi-cal**
4. You usually put the primary stress two syllables before these suffixes.	*-ary, -ate, -ize*	VO-cab / vo-CA-bu-**la-ry** CER-ti-fy / cer-TI-fi-**cate** lo-CA-tion / LO-cal-**ize**

A. For each pair of words, predict where the stress should go and circle that syllable. Then listen and check your answers.

1. a. manipulate   b. manipulation

2. a. alternate   b. alternative

3. a. deceive   b. deception

4. a. image   b. imaginary

5. a. technique   b. technically

6. a. mystery   b. mysterious

7. a. popular   b. popularity

8. a. psychology   b. psychological

9. a. terrify   b. terrific

10. a. visual   b. visualize

B. Work with a partner. Take turns reading these sentences. Listen for correct word stress on the underlined words.

1. Some children are <u>terrified</u> by magic, but others think it's <u>terrific</u>.

2. Magicians use different <u>techniques</u>, but <u>technically</u> their goals are the same.

3. The <u>mystery</u> of nature is revealed in <u>mysterious</u> ways.

4. The <u>subjects</u> all gave very <u>subjective</u> answers to the research questions.

5. The <u>images</u> in the book helped the children visualize the <u>imaginary</u> creatures.

6. They did <u>psychological</u> experiments to understand the <u>psychology</u> behind the illusions.

In a conversation, there are a number of ways to ask someone to clarify something that he or she has said.

Restating speaker's point

Do you mean that . . . ?

So are you saying that . . . ?

Let me see if I understand . . .

Asking speaker for clarification

What (exactly) do you mean by that?

Could you give an example?

Could you explain how that works?

Asking speaker to rephrase what was said

What do you mean by . . . ?

Could you explain that another way?

I'm not sure what that means.

CD 2
Track 12

Listen to how radio show host Marco Werman restates Dr. Kuhn's idea and then asks Dr. Kuhn for clarification.

Now, in your study, you argue that the time has come to create a science of magic. What exactly do you mean by that?

To clarify a point in response to a question, or to rephrase a difficult idea without being asked, a speaker often uses phrases like these.

What I mean to say is . . .

In other words, . . .

That is, . . .

Let me explain. . .

To make myself clear, . . .

Sorry, let me rephrase that.

Just to clarify, . . .

A. Work with a partner. Use phrases from the Speaking Skill box to complete this conversation. Then practice the conversation aloud. Take turns playing the tutor and the student.

Tutor: So you have a quiz on mimicry and camouflage tomorrow. Do you have any questions?

Student: I get camouflage, but _____ mimicry.
                                                              1

Tutor: Well, the technical definition for mimicry is when one organism can share characteristics and imitate sounds or actions of another.

Student: _____?
                              2

Tutor: Sure. An example would be a moth that makes a clicking sound to make it sound like something dangerous to bats so they won't come near. Remember, mimicry is part of a bigger concept called *crypsis*.

_____ mimicry falls into a larger category of
behavior along with evasion, camouflage, and just plain hiding.
    3

Student: _____ running away from something and
hiding are considered in the same category as camouflage and mimicry?
    4

Tutor: Exactly. So _____, they are all part of the same
protective behavior.
    5

B. Work with a partner. Role-play an interview between a reporter and
a scientist explaining one or more of the concepts below. Use phrases
from the skill box. Then practice the conversation aloud and present it
to the class.

> camouflage   misdirection   illusions   forcing

Unit Assignment | Give a group presentation on the uses of illusions

 In this section, you will deliver a group presentation on how optical illusions
are used. As you prepare your presentation, think about the Unit Question,
"How can the eyes deceive the mind?" and refer to the Self-Assessment
checklist on page 98.

For alternative unit assignments, see the *Q: Skills for Success Teacher's Handbook.*

CONSIDER THE IDEAS

Look at these PowerPoint slides from a lecture on optical illusions.
In a group, discuss the questions below.

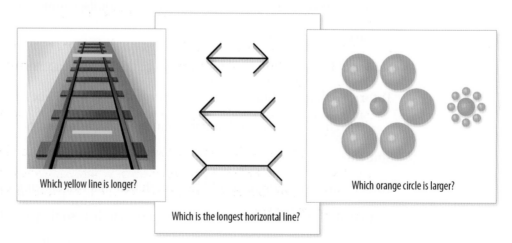

Which yellow line is longer?

Which is the longest horizontal line?

Which orange circle is larger?

1. In each illusion, one object appears longer or bigger than the others, but they are the same size. What creates the illusion in each case?

2. Do you always see what is really there, or do you sometimes see only what you want to see? Do you think some people can resist being fooled?

3. Do you think the study of optical illusions is important? Why or why not?

PREPARE AND SPEAK

A. **GATHER IDEAS** Work in a group. Brainstorm some ways illusions like the ones above are or could be used in each of the following fields. Take notes in the chart.

Field	Uses
Fashion	
Art	
Architecture	
Marketing	
Other	

B. **ORGANIZE IDEAS** Plan your group presentation.

1. Choose one of the fields above. As a group, discuss examples in the field that use the illusion. The examples can be ones you have seen or ones you imagine. Be creative.

2. Plan the report on your findings. Your presentation should include these parts:
   - a description of the illusion used and the field you chose and why
   - a description of three or four examples of how the illusion is or could be used. If possible, collect pictures from the Internet or magazines, or draw your own.

- a response to the question, "How easily do you think people are deceived by this illusion?"
- a conclusion that addresses implications of using optical illusions in this field

3. Divide the points and/or examples among the members of your group. Use a note card for each part of the report you will give, and write essential points to remind yourself what to say.

4. Practice presenting your information to your group. Use relative clauses to describe each optical illusion figure or drawing and explain how it is used in a particular field.

This optical illusion shows two lines that are the same length but don't appear that way.

People who want to look taller might wear a V-neck sweater rather than one with a round neck.

C. **SPEAK** **Present your ideas to the class. Answer questions from the audience at the end. When you listen to other presentations, ask questions to clarify information if you are not sure of the meaning. Refer to the Self-Assessment checklist below before you begin.**

CHECK AND REFLECT

A. **CHECK** **Think about the Unit Assignment as you complete the Self-Assessment checklist.**

SELF-ASSESSMENT		
Yes	No	
☐	☐	I was able to speak fluently about the topic.
☐	☐	My group and class understood me.
☐	☐	I used relative clauses correctly.
☐	☐	I used vocabulary from the unit to express my ideas.
☐	☐	I emphasized the correct syllable in words to indicate the word form.
☐	☐	I asked for clarification as necessary and clarified my speech for others when asked.

B. **REFLECT** **Discuss these questions with a partner.**

What is something new you learned in this unit?

 Look back at the Unit Question. Is your answer different now than when you started this unit? If yes, how is it different? Why?

Track Your Success

Circle the words and phrases you learned in this unit.

Nouns
camouflage
illusion
link 🔑 AWL
perception AWL
phenomenon AWL
predator
prey
survival AWL

Verbs
adapt 🔑 AWL
distract
manipulate AWL
mature AWL
mimic
resemble
utilize AWL

Phrasal Verbs
tap into
work out

Adjectives
cognitive
elaborate
infinite AWL
obvious 🔑 AWL
subjective
supernatural

Adverb
virtually 🔑 AWL

🔑 Oxford 3000™ words
AWL Academic Word List

Check (✓) the skills you learned. If you need more work on a skill, refer to the page(s) in parentheses.

LISTENING ●	I can recognize appositives that explain. (p. 82)
VOCABULARY ●	I can use word forms and suffixes. (p. 88)
GRAMMAR ●	I can use relative clauses. (pp. 90–91)
PRONUNCIATION ●	I can shift word stress with suffixes. (p. 93)
SPEAKING ●	I can clarify information. (p. 95)
LEARNING OUTCOME ●	I can deliver a presentation that describes and gives examples of how optical illusions are used and discusses implications of their use.

UNIT

5

Global Cooperation

LISTENING • organizing notes with a T-chart
VOCABULARY • collocations
GRAMMAR • reported speech
PRONUNCIATION • linking with final consonants
SPEAKING • citing sources

Unit QUESTION

What does it mean to be a global citizen?

PREVIEW THE UNIT

A Discuss these questions with your classmates.

Which of these concerns get the most attention: short-term disasters such as hurricane relief or long-term problems such as world hunger? Why?

Look at the photo. Have you or someone you know participated in an activity that reflects a desire to become a better global citizen?

B Discuss the Unit Question above with your classmates.

Listen to *The Q Classroom*, **Track 13** on **CD 2**, to hear other answers.

C Look at the photos. What problems do you see? Talk with a partner and write your ideas. Then think of four more problems you think the world faces today.

Problems the world faces today

_____

_____

_____

_____

_____

D Work with a group. For each problem in Activity C, decide who is primarily responsible for solving the problem. (There may be more than one answer.) Write the problem beside the correct heading.

Governments	
NGOs (non-governmental organizations)	
Businesses	
Individuals	

LISTENING

| ## The Campaign to Humanize the Coffee Trade

VOCABULARY

Here are some words from Listening 1. Read the sentences. Then write each bold word next to the correct definition.

1. Many celebrity **activists** worked together to bring attention to the effects of the tsunami and to raise money for countries affected by it.

2. If a local community effort, or grassroots campaign, gets a lot of media attention, it might **transform** into a national or even a global fight for change.

3. Many farmers are forced to find other jobs because they cannot **afford** the high costs of producing food.

4. Some businesspeople who like risk base their investments on **speculation** and luck rather than on past performance history.

5. There was a **massive** demand for sugar, but because of agricultural problems, the supply was very low.

6. Water is a basic **commodity** that is scarce in many parts of the world.

7. The grower sells his product to a **processor**, who then gets it ready for the market.

8. Human rights groups spend a lot of their energy trying to **devise** ways to improve labor laws around the world.

9. **Roughly** 884 million people worldwide have unsafe drinking water, and according to the humanitarian group Save the Children, this estimate is low.

10. In order to avoid the obstacles that can prevent small businesses from succeeding, some people prefer to join a **co-op** and work together with other small business owners.

11. The United Nations Global Compact wants businesses to **guarantee** that they will reduce their environmental impact, not just say they hope it will happen.

12. The importer didn't have a license to do business in that country, so she needed an **intermediary** to buy the products for her.

a. _speculation_ (n.) the activity of buying and selling goods or shares in a company in the hope of making a profit, but with the risk of losing money

b. _transform_ (v.) to change someone or something completely

c. _roughly_ (adv.) more or less; approximately

d. _guarantee_ (v.) to give a promise

e. _commodity_ (n.) a product or raw material that can be bought and sold

f. _intermediary_ (n.) someone who passes on information; a middleman

g. _processor_ (n.) something or someone that changes materials before they are sold

h. _devise_ (v.) to invent a plan or system

i. _activist_ (n.) someone who wants to achieve political or social change

j. _afford_ (v.) to be able to pay for something

k. _massive_ (adj.) very big

l. _co-op_ (n.) a community organization of people working together towards a shared goal

PREVIEW LISTENING 1

The Campaign to Humanize the Coffee Trade

You are going to listen to a report, "The Campaign to Humanize the Coffee Trade," by Daniel Zwerdling for American RadioWorks. It addresses an issue of global concern for a product consumed in almost every country.

Check (✓) your predictions of what the speaker will say about *humanizing* the coffee trade, improving the conditions for the workers.

☐ Coffee production in small villages is usually not controlled by the farmers themselves.

☐ Products that come from socially responsible businesses that protect workers and the environment cost less because they come from small companies.

☐ Coffee farmers earn less than one-tenth of the money from their beans sold in other countries.

LISTEN FOR MAIN IDEAS

Listen to the report. Then write a sentence for each topic to express the main idea.

1. The lives and homes of the coffee farmers

   - coffee farmer work hard, but still live in poverty without water + electricity

2. The role of the coyote, or middleman

   - coffee farmers sell to middlemen who pay them a little money.

3. The goal of the Fair Trade system

   - designed to make sure farmers get fair wage. In order for it to work consumers have to pay more for Fair Trade products

LISTEN FOR DETAILS

A. **Read the statements. Then listen again. Check (✓) the statements that are true according to the report.**

☐ 1. The coffee farmers introduced here say they send their coffee into town on trucks.

☑ 2. The coyotes, or middlemen, buy the coffee beans for 50 cents or less a pound.

☐ 3. Zwerdling says that in Washington, D.C., he spends less than $9.00 a pound for coffee.

☐ 4. Coffee is not a highly traded commodity.

☑ 5. Fair Trade was started by Europeans.

☑ 6. At the time of the report, over 300 groups of farmers around the world had joined the Fair Trade system.

☐ 7. Large corporate plantations can join Fair Trade if they promise to follow fair business practices.

☑ 8. Guillermo Denaux explains that under Fair Trade, farmers are basically guaranteed to earn enough money for food, education, clothes, and health care.

B. Who sells coffee to whom? Number the people in the order that they purchase coffee after the farmer offers it for sale. Then listen again and check your answers.

5   a coffee shop

1   a coyote, or middleman

2   a processor

4   a roaster

6   the consumer

3   an exporter

 **WHAT DO YOU THINK?**

Discuss the questions in a group.

1. Would you be willing to pay extra for Fair Trade products? Why or why not? How much more would you pay (than you do now) for a cup of coffee? A chocolate bar? A cotton T-shirt?

2. Zwerdling says that "consumers have to help, too." In what ways can consumers help in the development of the Fair Trade network?

3. Who should determine prices of luxury commodities (such as coffee or chocolate)? Who should determine the prices of necessities (such as vegetables)? What might happen if farmers were allowed to charge as much as they wanted for their products?

After you listen to a lecture, it's useful to **organize your notes**. This makes it easier to understand and remember the information and makes it easier to use your notes to write papers or study for tests.

Some lectures follow organizational patterns that are easily noted in a **T-chart**. Some common patterns include cause and effect, problem and solution, and discussions of differences before and after a particular event or time.

To use a T-chart, divide your paper into two columns and write one category at the top of each column. Write connected ideas across from each other; however, remember that there might be, for example, several effects from one cause or several problems for one solution. Drawing arrows can help you see the connections between ideas.

CD 2
Track 16

Listen to this excerpt from Listening 1, and see how a student noted the ideas in the chart:

Problems	Solutions
• Farmers are poor and powerless. • Farmers don't know who buys their coffee. • Many different people buy and sell the coffee beans before the consumer.	The Fair Trade system can help farmers earn more money and gain some power.

Remember that in a lecture, you might hear some of the information out of order. However, if you can note problems in the problem column and solutions in the solution column, you can reorder them later when you revise your notes. If you hear information that you don't have time to write down, draw a line; then you can ask your instructor or a classmate later. Sometimes your instructor might ask you to research the missing information or come up with your own ideas.

CD 2
Track 17

Listen to students talking about humanitarian organizations. Write the problems and solutions they discuss. Then compare notes with a partner.

Tip Critical Thinking

This activity asks you to **identify** the problems and solutions you hear the speakers talk about. Identifying ideas is one way to show you understand the information.

Problems	Solutions
1. poverty	buy Fair Trade products - tea, coffee, jewelry.
2. Water crisis	World Water organization, protect water
3. Environmental prob. like pollution	Leonardo Di Caprio Foundation - expand public awareness - grassroots campaign to end use of plastic bags.
4. Disaster Relief Group is new + small, so hard to raise $ for group	- they're improving outreach communication with their website?

Clean drinking water is a precious commodity.

LISTENING 2 | The UN Global Compact

VOCABULARY

Tip for Success

These noun phrases are all collocations. The field of business has many noun phrases that are collocations. See the Vocabulary Skill on page 113 for more information on collocations.

Here are some words and phrases from Listening 2. Read the sentences. Then write each bold word or phrase next to the correct definition.

1. India is recognized as a key **emerging economy** in the world. There is some risk in investing there, but potential for enormous profits and growth, too.

2. Many organizations try to ensure that proper **labor standards** exist so that employees have safe conditions at their jobs.

3. Businesses worry about the **confidence of investors** because if people don't invest, there won't be money to innovate and expand, or perhaps even to stay in business.

4. Institutions such as the World Bank provide loans to developing countries to improve their **social impact** in the world.

a. labour standards.   laws that protect workers

b. social impact   the effects of an organization or agency on others

c. emerging economy   a region that is experiencing rapid growth and industrialization

d. confidence of investors   a feeling or belief by people with money that it is safe to spend it in order to make a future profit

5. Businesses have easily identifiable assets, or property. They also have **intangible assets**, like a good reputation, that are not easily visible.

6. At the end of the year, a corporation's **accounting practices** might be examined to make sure the business reports are accurate and honest.

7. In tough economic times, families need to reduce unnecessary **household expenditures** such as eating in restaurants or going to the movies.

8. I am only interested in buying **ethical goods** for people as gifts this year. I don't want to support any businesses that don't treat workers fairly.

e. household expenditures   the costs of taking care of a home and family

f. accounting practices   methods of keeping financial records

g. ethical good   products that are judged to be morally acceptable and not harmful to society or the workers who produce them

h. intangible assets   things of value that cannot be seen, such as knowledge

9. Even though countries want to **exploit** their own natural resources, they have to consider the environmental impact of using those resources too quickly.

10. In recent years, businesses have tried to find ways of being **proactive** with problems so they can take action before being criticized.

11. The principles, or basic beliefs, of a company determine its **core strategies**.

12. The country's economic policies are focused on creating a **sustainable market** to attract and keep foreign investors.

i. ~~sustainable market~~ a system that can operate continuously while still meeting global economic, environmental, and social needs

j. ~~exploit~~ to use something well in order to gain as much from it as possble

k. ~~proactive~~ controlling a situation by making things happen rather than waiting for things to happen and then reacting to them

l. ~~core strategies~~ primary or fundamental plans of action for a business

The United Nations building

PREVIEW LISTENING 2

The UN Global Compact

The United Nations, itself a symbol of international cooperation, has many subgroups that work in specific areas. You are going to listen to a report on the UN Global Compact. The report discusses a special formal agreement, or compact, among businesses around the world on the issues that concern them.

Check (✓) the issues you expect to hear discussed in the report.

☐ corruption   ☐ investor confidence

☐ import and export prices   ☐ worker safety

☐ pollution   ☐ climate change

☐ treatment of employees   ☐ consumer spending

Handwritten note: U.N. Global Compact = U.N. policy initiative for businesses to operate following principles of human rights + respecting labour rights + the environment

LISTEN FOR MAIN IDEAS

Listen to the report on the Global Compact. Circle the answer that best completes each statement.

1. The *Exxon Valdez* disaster and the Enron collapse showed that businesses
    a. can act responsibly without regulations.
    b. are guilty of corporate irresponsibility.

2. Expansion into the global market brings more risk to the public because
    a. emerging markets have weaker regulations.
    b. emerging markets will increase competition.

3. In order to participate in the UN Global Compact, companies must promise to
    a. take responsibility for their own actions.
    b. report irresponsible actions by other businesses.

4. Two of the ten areas that the Global Compact is intended to safeguard are
    a. labor standards and business reputations.
    b. human rights and the environment.

5. Evidence of changes in public attitudes includes findings that people are
    a. spending more money on ethical goods.
    b. more concerned about the cost of a product than the reputation of the company that produced it.

6. Ban Ki-Moon's hopes for the future of the Global Compact include
    a. limiting global expansion and development.
    b. creating sustainable markets.

LISTEN FOR DETAILS

Track 19

Read this list of supporting details. Then listen again. Complete the chart with the correct numbers as you listen. Check your answers with a partner.

Details	Numbers
1. The year of the *Exxon Valdez* disaster	1989
2. The number of gallons of crude oil spilled into the water by the *Exxon Valdez*	11 million
3. The number of dollars in foreign direct investment at the time of this report	one trillion
4. The year the UN started the Global Compact	2000
5. The number of Global Compact principles the participating companies agree to uphold	10
6. The percentage of a company's market value that is determined by its reputation and intangible assets	70%
7. The share price of Enron before its bad reputation caused the price to fall to less than 50 cents	$90
8. The percentage of CEOs who report doing more now to incorporate environmental, social, and political issues into their core strategies	90%
9. The number of companies in the Global Compact when it first started	38
10. The number of countries in the Global Compact at the time of this report	120

 WHAT DO YOU THINK?

A. Discuss the questions in a group.

1. What do you think are the most serious problems caused by businesses and corporations that the Global Compact should force them to address?

2. Do you think corporations that follow the Global Compact are motivated more by the desire for profits, the desire to be better global citizens, or something else?

3. What are some examples you've seen of efforts by businesses or individuals to be better global citizens?

B. Think about both Listening 1 and Listening 2 as you discuss the questions.

1. Did the two recordings change your mind about global citizenship and cooperation, or did they confirm views you already had? In what ways?

2. What are some current problems that would benefit from global solutions on a small scale or a grassroots level?

Vocabulary Skill | Collocations

To increase your fluency and expand your vocabulary, it is important to know about **collocation**, or the way two or more words are commonly combined when written or spoken. Compound words, idioms, lexical phrases, and phrasal verbs, as well as adjective-noun combinations, are examples of collocations.

Collocations are based on common usage and not usually on grammatical rules.

We say . . .	but not . . .
crude oil	rough oil
Fair Trade products	Kind Trade products
climb the corporate ladder	climb the business ladder

Learners' and collocations dictionaries are good tools for finding out which word collocates with another. A thesaurus might lead you in the wrong direction, however, because even though two words are synonyms, they will probably not collocate with the same words.

Synonyms	global	international
Collocations	global warming	international borders

Tip for Success

One way to check for common collocations is to use the Internet to search for a phrase in quotations. For example, "emerging market" gives over two million hits, but "emerging economy" fewer than 200,000.

A. Choose the phrase that has the correct collocation. Check a collocations dictionary if necessary.

1. Agencies like Amnesty International help protect (personal rights / human rights) around the world.

2. We need to write the (final draft / end draft) of our proposal.

3. The (prices rose / prices ascended) when the corporation took over.

4. They carried the coffee (down and up / up and down) the mountain.

5. The (short supply of / little supply of) that commodity affected prices.

6. My favorite charity is one that brings (disaster comfort / disaster relief) to victims of hurricanes.

7. We need to (make some research / do some research) on that project before we invest in it.

8. (Startup markets / Emerging markets) are those in developing countries where businesses see the possibility for growth and are making new investments.

9. The (coffee shop / coffee store) bought most of its coffee from Fair Trade organizations.

10. Businesses that abuse the environment are partly responsible for the problem of (weather change / climate change).

B. Work with a partner. Circle the two words or phrases that collocate with the bold word or expression. Check a learners' or collocations dictionary if necessary.

1. **business**   a. run a . . .   b. make a . . .   c. go into . . .

2. **money**   a. make . . .   b. spend . . .   c. afford . . .

3. **costs**   a. get rid of . . .   b. run up . . .   c. cover . . .

4. **confidence**   a. grow . . . in   b. have. . . in   c. lose. . . in

5. **responsibility** a. take . . . for   b. discover   c. have . . . for
                                               . . . for

6. **chief . . . officer** a. financial   b. executive   c. management

C. With your partner, write at least six sentences using collocations from Activity B.

_____

_____

_____

_____

_____

SPEAKING

In **reported speech** (or indirect speech), you restate what someone else has said or written. It is often used to incorporate information from another source into a presentation. In reported speech, it is important to keep the same meaning as the original source, although it is not necessary to use the exact words.

Reported speech	Examples
requires a backshift in verb tense when talking about things said in and about the past simple present → simple past present continuous → past continuous simple past → present perfect present perfect → past perfect *will* → *would* *can* → *could* *may* → *might*	The farmer said, "We <u>need</u> to get a higher price." The farmer said that **they needed** to get a higher price. The board said, "We <u>will invest</u> more in emerging markets in the future." The board said **they would invest** more in emerging markets.
keeps the same verb tense if the speaker's words involve a timeless or current situation or event	He said, "Climate change <u>is</u> a reality." He said (that) climate change **is** a reality.
uses statement word order, even if the original source is a question	The executive asked, "<u>What's the agenda</u>?" The executive asked **what the agenda was**.
starts with a reporting verb such as *say, tell, ask, add, assert, point out, state, remark, respond,* and *warn* has an optional *that* for statements	"The environmental crisis is a global problem." (Barry Commoner) Barry Commoner **asserts (that)** the environmental crisis is a global problem.
may require a change in pronoun from *I/we/you* to clarify the reporter's relationship to what is said	I told her, "<u>You and I</u> can do more." I told her **she and I** could do more.
uses *if* or *whether* to introduce a *Yes/No* question, or an infinitive to introduce a command	The UN speaker asked, "<u>Are you</u> ready to make a global commitment? Then <u>do</u> it." The UN speaker asked **whether** they were ready to make a global commitment and told them **to do** it.

A. Work with a partner and take turns. One person reads the quotation, and the other changes it to reported speech. Remember to begin with a reporting verb.

1. The farmer, about growing coffee: "It's a lot of work, and sometimes we can't even cover our costs."

   The farmer stated that growing coffee was a lot of work, and . . .

2. Deborah Amos, to the radio audience: "Do you ever think about the farmers who grew that coffee?" *Deborah .. asked the audience if they thought* ✓ ✓

3. Georg Kell, about the Global Compact: "Initially we started off with a moral core." *George said that Global Compact had initially .."*

4. Ban Ki-Moon, UN Secretary General: "Together we can achieve a new face of globalization." *Dan pointed out that together .."*

5. Dan Zwerdling, about the coffee farmers: "These farmers are the poorest and most powerless part of the global coffee trade." *Dan said that those farmers were the poorest..."*

6. Daniel Zwerdling, about Fair Trade: "Still, the Fair Trade network can't raise all the money that farmers need just by cutting out middlemen. Consumers have to help, too." *Dan said that Fair Trade network can't raise ...*

B. Work in a group. Sit in a circle. Share a fact or ask a question about a global issue. The person to your right will report what you said and then add another fact or question. Continue around the circle until everyone has had a chance to share and report.

> A: *In Cambodia last year, heavy rains caused flooding, and many farmers' crops were destroyed.*
>
> B: *Student A reported that in Cambodia last year, heavy rains had caused flooding and many crops had been destroyed. Do any international organizations help farmers in different countries?*
>
> C: *Student B asked if any international organizations help farmers in different countries. I think the United Nations . . .*

In order to improve fluency, it is important to connect the final sound of one word or syllable to the initial sound of the next, especially in the same thought group. If you say each sound perfectly, but in isolation, your speech will sound unnatural.

It is important not to drop final consonants, or your speech will be unclear because one word may be confused with another. *Time is money* should *not* sound like *Tie is money*.

Do not link a word that ends with a consonant to one that begins with another consonant by inserting a vowel sound between them. This will cause you to add an extra syllable that will confuse your listener. *The date began with a three* should *not* sound like *The data began with a three*.

CD 2
Track 20

Read the principles of linking with final consonants and study the examples in the chart. Then listen to the example sentences.

Principles of linking	Examples
1. Join a final consonant sound to the vowel sound at the beginning of the next word.	They sold items made in Africa thousands of miles away.
2. When the same consonant ends one word and begins the next, do not insert a vowel sound. Hold the consonant longer instead of repeating it.	They want to take control of production.
3. When a word ends in the consonant sounds *t, k, d, p, g,* or *b,* do not release the first sound, but say the second one right away.	They grow some of the best coffee you can drink.

CD 2
Track 21

A. Link the final consonants in these phrases. Write ⌣ where the sounds are joined, ___ where the same sound is held longer, and) where the final consonant sound is not released. Then listen and repeat to check your work. Practice saying the phrases aloud with a partner.

1. an economist
2. growing coffee
3. special label
4. stuck in poverty
5. can't cover costs

6. basic commodity
7. household expenditure
8. global expansion
9. climate change
10. environmental issues

B. Mark the places where sounds should be linked. Then ask and answer the questions with a partner. Help each other improve linking sounds by listening carefully and pointing out problems.

1. What time is the conference on the global economy?

2. What kind of help does a refugee camp provide?

3. How can countries demonstrate international unity?

4. What are some ways to help earthquake victims?

5. How can companies promise to reduce their environmental impact?

6. What are some nonprofit organizations that collect food donations for the hungry?

7. What are some ways you take care of the people in your community?

8. How might an economist describe fair trade?

When giving academic presentations, you need to tell the audience where your information comes from. Giving credit to authorities or outside sources will make your presentation more believable and informative. You can show that you have studied background information and up-to-date material.

In speaking, you can cite information by:

- introducing the person who wrote or said something important about your topic.
- telling where and when it was published or said.
- using reported speech to restate the speaker's idea.

When citing a speaker's words from a specific point in the past, related to past activities or ideas, use a reporting verb in the past form (he *stated*, she *explained*, they *claimed*).

When citing written material, a quotation that is closely related in time to the speaker, or a statement of a universally accepted idea, it is common to use either the present perfect form (*he has asserted*) or the citational present (*the report proves*; *research shows*).

Here are some common phrases for citing sources:

> According to X, . . .
> As X says / explains / reports, . . .
> X's article shows . . .
> In [year], X proved that . . .
> In a survey published in [year], the results showed . . .
> At a conference on [date], X explained how . . .

A. Add a different opening for each sentence to introduce the source provided in parentheses. Read your sentences to a partner and compare your choices.

1. According to Wikipedia Fair Trade is a social movement that has been organized to give power to developing countries. (Wikipedia)

2. In 2005, the BBC reported that 200,000 people attended a series of Live 8 concerts in London's Hyde Park to combat poverty in Africa. (BBC News, July 3, 2005)

3. Rose Tran Bach Yen, an orphange director in Vietnam, reports that the Heifer Foundation has provided an orphanage in Vietnam with an animal farm, so children learn how to raise and care for animals. (Rose Tran Bach Yen, orphanage director, Vietnam)

4. In a Mckinsey survey report more than 90 percent of CEOs are doing more about environmental, social, and political issues now. (2007, McKinsey survey)

Tip for Success

Try to use a variety of reporting verbs or phrases, and don't always use them at the beginning of a sentence. For example: *The New York Fair Trade Day this year was an enormous success,* **according to Scott Codey.** *The interest in buying Fair Trade products for gifts,* **Codey added,** *increases every year.*

5. *When accepting his Academy Award in 2007, Al Gore said* _____ "My fellow Americans, people all over the world, we need to solve the climate crisis. It's not a political issue; it's a moral issue." (Al Gore, Academy Award acceptance speech, February 2007)

6. *Pediatrician Susan Shepard in the Jan. 30 2008 New York Times article stated that* _____ colleagues at Doctors Without Borders treated more than 150,000 children suffering from hunger around the world. (Susan Shepherd, pediatrician, *The New York Times*, January 30, 2008)

B. Work with a partner. Read these descriptions of organizations that have made a difference. Take turns asking questions about them and citing the information.

1. Save the Children is the leading independent organization creating lasting change for children in need in the United States and around the world. For more than 75 years, Save the Children has been helping children survive and thrive by improving their health, education and economic opportunities and, in times of acute crisis, mobilizing rapid life-saving assistance to help children recover from the effects of war, conflict and natural disasters. (Save the Children, Causecast.org, http://www.causecast.org)

2. More than 1,400 people, both specialized staff and delegates, are currently on field missions for the [International Committee of the Red Cross] across the globe. This work is backed up by some 11,000 local employees and supported and coordinated by around 800 staff at its Geneva headquarters. (International Committee of the Red Cross, http://www.cicr.org)

Unit Assignment | **Report on a global problem**

 In this section, you will deliver a group presentation on a global problem. As you prepare your presentation, think about the Unit Question, "What does it mean to be a global citizen?" and refer to the Self-Assessment checklist on page 122.

For alternative unit assignments, see the *Q: Skills for Success Teacher's Handbook*.

CONSIDER THE IDEAS

In a group, discuss this campus flyer that introduces students to ways they can get involved in grassroots campaigns and become better global citizens on their own campus.

Informed Students ▶▶ Global Citizens

New students! Welcome to this month's edition of *Informed Students* ▶▶ **Global Citizens**.

You're in college now, and doors are open to the following organizations! Join up and make a difference.

Greenpeace: You've probably seen Greenpeace volunteers and recruiters around campus. They're here to encourage you to sign petitions to protect the whales and other endangered species. If you want to do more, why not sign up to be a volunteer yourself?

Habitat for Humanity: Although spring break is months away, check out a Habitat for Humanity working vacation to an area where hurricane victims get needed homes.

Humanities Out There: No need to go far from home to lend a hand. Underprivileged students nearby need tutors in English and math. Volunteer to help!

Campus Recyclers: Work at the recycling center collecting plastic bottles and paper and helping to raise awareness on campus about the need to recycle. Every little bit helps!

1. Discuss the issues these groups are involved in and the problems they are working to solve. What solutions do they offer?

2. Many grassroots organizations like these try to raise money, write letters to political leaders, or work on small projects that help people in need. What kind of work would you be willing to volunteer to do? How could an organization persuade others to volunteer?

PREPARE AND SPEAK

A. GATHER IDEAS **Work in a group. Think about the global problems and solutions discussed in this unit. Choose an issue related to the environment, health, education, energy, poverty, or a similar topic. Complete the chart with your group's ideas.**

What is the problem or issue?	
What are some of the causes of the problem?	
What are some of its effects?	
What are some possible solutions?	
What solutions or suggestions can your group offer?	

B. ORGANIZE IDEAS **Plan your group presentation.**

1. Divide the following parts of your presentation among your group members:
   a. Introduce and explain the problem
   b. Explain possible causes
   c. Discuss effects
   d. Present possible solutions

2. If possible, use information from outside sources in your presentation (you can research outside of class or use information from this unit).

3. Make note cards to remind you of what to cover during the presentation.

4. Practice your presentation. Time yourselves so that you keep to the limit set by your instructor. Give each other feedback on your sections of the presentation, and exchange suggestions for improvement.

C. SPEAK **Give your presentation to the class. Refer to the Self-Assessment checklist below before you begin.**

CHECK AND REFLECT

A. CHECK **Think about the Unit Assignment as you complete the Self-Assessment checklist.**

Yes	No	SELF-ASSESSMENT
☐	☐	I was able to speak fluently about the topic.
☐	☐	My group and class understood me.
☐	☐	I used vocabulary and collocations from the unit to express my ideas.
☐	☐	I used reported speech to cite information from others.
☐	☐	I linked final sounds to make my speech more fluent and understandable.
☐	☐	I cited sources appropriately and effectively.

B. REFLECT **Discuss these questions with a partner.**

What is something new you learned in this unit?

Look back at the Unit Question. Is your answer different now than when you started this unit? If yes, how is it different? Why?

Circle the words and phrases you learned in this unit.

Nouns	Verbs	Adverb
accounting	afford 🔑	roughly 🔑
activist 🔑	devise	**Phrases**
commodity AWL	exploit AWL	accounting practices
co-op	guarantee 🔑 AWL	confidence of investors
economy 🔑 AWL	transform 🔑 AWL	core strategies
expenditure	**Adjectives**	emerging economy
intermediary	core 🔑 AWL	ethical goods
investor AWL	ethical AWL	household expenditures
processor	intangible	intangible assets
speculation	massive 🔑	labor standards
standard 🔑	proactive	social impact
	sustainable AWL	sustainable market

🔑 Oxford 3000™ words

AWL Academic Word List

Check (✓) the skills you learned. If you need more work on a skill, refer to the page(s) in parentheses.

LISTENING	●	I can organize notes with a T-chart. (p. 107)
VOCABULARY	●	I can use collocations. (p. 113)
GRAMMAR	●	I can use reported speech. (p. 115)
PRONUNCIATION	●	I can understand and use linking with final consonants. (p. 117)
SPEAKING	●	I can cite sources. (p. 119)
LEARNING OUTCOME	●	I can identify and report on aspects of a global problem.

UNIT

6

Personal Space

LISTENING ● recognizing organizational cues
VOCABULARY ● words with multiple meanings
GRAMMAR ● conditionals
PRONUNCIATION ● thought groups
SPEAKING ● giving advice

LEARNING OUTCOME ●

Role-play a talk show focused on identifying and solving conflicts centered on issues of personal space.

Unit QUESTION

How do you make a space your own?

PREVIEW THE UNIT

A Discuss these questions with your classmates.

What places or spaces do you have that you consider "yours"? How do other people know that these spaces belong to you?

What are some differences in the way different groups, such as males, female, adults, or children personalize their space?

Look at the photo. Do you think the people who live in the house have made the space their own? Why?

B Discuss the Unit Question above with your classmates.

Listen to *The Q Classroom*, Track 22 on CD 2, to hear other answers.

C Look at the pictures of different kinds of space. What does each space tell you about the person? Share your ideas with a partner.

D Work in a group. Think of one of your personal spaces. Take turns describing your space and explaining what it shows about you.

My room is usually a little messy, but it is filled with things I really enjoy. In one corner is a pile of sports equipment: my tennis racket, some balls, a Frisbee, and a baseball glove. On the wall are posters of movies I really like. I've got a lot of CDs on the shelves. There's a plant on my windowsill.

LISTENING 1 | Environmental Psychology

VOCABULARY

Here are some words and phrases from Listening 1. Read the sentences. Circle the answer that best matches the meaning of each bold word or phrase.

1. **Gender** differences between boys and girls can be seen at an early age.
   a. classification by age
   b. classification by sex
   c. classification by name

2. To work with your partner on this dialog, sit in chairs that are face-to-face or in ones that are **adjacent** so you can communicate easily.
   a. next to each other
   b. away from the door
   c. far from each other

3. People usually **affiliate with** others who are similar to themselves. They like to feel that they belong to a group of like-minded friends.
   a. connect to
   b. are curious about
   c. are afraid of

4. The teachers are going to **engage in** a discussion on social psychology, so I'd like to stay and hear what they have to say.
   a. schedule
   b. take part in
   c. call off

5. He keeps all of his **belongings**, including his books and clothes, in one small cabinet in his dorm room.
   a. things you want
   b. things you don't want
   c. things you own

6. It's **remarkable** how often people will choose to sit at the same table in a restaurant, even when better tables are available.
   a. very interesting
   b. very difficult to believe
   c. very uncomfortable

7. Territorial behavior, or wanting to protect a personal space, is **ingrained in** us, and it is hard to change our attitude.
   a. all around
   b. unfamiliar to
   c. deeply a part of

8. When my little sister **invades** my room, she throws her toys all over my bed.
   a. forgets about; ignores
   b. protects; takes good care of
   c. marches into; enters by force

9. Most pizza places only deliver within a three-mile **radius**.
   a. circular area
   b. city center
   c. diameter

10. Please **refrain from** using your cell phone in class because it distracts other students.
    a. think about
    b. continue
    c. avoid

11. They prefer to commute to work in the city every day but live in a **suburban** area, because life is less stressful there.
    a. in a city
    b. near a city
    c. very far from a city

12. Although visitors are not likely to enter a house without knocking, they are **moderately** likely to stop by for a visit without being invited. It happens sometimes.
    a. always
    b. a little
    c. very

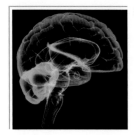

PREVIEW LISTENING 1

Environmental Psychology

You are going to listen to an excerpt from a lecture by Dr. Traci Craig, a psychology professor at the University of Idaho. It will introduce you to the field of environmental psychology.

Behavioral psychology is the study of how humans react to stimuli from outside and within themselves. *Educational psychology* is the study of how humans learn. Look at the pictures below. What do you think *environmental psychology* is? Write a short definition.

_____

_____

_____

Tip for Success

Learning the special vocabulary of academic fields will help you understand discussions and lectures and make you more comfortable communicating at school. Keep lists of vocabulary you learn in different subjects.

LISTEN FOR MAIN IDEAS

 CD 2
Track 23

A. **Listen to the lecture. Take notes to complete the main ideas in the outline.**

Tip Critical Thinking

In Activity A, you will complete an outline. **Outlining** is one way of breaking down information into its component parts.

I. Environmental psychology

   A. Definition: _____

      _____

   B. Areas the lecture will focus on:

      1. _____

      2. _____

      3. _____

II. Male and female _____ behavior

    A. Feelings of invasion

        1. Face-to-face invasion (males)

        2. _____ invasion (females)

    B. Placement of belongings

        1. The _____ study

        2. Placement of _____

    C. Exploring territories on bikes

        1. Smaller territories for girls

        2. Larger territories for boys

    D. Touching _____ in _____

a server and customer
in a restaurant

III. Eye contact: Post office experiment

    A. _____ likely to make eye

    contact in a _____

    B. _____ likely to make eye

    contact in a _____

IV. Visual intrusion and privacy—stressful places

    A. Visual intrusion—to see and be seen

        1. Restaurants

        2. _____

    B. Privacy—dorm rooms

B. Use your notes from the outline in Activity A to write answers to these questions. Compare your answers with a partner.

1. What is environmental psychology?

_____

2. In what ways does Dr. Craig believe males and females are similar or different in their territorial behavior?

_____

3. According to Dr. Craig, what is the connection between eye contact and personal space?

_____

4. What effects can a feeling of lack of privacy have on an individual?

_____

LISTEN FOR DETAILS

CD 2
Track 24

A. Read the statements. Then listen again. Write *T* (true) or *F* (false). Compare your answers with a partner.

_____ 1. Men are more offended by someone sitting adjacent to them than someone sitting across from them.

_____ 2. Males and females often miscommunicate because they are both competitive.

_____ 3. The statement "Women are expected to affiliate" means women feel they have to make contact with someone they sit next to.

_____ 4. In a large lecture class, the majority of students sit in the same seat all semester.

_____ 5. Visitors to a man's office will touch his belongings displayed on the desk more freely than they would if the office belonged to a woman.

_____ 6. In the jacket study, people moved a jacket that clearly belonged to a woman, but refrained from moving one that belonged to a man.

_____ 7. Territorial behavior does not begin until we are teenagers.

_____ 8. Even at a young age, females explore larger territories than males.

_____ 9. Touching your plate in a restaurant is a sign of marking the plate as your own.

_____ 10. It is more acceptable and expected for people to make eye contact in a post office in a large city than in a small town.

WHAT DO YOU THINK?

Discuss the questions in a group.

1. How do the details that you marked as true in the previous exercise fit your own actions or your observations of others? Do you always choose to sit in the same chair in class, for example?

2. Has Dr. Craig convinced you that males and females have very different reactions to personal space? Why or why not?

3. In what ways do you think the rules for respecting personal space and personalizing territories vary in different countries and cultures?

| Listening Skill | Recognizing organizational cues | |

Organizational cues are words or phrases a speaker uses to signal the type of information that follows. Recognizing organizational cues can help you predict what speakers will say next.

Organizational cues	What they signal	Examples
most importantly, in fact, actually, what we will focus on here is, I want to stress	importance, emphasis	What we will focus on here is a definition of territoriality.
for example, such as, for instance, specifically, in particular, that is	examples, illustrations	There are many ways to invade someone's space. For example, if you . . .
furthermore, in addition, moreover, besides, additionally, also	additional support or evidence	Women try to talk to those sitting next to them. In addition, they feel they have to affiliate with them.
now let's turn to, moving on, let's now look at, related to that	shifting topics	Now let's turn to the statistical evidence.
in short, to sum up, in conclusion, we've seen that, in the end	conclusions	In short, gender affects our sense of space.

A. Listen to this excerpt from Listening 1 and write down the six organizational cues that you hear. Then work with a partner and discuss the reasons the lecturer used them in each case.

1. _____

2. _____

3. _____

4. _____

5. _____

6. _____

CD 2
Track 26

B. Listen to the beginnings of these sentences and circle the correct ending for each, based on the organizational cues that you hear.

1. a students who take the time to put up posters feel more at home.
   b. their attendance in class is better and their grades are higher.

2. a. we found some posts by teenagers about how they got out of doing some school assignments.
   b. we found some detailed resumes of businessmen.

3. a. women don't usually consider their cars as a personal space to spend time on.
   b. it is believed that most men would rather watch football on their day off than go out to eat.

4. a. our car is just one piece of evidence of who we are.
   b. a car is enough information on which to base an opinion of a person.

5. a. eye contact does not appear to be a gender-related issue.
   b. men usually put a jacket on a seat in front of them rather than next to them.

6. a. staring at people is considered inappropriate and makes them feel uncomfortable.
   b. psychologists use all of this information to help people understand why they behave the way they do.

What Your Stuff Says About You

VOCABULARY

Here are some words from Listening 2. Read the paragraphs. Then write each bold word next to the correct definition.

Each of our actions and all of the spaces within our **domain** say something about us, whether we make those statements on purpose or not. Our personality **traits** are revealed by the ways we behave and the things we use to define our spaces. Anyone who spends time with us usually can walk away with a **profile** of us based on the things we own and the way we act with others. Although this information may provide **clues** to help others judge our personalities, it can also mislead them if one action or object makes them jump to the wrong conclusion. Then they have to **modify** their perception and try again to figure us out.

Two traits of the human personality that psychologists use as a **framework** to study human behavior are *introversion* and *extroversion*. Through observations and experiments, they try to **clarify** the differences between groups with these traits. An **introvert** generally prefers not to make eye contact and prefers to be alone, while an **extrovert** seeks opportunities to invite people in and start up a conversation. An introvert does not want to make eye contact because he wants to maintain his own personal space. He enters a room **tentatively** and might stand in the corner observing others before talking to them. Privacy is **crucial** to him. In contrast, an extrovert invites people to learn more about her; she may quickly **propose** getting together for some kind of activity even if she has just met someone. She may even make her private life more widely known in a virtual environment such as a website or a Facebook page.

1. _____ *(v.)* to change slightly

2. _____ *(v.)* to suggest a plan or an action

3. _____ *(n.)* a quiet person not interested in spending time with others

4. _____ *(n.)* pieces of information that help solve a puzzle

5. _____ *(v.)* to make something clear and easy to understand

6. _____ *(n.)* a description of somebody or something that gives useful information

7. _____ *(adv.)* without confidence or certainty

8. _____ *(n.)* qualities of a person's character

9. _____ *(n.)* a lively, confident person who enjoys being
with others

10. _____ *(n.)* an area owned or ruled by a person
or government

11. _____ *(adj.)* extremely important

12. _____ *(n.)* a system of ideas or rules

PREVIEW LISTENING 2

What Your Stuff Says About You

You are going to listen to part of a radio interview and call-in show from
NPR's *Talk of the Nation*. On the show, Dr. Sam Gosling, a psychology
professor, discusses his book, *Snoop: What Your Stuff Says About You*.

Dr. Gosling says that he looks for information about people in many places—
and that he uses the word *places* very broadly, to refer not only to physical
areas. Talk with a partner. What kinds of places or things do you think
Dr. Gosling might be interested in?

LISTEN FOR MAIN IDEAS

 CD 2
Track 27

**A. Read the questions. Then listen to the interview. Write short answers.
Compare your ideas with a partner.**

1. What are some places Dr. Gosling snoops around that reveal a great deal
about people?

   _____

   _____

2. Does Dr. Gosling believe that people are always correct in the conclusions
they come to about the possessions and actions of others? Why or why not?

   _____

   _____

3. How does psychology play a role in figuring out "what your stuff says
about you"?

   _____

   _____

LISTEN FOR DETAILS

CD 2
Track 28

B. Listen again. Complete the sentences.

1. Two personal objects the host, Neal Conan, has in his office are

   _____.

2. In addition to the actual objects people display, Dr. Gosling says it is

   important to notice _____.

3. The objects Dr. Gosling indicates as revealing the most about people are

   _____.

4. One example of an oral or virtual environment would be

   _____.

5. The two personality types the psychologist often refers to are

   _____.

6. The experiment mentioned in the interview that affected people's

   impressions of others involved _____.

7. When we are asked, "What does this stuff say about someone?"

   Dr. Gosling believes that the mistake we make is that we might

   _____.

8. In the end, Dr. Gosling decides that the adjective he would use to describe

   the host, Neal Conan, is _____.

WHAT DO YOU THINK?

A. Discuss the questions in a group.

1. Do you agree with Dr. Gosling that we are all natural-born snoops? Why or why not? Use examples from your own life to support your opinion.

2. Look around your classroom. What conclusions might Dr. Gosling draw from what he could see there?

B. Think about both Listening 1 and Listening 2 as you discuss the questions.

1. What different answers might Dr. Gosling and Dr. Craig have to this question that was sent in to *Talk of the Nation*: "What would you say about people who do not include personal items in their offices or cars?"

2. What other professions would be interested in the findings of psychologists and their studies of personal space and privacy? Why?

Vocabulary Skill | Words with multiple meanings

Many words in English have more than one meaning, so you cannot assume that the one definition you know will fit every situation. For example, the following definitions can be found in the dictionary for the word *chair*.

> **chair** 🔑 /tʃer/ *noun, verb*
> ● **noun** **1** [C] a piece of furniture for one person to sit on, with a back, a seat, and four legs: *a table and chairs* ◆ *Sit on your chair!* ◆ *an old man asleep in a chair* (= an ARMCHAIR) ➲ picture on page 235 ➲ see also ARMCHAIR, DECK CHAIR, EASY CHAIR, HIGH CHAIR, MUSICAL CHAIRS, ROCKING CHAIR, WHEELCHAIR **2** [C] = CHAIRMAN, CHAIRPERSON **3** [C] the person in charge of a department in a university: *He is the chair of philosophy at Stanford.* **4** **the chair** [sing.] (*informal*) = THE ELECTRIC CHAIR
> ● **verb ~ sth** to act as the chairman or chairwoman of a meeting, discussion, etc.: *Who's chairing the meeting?*

The dictionary can help you choose the correct definition if you:

1. check the part of speech to eliminate any definitions that do not fit the grammar of the sentence.
2. check the first definition, which is usually the most common definition.
3. look at the sample sentences to determine which best fits the context.

The third step would confirm that the best definition of *chair* in the sentence "She is the chair of the psychology department" is the third definition listed, "the person in charge of a department in a university."

All dictionary entries are from the *Oxford Advanced American Dictionary for learners of English* © Oxford University Press 2011.

A. Read the sentences and write the letter of the correct definition of the underlined words. Use the context and a dictionary to help you.

_____ 1. They didn't understand that the jacket was a <u>marker</u> to save a seat.

_____ 2. She bought a <u>marker</u> to write her name in her books.

    a.   *(n.)* a type of pen that draws thick lines

    b.   *(n.)* an object or sign that shows the position of something

    c.   *(n.)* a sign that something exists or that shows what it is like

_____ 3. In the video game <u>Space</u> Invasion, players engage in wars between the planets.

_____ 4. We try to respect the desk, office <u>space</u>, and seating arrangements.

_____ 5. Can you <u>space</u> the chairs so that they don't touch one another?

    d.   *(n.)* an area or room

    e.   *(n.)* an unused or empty area

    f.   *(n.)* the area around the Earth

    g.   *(n.)* a period of time

    h.   *(v.)* to arrange things with areas or gaps between

_____ 6. Did you <u>mean</u> to leave your jacket on my desk?

_____ 7. The <u>mean</u> number of students who take that psychology class each year is 75.

_____ 8. Radius can <u>mean</u> one-half of a diameter or an area surrounding a point.

    i.   *(v.)* to intend to say or do something

    j.   *(v.)* to have something as a meaning

    k.   *(adj.)* average

    l.   *(adj.)* (of people or their behavior) unkind

_____ 9. She couldn't <u>refrain</u> from trying to make eye contact with him.

_____ 10. The teacher said the same <u>refrain</u> again and again: "Keep your eyes to yourself."

    m. *(n.)* a part of a poem or song that is repeated

    n. *(n.)* a comment or complaint that is often repeated

    o. *(v.)* to stop yourself from doing something

B. Use your dictionary to look up the definitions for one of these words. Copy three definitions and label them *a*, *b*, and *c*. Then write three sentences that reflect the different definitions for each of your words, as in Activity A.

contact	place	stress	stuff	type

Word: _____

Definitions:

a. _____

b. _____

c. _____

Sentences:

a. _____

_____

b. _____

_____

c. _____

_____

C. Take turns reading one of your sentences from Activity B to a partner. See if your partner can choose the correct definition of the word for that sentence.

Grammar Conditionals

The verbs in conditional sentences show:

- the time frame (present, present/future, or past).
- whether the conditions are real (true) or unreal (not true; imaginary).

Present/future real conditionals: There is a real possibility the condition will happen, or it can, should, or might happen.

If clause = present tense form

Result = *will, can, might, should* + base verb

> If he **wants** to make friends, he **should join** a club.
> He **will not enjoy** parties if he **is** an introvert.

Present/future unreal conditionals: The condition is not true now, so the results are not true either.

If clause = past tense form

Result = *would, might* + base verb

> If she **wanted** to reveal more about her personality, she **would display** photos.
> He **might sit** at the front of the classroom if he **weren't** so shy.

Past unreal conditionals: The condition was not true before; the result in the past or the present is not true either.

If clause = past perfect form

Result = *would, could, might* + base verb (present results) *would have, could have, might have* + past participle (past results)

> If they **had asked** everyone about painting the room, no one **would be** angry now.
> If everyone **had contributed** some money, we **could have redecorated**.

 for Success

In present unreal conditionals, the form *were* is used instead of *was* for all speakers: *If I **were** rich, I'd give more money to charity.* However, in informal situations, you may hear people use ***was***.

A. Read the conditional sentence. Then circle the correct conclusion that you can draw.

1. If I'd seen him, I would've said "hello."
   a. I saw the man.
   b. I didn't say "hello."

2. She will probably be standing in a crowd of friends if she is an extrovert.
   a. She isn't standing in a crowd of friends now.
   b. She may be an extrovert, but I'm not sure.

3. If privacy had been so important to her, she wouldn't have left the door open.
   a. Privacy was important to her.
   b. She left the door open.

4. Shouldn't you label your stuff if you want us to know it's yours?
   a. We know it's your stuff.
   b. Your stuff is not labeled.

5. If he weren't so afraid of making new friends, he'd hang out in the library more.
   a. He doesn't hang out in the library much now.
   b. He isn't afraid of making new friends.

6. I would be sitting on that chair if he hadn't left his coat on it.
   a. I am sitting on the chair.
   b. He left his coat on the chair.

B. **Complete the sentences. Then compare them with a partner. Check each other's verb forms.**

1. If I had known you were an extrovert, _____.

2. If I could redecorate my room, _____.

3. If I am going into a new classroom for the first time, _____.

4. If I didn't want to share my space, _____.

5. _____ he might lock the door.

6. _____ I would get a roommate.

7. _____ I wouldn't have gone home early.

8. _____ I would have been angry.

Thought groups are meaningful phrases (groups of words) or clauses (sentence parts that have a subject and a verb) that express an idea. Just as writers use punctuation to separate sentence elements, speakers use intonation and pauses to help listeners process what they are hearing.

If listeners make the wrong connections between your words, this can lead to an error in understanding.

CD 2
Track 29

For example, read and listen to these two sentences. Notice how the different thought groups (indicated with slashes /) change the meaning.

The psychologist / said the lecturer / tries to understand social behavior.
"The psychologist," said the lecturer, "tries to understand social behavior."

The psychologist said / the lecturer / tries to understand social behavior.
The psychologist said, "The lecturer tries to understand social behavior."

To make effective thought groups, remember to:

- divide sentences into meaningful units (don't separate an adjective and a noun, for example).
- put the most stress on the final key word in each thought group.
- end a thought group with a slight fall or a fall-rise in intonation.
- pause slightly at the end of each thought group.
- not drop your pitch too low until the end of a sentence.

CD 2
Track 30

A. Listen to this excerpt from Listening 2. Mark the thought groups you hear by drawing lines between them. Compare your work with a partner. The first sentence is done for you.

Dr. Gosling: That's right / because it's really important / you know / if I had

one wish / one wish in the world / it would be that one clue / told you

something / about a person. If you had a stuffed teddy on your bed it

meant something you know. But the world is more complicated than that.

So unfortunately it doesn't work like that because there are many reasons

why we might have say a stuffed animal on our bed or something like

that. And so really you can't use a codebook approach where *x* means *y*.

What you have to do is you have to build up a picture piece by piece

and sometimes you only have a very little piece and you have to hold

your view very tentatively. But that will that will guide your search for

more information.

As you become a more proficient speaker, try to make your thought groups longer so your speaking is less choppy and more fluent.

B. With your partner, take turns reading one of the following sentences in each set. See if your partner can identify which sentence, *a* or *b*, you are reading.

1. a. So if we really wanted to understand kids, that's the question we would ask.

   b. So, if we really wanted to understand, kids, that's the question we would ask.

2. a. "The lecturer," said the students, "couldn't explain environmental psychology very well."

   b. The lecturer said, "The students couldn't explain environmental psychology very well."

3. a. This is a way of maintaining space. In a rural area, you often feel you have enough space.

   b. This is a way of maintaining space in a rural area. You often feel you have enough space.

4. a. "The psychologist," claims my sister, "is an extrovert," but I don't believe it.

   b. The psychologist claims my sister is an extrovert, but I don't believe it.

Speaking Skill | Giving advice

Knowing how to make suggestions and give advice without sounding pushy or demanding is an important conversational skill.

In each column in the chart, the expressions are listed from the weakest to the strongest forms of advice.

Advice with modals in the present/future	Advice with modals in the past	Advice using *if*	Other expressions
You might want to . . .	You could have . . .	If I were you, I would . . .	Why don't you . . . ?
You can/could . . .	You might have . . .	(Notice that we use *if I were you* to show that the speaker is not really that person.)	Have you thought about . . . ?
You should . . .			
You ought to . . .	You should have . . .		Whatever you do, don't . . . !
You had better (You'd better) . . .	You had to . . .		Whatever you do, make sure to . . . !
You must (not) . . .			

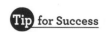

A. Work in a group. Take turns reading the problems below and giving advice to the speaker according to the situation. Share and discuss your sentences in a group.

A: *My sister thinks I'm a slob because I don't wash or clean my car.*

B: *I think you should clean it if you want to change her attitude.*

C: *Yeah, if I were you, I'd clean it. Otherwise she won't want to go anywhere with you.*

D: *Why don't you ask a couple of friends to help you clean it?*

1. People make fun of me for wearing crazy clothes.

2. My room is so full of stuff I can't get any work done.

3. Our neighbors are going to build a tall fence around their property.

4. I'd like to ask my instructor for help, but I feel too shy.

5. I sat next to someone on the subway this morning, and he gave me a terrible look.

6. My roommate is always using my computer.

B. Work with a partner. Role-play a conversation with a friend who is moving into an empty office space for his or her first job. Take turns asking for and giving advice on ways to personalize the space and mark it as his or her own.

Unit Assignment | Role-play a talk show

 In this section, you will role-play a talk show. As you prepare your role-play, think about the Unit Question, "How do you make a space your own?" and refer to the Self-Assessment checklist on page 146.

For alternative unit assignments, see the *Q: Skills for Success Teacher's Handbook.*

CONSIDER THE IDEAS

Listen to this excerpt from a radio call-in show, in which a psychologist helps two college roommates who need advice about sharing a space. Discuss the questions below in a group.

1. What is the main issue that is causing the problem between the roommates? What kind of advice do you think Dr. Hill will offer?

2. Talk about a time when your own feelings about personal space caused you to come into conflict with someone else. What happened? How did you resolve the conflict? What did you learn from it?

PREPARE AND SPEAK

A. **GATHER IDEAS** In a group, talk about the kinds of conflicts that can develop when people live together. Brainstorm different types of relationships, the conflicts that might come up between people regarding personal space, and solutions. Write your ideas in the chart.

Relationship	Conflict	Advice / Solution

B. `ORGANIZE IDEAS` In pairs or groups of three, write a script for a role-play of a talk show, using one of the conflicts you came up with in Activity A. One or two of you will play the role(s) of someone with a problem related to space. One of you will be the expert who offers advice and solutions. Follow these steps.

1. Introduce yourselves and describe your situation and relationship.

2. Explain the problem or conflict over personal space.

3. Offer solutions and advice, both real and imaginary.

4. Give your reactions to the advice.

Tip for Success

In order to avoid monotone intonation or flat speaking, make sure to show enthusiasm and interest by stressing key words so they stand out.

C. `SPEAK` Practice your role-play in your group, and then present it to the class. Ask the class if they can think of any other solutions to the problem you presented. Refer to the Self-Assessment checklist below before you begin.

CHECK AND REFLECT

A. `CHECK` Think about the Unit Assignment as you complete the Self-Assessment checklist.

Yes	No	SELF-ASSESSMENT
☐	☐	I was able to speak fluently about the topic.
☐	☐	My group and class understood me.
☐	☐	I used conditionals correctly.
☐	☐	I used vocabulary from the unit to express my ideas.
☐	☐	I phrased my sentences in thought groups to help my speech sound more natural.
☐	☐	I was able to give advice.

B. `REFLECT` Discuss these questions with a partner.

What is something new you learned in this unit?

 Look back at the Unit Question. Is your answer different now than when you started this unit? If yes, how is it different? Why?

Track Your Success

Circle the words and phrases you learned in this unit.

Nouns	Verbs	Adverbs
belongings	clarify AWL	moderately
clue	invade	tentatively
domain AWL	modify AWL	**Phrases**
extrovert	propose 🔑	affiliate with
framework AWL	**Adjectives**	ingrained in
gender AWL	adjacent AWL	**Phrasal Verbs**
introvert	crucial 🔑 AWL	engage in 🔑
profile 🔑	remarkable 🔑	refrain from
radius	suburban	
trait		

🔑 Oxford 3000™ words

AWL Academic Word List

Check (✓) the skills you learned. If you need more work on a skill, refer to the page(s) in parentheses.

LISTENING	●	I can recognize organizational cues. (p. 132)
VOCABULARY	●	I can use words with multiple meanings. (p. 137)
GRAMMAR	●	I can use conditionals. (p. 140)
PRONUNCIATION	●	I can use thought groups. (p. 142)
SPEAKING	●	I can give advice. (p. 143)
LEARNING OUTCOME	●	I can role-play a talk show focused on identifying and solving conflicts centered on issues of personal space.

UNIT 7

Alternative Thinking

LISTENING ● distinguishing between facts and opinions
VOCABULARY ● idioms and informal expressions
GRAMMAR ● noun clauses
PRONUNCIATION ● conditional modals: affirmative and negative
SPEAKING ● using formal and informal language

LEARNING OUTCOME ●

Develop a marketing presentation
designed to sell a new invention
or idea.

Unit QUESTION

Where do new ideas come from?

PREVIEW THE UNIT

A Discuss these questions with your classmates.

How do you come up with new ideas or solve problems?
Where do you look for inspiration?

What do you think have been some of the best inventions in
the past ten years?

Look at the photo. What do you think the two women are
mapping out on the wall?

B Discuss the Unit Question above with your classmates.

🔊 Listen to *The Q Classroom*, Track 2 on CD 3, to hear other answers.

C Complete the survey. Then share and explain your responses in a group. Give specific examples where you can. Discuss what your answers show about your personality.

When you . . . ,
. . . what do you do?

1. want to decide what movie to see
   - ☐ read the newspaper or a magazine
   - ☐ talk to friends
   - ☐ read online reviews

2. are sick
   - ☐ use traditional or folk remedies
   - ☐ rely on mainstream medicine
   - ☐ try a new-age or alternative therapy

3. prepare a meal for friends
   - ☐ make a favorite family dish
   - ☐ try a new recipe from a magazine
   - ☐ check the refrigerator and use what's there

4. imagine where you'll live in the future
   - ☐ imagine a house like where you grew up
   - ☐ imagine a home like one you have visited or seen on TV
   - ☐ imagine a futuristic home

5. need a new cell phone
   - ☐ get a similar model to the one you have
   - ☐ carefully research new phones and their features
   - ☐ buy a popular model or one your friends recommend

6. fail at a task
   - ☐ give up on the task and do something else instead
   - ☐ ask someone for help
   - ☐ rethink your plan and start over

7. are faced with a problem
   - ☐ use a solution that worked in the past
   - ☐ think up a new solution
   - ☐ brainstorm several possible solutions

LISTENING 1 | Alternative Ideas in Medicine

VOCABULARY

Here are some words and phrases from Listening 1. Read the sentences. Cross out the word or phrase with a different meaning from the bold word or phrase.

1. Housing prices have increased because of the **shortage** of wood and other raw materials.
    a. poor quality   b. scarcity   c. lack

2. The appliances were packed in a large **container** for shipping.
    a. box   b. carton   c. house

3. Before you travel to France, you should **convert** your dollars to euros.
    a. change   b. preserve   c. transform

4. The space center built a **prototype** of the spacecraft to test it in a controlled environment.
    a. model   b. diagram   c. example

5. I'm **reluctant** to spend any more money on this failing project.
    a. hesitant   b. excited   c. unwilling

6. Please take a minute to **verify** the correct spelling of your name and address.
    a. confirm   b. check   c. hide

7. After adding two simple elements together, the scientist told us she had discovered a new **compound** that would cure a common cold.
    a. chemical   b. alternative   c. bonded
       reaction   medicine   mixture

8. You must follow the proper **protocol** for your experiment to be valid.
    a. procedure   b. set of rules   c. trend

9. My cousin applied for a visa, but unfortunately, he was **denied**.
    a. rejected   b. refused   c. reminded

10. I've heard **anecdotal evidence** that vitamin E helps cuts heal faster, but I've never read any research that supports that.
    a. scientific proof   b. personal reports   c. individual observations

11. It's important to review your investments **periodically**; my advisor recommends checking every three or four months.
   a. occasionally   b. constantly   c. regularly

12. All of his clever arguments still didn't **convince** me to change my mind.
   a. persuade   b. prevent   c. influence

PREVIEW LISTENING 1

Alternative Ideas in Medicine

Doc-in-a-Box, exterior

You are going to listen to two reports: "Doc-in-a-Box?" from WorldVision.org and "Bee Sting Therapy" from North Carolina Public Radio. They present innovative ideas that may benefit people's health.

With a partner, look at the photos. In the chart, list some typical uses of bees and of shipping containers. Then brainstorm some unconventional uses for them. Write down your ideas, and then share them with another pair.

Doc-in-a-Box, interior

a beekeeper

	Conventional uses	Unconventional uses
1. Bees		
2. Shipping containers		

LISTEN FOR MAIN IDEAS

A. Listen to the reports. Use the chart to take notes. Then compare notes with a partner and add any missing information.

	Report 1: Doc-in-a-Box	Report 2: Bee Sting Therapy
1. Meaning of the term and where it came from	- Doc. in a box; comes from dr's office in box-shaped shipping containers	medical therapy using bees; comes from apis which means bee in Latin + therapy
2. Problem it is trying to solve	- provide cheap medical services to remote, poor villages	- trying to cure disease in a new, alternative way and/or relieve pain
3. Analysis of the solution: Benefits	① reasonable price ② use old abandoned shipping containers ③ easy transport to remote villages	① cheap ② works according to anecdotal evidence ③ can be used by patients w/ doc
4. Analysis of the solution: Obstacles	① expense ② idea still in early stages ③ prototype clinic was expensive ($5000) but could be built for less	① not a lot of research ② not accepted yet by mainstream dr. ③ people may have trouble accepting the idea — cortisol from adrenal gland

B. Listen again. Then ask and answer the questions in pairs. Use your notes from Activity A to help you.

Report 1: Doc-in-a-Box?

1. What is the meaning of *Doc-in-a-Box*? — dr's working in a box-shaped office made out of shipping containers

2. What problem is the Doc-in-a-Box program trying to solve? How is the program trying to solve it? — In some remote villages there are no drs. Doc in a box can be built cheaply & transported easily

Report 2: Bee Sting Therapy

3. What is apitherapy and why does it work? — using bee sting to alleviate pain. Something in bee venom may release an anti-inflammatory

4. Why are the speakers so enthusiastic about this type of therapy? — good healing powers at low cost of treatment — venom may change how body transmits pain

Both Reports:

5. What are the main obstacles faced by those who try to present alternative ideas in medicine to the medical community? — ① acceptance by public ② funding for research + dev'l.

| Listening and Speaking   153

LISTEN FOR DETAILS

CD 3
Track 4

Read the statements. Then listen again. Write *T* (true) or *F* (false). Correct the false statements.

Report 1

_F_ 1. Laurie Garrett, founder of the Doc-in-a-Box idea, works for the Ministry of Health. *(Pulitzer Prize - winning science writer)*

_F_ 2. Doc-in-a-Box medical centers could only offer medical care to poor people in cities near ports where ships could unload the containers. *bee or (hoop clos)*

_T_ 3. Ministries of Health or non-governmental agencies would operate the Doc-in-a-Box clinics.

_F_ 4. Garrett hopes that the Doc-in-a-Box clinics will mostly be staffed by doctors and paramedics from famous hospitals around the world. *- staffed by local village paramedics + midwives*

_T_ 5. Garrett believes the container price could eventually go down from $5,000 to $1,500.

Report 2

_F_ 6. Frederique Keller is a nurse and an acupuncturist. *beekeeper*

_T_ 7. It is difficult to travel with the bees.

_F_ 8. The idea behind apipuncture is to use the venom of dead bees to treat pain or discomfort. *live*

_F_ 9. Andrew Cokin, a pain management doctor, says that the use of bee products already has a strong tradition in Asia and South America. *Eastern Europe*

_T_ 10. According to former state legislator Fountain Odom, alternatives such as bee therapy are inexpensive and worth supporting.

Q WHAT DO YOU THINK?

Discuss the questions in a group.

1. In both of the reports in Listening 1, people have come up with a new use for something that has been around a long time. Can you think of any other inventions or therapies that are examples of the same principles?

2. Would you go to a doctor whose office was in a shipping container? Would you trust a bee to cure your pain? Why or why not?

(handwritten margin note: fact or opinion)

3. In each of the two reports, do you feel that the narrator is taking a neutral position, or is he or she trying to persuade the listeners to accept or reject the idea? Explain your reasons.

(handwritten margin notes: fact can be proven; opinion personal belief; speakers should support opinions w/ logic, examples + facts)

A **fact** is something that is known to be true or that can be proven or disproven. An **opinion** is someone's personal belief. It cannot be proven or disproven. The ability to distinguish between facts and opinions helps you analyze the strength of a speaker's argument. It also helps you determine if the information provided is reliable. For example, we expect speakers to offer *support* for their opinions through their use of logic, examples, or facts.

Noticing certain words or phrases while you listen can help you identify whether a statement is a fact or an opinion.

Words or phrases identifying facts

- **Verbs that signal information or research:** *show, prove, verify, support, cause*
- **Numbers, statistics, or time periods to introduce facts:** *40 percent of, 15 students, for 200 years, since the early 20th century*
- **Expressions to introduce factual support:** *studies conducted, eyewitness reports, from the evidence, data reveal, studies have shown*

Words or phrases identifying opinions

- **Expressions to signal a belief, perception, or interpretation:** *I think, we believe, it seems, it appears*
- **Modals to signal advice, certainty, or possible solutions:** *should, must, could, might*
- **Adjectives that express judgments:** *best, worst, most important*
- **Adverbs and other words that show uncertainty:** *likely, probably, possibly, maybe, perhaps*

CD 3 Track 5

Listen to these examples from Listening 1.

Facts: Bee venom has been used as a treatment since the time of the Greeks and for at least 2,000, 3,000 years in Chinese medicine.

Opinions: We believe that there are tremendous opportunities for the beekeepers of this state to develop some of the ancient modalities for medical treatment of pain and other uses. These are some alternatives that are very, very inexpensive.

CD 3 Track 6

A. Listen to the sentences. Identify them as *F* (fact) or *O* (opinion). Write the word or phrase that helps you decide. Then compare answers with a partner. The first one is done for you.

Sentence	Fact or Opinion?	Words / Phrases
1	O	I think, unreliable
2	F	can find online
3	F	was developed, cost 5000
4	O	believes, could
5	O	should
6	F	reports
7	F	is based on
8	O	so expensive, probably
9	O	best
10	F	is sometimes used

CD 3 Track 7

B. Listen to this advertisement for an alternative medicine and complete the sentences with the words and phrases the speakers use. With a partner, talk about whether the ad relies mostly on fact or opinion to convince the audience. Then explain why you would or wouldn't buy the product.

Go-Cream

Speaker: Have you noticed that your legs get tired in the middle of the day?

Do you wish you could keep going when your body wants you to sit down?

Do you have trouble keeping up with other people—or with life in general?

Our __amazing__ product, Go-Cream, is the answer you've been
₁
looking for. It offers the __absolute best__ solution for tired legs and
₂
low energy. After just one application of this energizing leg cream, you

__should be__ convinced. Made from the oils of the Brazil nut and
₃
sand from the beaches of Hawaii, Go-Cream soothes and energizes at the

same time. __Thousands__ of people suffer from tired legs, but now
₄
there is relief. Listen to what some of our satisfied customers have to say.

Customer 1: I'm a busy mother of four, and I've been using this product

__For two years__. I've tried vitamins and other alternative therapies,
₅

156

UNIT 7 | Where do new ideas come from?

but nothing worked—until Go-Cream. It's definitely _the most effective_
6
product out there and a deal at only $9.99 a jar.

Customer 2: _I believe_ Go-Cream is for people of all ages.
7
My friends and I are students, and we're always on the go. We've all

tried Go-Cream and noticed a big difference in our energy. And it

probably even helps make your skin smoother and
8
healthier, too.

Speaker: Don't get left behind. Order your Go-Cream today!

LISTENING 2 | Boulder Bike-to-School Program Goes International

VOCABULARY

Here are some words and a phrase from Listening 2. Read the sentences. Then write each bold word or phrase next to the correct definition.

1. I ride a bike to school occasionally, but my doctor says I really need to exercise **consistently** to improve my health.

2. When you have to give an **impromptu** speech, it's easy to make mistakes and forget to cover all the crucial information.

3. The **incentive** for trying out acupuncture is one month of free treatments.

4. Some supermarkets have automatic checkouts, where you scan the **bar codes** on your groceries yourself.

5. The organization made a **substantial** donation to our school, so we were able to buy 500 new computers.

6. The marketing department made some **outrageous** claims about the product that could not be proven.

7. What's the latest **buzzword** to get young adults excited about a new product?

8. A motor **propels** a car, but a bike is propelled by foot power.

9. Land in the countryside is cheaper to buy, but there is no existing **infrastructure**, such as water pipes and electric cables.

10. The committee **submitted** several plans to encourage children to participate in healthy activities.

11. The school district tried to get a **grant** to pay for bikes for children who couldn't afford one.

12. Before we can **implement** the new plan, we must get approval from management.

a. _bar code_ (n.) a pattern of lines that contains information read by a computer

b. _infrastructure_ (n.) the basic systems and services necessary for a country or city to run

c. _submit_ (v.) to give to somebody in authority for consideration; to hand in

d. _propel_ (v.) to move, drive, or push forward

e. _substantial_ (adj.) large in value or importance

f. _outrageous_ (adj.) very unusual and slightly shocking

g. _implement_ (v.) to make something start to happen

h. _consistently_ (adv.) repeatedly and in the same way

i. _grant_ (n.) a sum of money to be used for a specific purpose

j. _incentive_ (n.) something that encourages somebody to do something; a reward

k. _impromptu_ (adj.) done without preparation or planning

l. _buzzword_ (n.) an expression or phrase that has become popular

PREVIEW LISTENING 2

Boulder Bike-to-School Program Goes International

You are going to listen to a *Colorado Matters* radio interview with
Tim Carlin, the executive director of a program called "Freiker." Carlin
describes the idea he and his partner came up with to encourage children
to ride bikes to school.

Check (✓) the ways you think kids could be encouraged to bike to school.
Then listen to find out if any of them are mentioned as part of Carlin's plan.

☐ get praised by teachers and parents

☐ get an iPod

☐ get a water bottle

☐ get a certificate from the school

☐ get stickers

☐ get extra credit in a school class

☐ get healthy

☐ get a cash gift

LISTEN FOR MAIN IDEAS

CD 3
Track 8

**Listen to the interview. Write short answers. Then discuss them with a
partner.**

combines frequent + biker
frequent biker program

1. Where did the word "Freiker" come from, and why does the name of the
   program have to change?

   — has to change name because walkers are
   now included.

2. How has the application of old and new technologies improved the way
   that the parents keep track of who is biking to school?

   radio frequency i.d.

   started w punch cards → bar codes → RFID tags
   now freikometer (it registers their ride so
   parents can help in class instead of monitoring

3. How does this program connect health, active transportation, and safety?

   buzz word.

   active tran = kids get themselves to school
   they ≠ get rides from parents.
   —riding bike is healthful activity
   —helps dev'l Freiker "safe routes to school."

   "ipod a day"

LISTEN FOR DETAILS

A. Listen again for the facts and complete the sentences with the correct information. Compare your answers with a partner.

1. The Freiker program at Crestview was started by two dads, and now about *1/2 the kids who can* _____ *50* _____ percent of the schoolchildren bike to that school.

2. The Freiker program has expanded to the states of Oregon and California in the U.S., and internationally to *Canada* _____.

3. The incentive offered to children who rode to school over 90 percent of the days was a(n) *iPod* _____.

4. The three main sources of funding for the Freiker program are

① Safe Routes to School, ② local bike shops, ③ community groups.

B. Which of these two opinions might Carlin have? Discuss your choice with a partner.

1. It seems the incentives aren't working because fewer students are biking to school.

2. The Freiker program has been successful because technology has made it easier.

WHAT DO YOU THINK?

A. Discuss the questions in a group.

1. What are some advantages and disadvantages of offering children incentives to improve their health? What are some other ways to achieve the same goal?

2. Do you think it is possible to implement the Freiker program in every type of community? In what types of communities would it be easier? More difficult?

B. Think about both Listening 1 and Listening 2 as you discuss the questions.

1. Why is it challenging for some people to give up traditional methods for newer, innovative ones? What are some reasons others find it easy to make those changes?

2. Where should the money come from to support new ideas like the ones presented in this unit? How can people raise money or support for new ideas like these?

| Vocabulary Skill | Idioms and informal expressions | |

Informal expressions can enrich your language when used correctly. However, informal language also affects the tone of the conversation or speech, and you should be very careful not to use informal language in the wrong situation. Here are some reasons people use informal language.

- To show that they belong to a certain group, such as young people or a certain club
- To show other people they are friendly, relaxed, or approachable
- To make a serious subject seem easier to understand

Most dictionaries indicate when words have an informal meaning (**kid** ▪ noun, *informal*) or are considered **slang** (**dude** ▪ noun, *slang*), meaning too informal and used only in conversation. Many **idioms** or set expressions are considered informal and are usually labeled (**IDM**) and listed in learners' dictionaries in a separate section at the end of an entry. Check the meaning of idioms and informal or slang expressions carefully before using them.

You can find an idiom by looking up the keyword—usually a noun or a verb—such as *think* in *think outside the box*. The keyword may not always be the first word in the expression. In addition, the idiom or informal expression may not always be the first meaning listed for a word. Look at these examples of idioms using the keyword *think*.

> *nothing of walking thirty miles a day.* **think on your feet** to be able to think and react to things very quickly and effectively without any preparation **think outside (of) the box** to think about something, or how to do something, in a way that is new, different, or shows imagination **think straight** to think in a clear or logical way **think twice about sth/**

All dictionary entries are from the *Oxford Advanced American Dictionary for learners of English* © Oxford University Press 2011.

A. Circle the keywords of these expressions. Then write a more formal expression for each one.

[handwritten: distance]

[handwritten annotation on left margin: for understand]

Informal expression	More formal alternative
1. the (buzz)	news; rumors
2. just around the corner	*[handwritten: will happen very soon]*
3. the deal is / here's the deal	*[handwritten: here is the situation]*
4. to catch on	*[handwritten: to gain popularity, to understand]*
5. to get (something) off the ground	*[handwritten: to implement something]*
6. a cut above (something)	*[handwritten: superior to, of better quality than]*
7. to wrap (something) up	*[handwritten: to conclude, to complete, to finish]*
8. wild about (something)	*[handwritten: thrilled with, delighted with, very enthusiastic]*

CD 3
Track 10

B. Listen to these excerpts from Listening 1 and Listening 2. Complete the sentences with the idiom or informal expression you hear. Discuss the meanings of each expression with a partner. Check a dictionary if necessary.

1. **Rose Hoban:** But now Odom's a true believer. He says getting stung is the only thing that helps him with his pain. He's also convinced his wife, and that's _a big deal_, since she's the state secretary for Health and Human Services.

   Meaning: _Something that is important or exciting_

2. **Rose Hoban:** Keller was here for the annual meeting of the American Apitherapy Society in Durham a couple of weeks ago. She demonstrated bee venom therapy during a session for about a dozen people who practically _buzzed with_ excitement as they waited to get stung.

   Meaning: _to be full of excitement, activity_

3. **Fountain Odom:** They might look at you askance or say, "Uh, you know, you are ~~Kind of flaky~~, aren't you? I mean, why would you want to be stung by a bee?"

   [handwritten above askance: look of suspicion or disapproval]

   Meaning: ~~odd or eccentric; a bit crazy~~

4. **Laurie Garrett:** There was a description of a place called "Container City" in London in which shipping containers, painted in primary colors, had been stacked in unusual ways to create apartment buildings. And I, I simply thought of it at that moment and a little sort of "bingo" ~~light bulb went off~~ in my head.

   Meaning: ~~to get a good idea.~~

5. **Narrator:** Laurie Garrett, who now works with the Council on Foreign Relations, hopes governments and aid organizations will take her idea and ~~run with it~~. She believes the container clinics, ultimately, could make portable medicine a reality for people in countries that need it most.

   Meaning: ~~to accept or start to use a new idea.~~

6. **Tim Carlin:** So, once we felt that we had a really good day-to-day tracking system, we, um, well, Rob, the guy who, ah, really started the program, decided that, um, "Why don't we ~~shoot for the moon~~ and offer a crazy incentive?" And, ah, his crazy incentive was an iPod.

   Meaning: ~~try to achieve or attain a goal that seems out of reach; to take a great risk in order to gain a great reward~~

SPEAKING

A **noun clause** is a group of words that functions as a noun. Like a noun, it can be a subject or a direct object in a sentence. It is a dependent clause and cannot stand alone as a sentence.

Noun clauses can combine two clauses, showing a connection between the ideas. To combine two statements, use *that*. Notice how the entire noun clause in the second sentence functions in the same way as the simpler noun in the first sentence.

The researchers explained the problem.
subject   verb   direct object

The government didn't support the protocol.
subject   verb   direct object

main clause   noun clause
The researchers explained **that** the government didn't support the protocol.
subject   verb   subject   verb

To combine a statement and a *Yes/No* question, use *if* or *whether*.

They don't know the answer. Can they verify the information in time?
They don't know **if they can verify the information in time**.

To combine a statement and a *wh-* question, use the *wh-* question word (*who, what, where, when, why,* or *how*).

I want to understand the issue. How do they change a container into a clinic?
I want to understand **how they change a container into a clinic**.

In a noun clause that begins with *if/whether* or a *wh-* question word, use sentence word order, not question word order.

✓ Scientists don't understand exactly <u>why</u> **bee sting therapy works**.
✗ Scientists don't understand exactly why does bee sting therapy work.

A noun clause can also be the subject of a verb, though this sounds very formal.

Where this program goes next is up to you to decide.
subject

A. Underline the noun clause in each sentence.

1. She believes the container clinics, ultimately, could make portable medicine a reality for people in countries that need it most.

2. I've had patients in the last 20 years who told me that relatives of theirs, older relatives working in the garden, had accidently got stung on their hands by a bee, and their arthritis got better.

3. And I might also add that we also include walkers now, um, as part of the program.

4. We see no reason why, if retrofitting is done on a mass scale . . . , these containers couldn't come in for well under $1,500 apiece.

5. Some compounds in bee venom might affect how the body transmits pain signals to the brain, but it's hard to know for sure.

6. He told me how this grew from a handful of kids at Crestview Elementary School in Boulder into an international program.

Tip for Success

It is common to delete the word *that* before noun clauses in speaking, but not in writing. *Garrett says [that] the cost of the clinics could be less.*

B. Work with a partner. Take turns reading the sets of two short sentences and combining them by using a noun clause.

> **A:** *Should I invest in that new product? I'm not sure.*
> **B:** *I'm not sure if I should invest in that new product.*

1. He thought that his coworker had stolen his idea. He told his boss.

2. Do we want to sell it online? We aren't sure.

3. Where did they develop the prototype? I need to find out.

4. How did they raise enough money to give away iPods? It's not clear.

5. Why can't we convince people to get stung by bees? I don't understand.

6. Can they convince the public to buy it? They are trying to decide.

7. When was the product featured on the air? We are trying to find out.

8. The incentive could be seen as too outrageous. The group was worried.

The auxiliary verbs *have* and *has* in conditional modal expressions such as *could have*, *would have*, and *should have* have a weakened **reduced form** when spoken. You may hear only the /v/ sound or what sounds like the word *of*.

In addition, in the negative contracted forms *couldn't have*, *wouldn't have*, and *shouldn't have*, the /t/ sound is not said distinctly. Therefore, it can be difficult to know whether you have heard *could have* or *couldn't have*!

To tell the difference, listen for the number of syllables (beats). *Could have*, even when the *have* is reduced, has two syllables. *Couldn't have* has three syllables.

CD 3 Track 11

Listen and repeat these sentences.

> I could have told her.
> I couldn't have told her.
> You should have come on Sunday.
> You shouldn't have come on Sunday.
> We would have been happy with that answer.
> We wouldn't have been happy with that answer.

CD 3 Track 12

A. Listen to the sentences. For each, circle *A* (affirmative) or *N* (negative).

1. A   N   5. A   N

2. A   N   6. A   N

3. A   N   7. A   N

4. A   N   8. A   N

CD 3 Track 13

B. Practice the conversations with a partner. Pay attention to the modal expressions. Then listen to check your pronunciation.

1. **A:** Did you read about that woman who tried bee sting therapy? That's crazy! I wouldn't have done something like that. Would you?

   B: Well, I'm not sure. I would have researched it first, of course. I wouldn't have dismissed it without finding out about it, though.

   A: I wonder if it helped her at all. Perhaps she should have gone to a conventional doctor.

   B: But the article said that her arthritis was completely cured. Maybe you should have finished reading it.

2. **A:** I went to an amazing conference on alternative medicine yesterday. You should have been there. You would have loved it.

   B: I know, but I had a big test to study for. If I hadn't studied, I wouldn't have passed. What did I miss?

   A: Well, the best part was this guy who talked about using shark fin extract to help boost your immune system. I wouldn't have imagined that was possible. But he convinced me and even gave out some free samples.

   B: Really? Maybe if I had been there, I could have tried one of those shark fin samples. I think I'm getting a cold.

Speaking Skill   Using formal and informal language

Deciding when to use formal and informal language, or appropriate **register**, is an important speaking skill. Register is reflected in the words, expressions, and pronunciation that speakers use.

What determines different

Different situations and different audiences determine the register you should use. For example, it is too informal to use words like *stuff* and *awesome* when giving an academic presentation. However, it is too formal to try to convince a friend to look at your new cell phone by saying, "I would like you to examine this phone." You would probably just say, "Hey, check this out!"

In general, English speakers use more formal language with people they don't know or people of a higher social status and more informal language with friends or family members. However, the situation itself is also important. You might use informal language with an older, unfamiliar person in a relaxed social situation such as a party or a picnic. You might use more formal language if you were asking a close friend for a large favor or delivering some difficult or bad news.

Formal register uses . . .	Informal register uses . . .
uncontracted forms such as *cannot, did not, he would*	more contractions such as *can't, didn't, he'd*
discourse markers such as *I see, Yes, Actually, Exactly*	discourse markers such as *OK, Yeah, Sure, Well, Oh*
more passive voice	more active voice
standard English vocabulary	idioms, informal expressions, and slang
more one-word verbs	more phrasal verbs
longer, more complex sentences	shorter sentences

A. In what ways would your use of formal or informal language differ in these three situations? Discuss your points with a partner.

1. Explaining to your friend how you damaged his car in an accident / Reporting an accident in your friend's car to your insurance company

2. Explaining to your sister or brother why you had to buy the latest technology gadget / Explaining to your parents why you needed a new technology device

3. Telling your friend about a new social networking site you found. / Giving a report to your class about a social networking site

B. Work with a partner. Choose one of the situations in Activity A or a similar one. Write a conversation. Make sure you use appropriately formal or informal language. Practice your conversation, and then present it to another pair or the class.

Unit Assignment | **Market a new idea**

 In this section, you are going to prepare a short presentation to "sell" a new invention or idea. As you prepare your presentation, think about the Unit Question, "Where do new ideas come from?" and refer to the Self-Assessment checklist on page 170.

For alternative unit assignments, see the *Q: Skills for Success Teacher's Handbook*.

CONSIDER THE IDEAS

 CD 3
Track 14

A. Listen to these two marketing presentations for a new product, the Vibrating Wallet. One presentation is for an audience of businesspeople looking to invest in a new product. The other is for an audience of young adult consumers. Take notes on types of language the speakers use in each ad. Listen for formal and informal expressions, facts and opinions, and reduced forms. Compare notes with a partner.

B. Discuss these questions in a group.

1. What problem is this invention trying to solve?

2. Does this product recycle old ideas, demonstrate alternative thinking, or combine old and new ideas?

3. How does each marketing presentation attempt to appeal to the two different audiences? Are the presentations effective? What other suggestions might you offer to help sell this product to these audiences?

4. Would you buy this product? Why or why not?

PREPARE AND SPEAK

Tip Critical Thinking

In this Unit Assignment, you will discuss possible inventions that can solve a problem. When you **invent** solutions, even in your imagination, you are applying knowledge to create something new.

A. GATHER IDEAS Work with a partner. Discuss possible inventions or solutions to these problems or one of your own. Be creative.

Problem	Invention / Solution
1. remembering to take back your credit card	
2. losing your cell phone or mp3 player	
3. forgetting all of your Internet passwords	
4. not having enough time to clean your house	
5. spending too much money for public transportation	
6. (your own idea)	

B. ORGANIZE IDEAS Follow these steps to organize your ideas.

1. Work with your partner. Choose one problem and invention or solution from Activity A. You will make a presentation to a large group of business investors or a small gathering of young customers. Decide whether your presentation will be formal or informal.

2. Write an outline with notes for your presentation. Use this format.

    I. Introduction

    II. Problem / existing situation

    III. Description of invention / solution

    IV. Benefits or advantages of invention / solution

    V. Conclusion

3. Write note cards with your key ideas and any special language you want to use. Divide the presentation material so that each partner speaks for about the same amount of time.

C. SPEAK Practice your presentation a few times. Then give it to a group or the whole class. Refer to the Self-Assessment checklist below before you begin.

CHECK AND REFLECT

A. CHECK Think about the Unit Assignment as you complete the Self-Assessment checklist.

	SELF-ASSESSMENT

Yes	No	
☐	☐	I was able to speak fluently about the topic.
☐	☐	My partner and my group or class understood me.
☐	☐	I used noun clauses correctly.
☐	☐	I used vocabulary to talk about innovations, problems, and solutions.
☐	☐	I pronounced affirmative and negative conditional modals correctly.
☐	☐	I distinguished between facts and opinions and used them appropriately.
☐	☐	I used formal and informal language correctly.

B. REFLECT Discuss these questions with a partner.

What is something new you learned in this unit?

 Look back at the Unit Question. Is your answer different now than when you started this unit? If yes, how is it different? Why?

Track Your Success

Circle the words and phrases you learned in this unit.

Nouns
bar code
buzzword
compound
container 🔑
grant 🔑 AWL
idiom
incentive AWL
infrastructure AWL
protocol AWL
prototype

Verbs
convert 🔑 AWL
convince 🔑 AWL
deny 🔑 AWL
implement AWL
propel
submit AWL
verify

Adjectives
impromptu
outrageous

reluctant AWL
substantial 🔑

Adverbs
consistently AWL
periodically AWL

Phrases
anecdotal evidence
shortage of

🔑 Oxford 3000™ words
AWL Academic Word List

Check (✓) the skills you learned. If you need more work on a skill, refer to the page(s) in parentheses.

LISTENING	●	I can distinguish between facts and opinions. (p. 155)
VOCABULARY	●	I can use idioms and informal expressions. (p. 161)
GRAMMAR	●	I can use noun clauses. (p. 164)
PRONUNCIATION	●	I can pronounce reduced forms. (p. 166)
SPEAKING	●	I can use formal and informal language appropriately. (p. 167)
LEARNING OUTCOME	●	I can develop a marketing presentation designed to sell a new invention or idea.

LISTENING	recognizing attitudes
VOCABULARY	phrasal verbs
GRAMMAR	gerunds and infinitives
PRONUNCIATION	consonant variations
SPEAKING	paraphrasing

UNIT **8**

Change

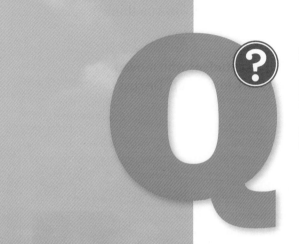

Unit QUESTION

How do people react to change?

PREVIEW THE UNIT

A **Discuss these questions with your classmates.**

How many times has your family moved? Have you or your family moved for work, education, or other reasons?

List a few major changes in your life. Are you a person who welcomes new opportunities or one who avoids change?

Look at the photo. How is this an example of someone reacting to change?

B **Discuss the Unit Question above with your classmates.**

Listen to *The Q Classroom*, Track 15 on CD 3, to hear other answers.

C According to recent United Nations statistics, people are migrating more than ever. Look at the statistics and discuss the question.

Percentage of population that are immigrants:		Actual numbers of immigrants in specific region:	
United States	13	Western Asia	22 million
Canada	18.9	North America	45 million
Australia	19.6	Europe	64 million

Do these statistics surprise you? In a group, discuss why you think people move so often.

D Read this blog post written by a university student who moved from China to Canada as a child. Then work in a group. Discuss the questions below.

Good News, Bad News
By Huang Yubin   Wednesday, May 5 at 11:22 a.m.

In China we have a story about a farmer whose theme is "Good news, bad news—who knows?" What we sometimes think is bad news may turn out to be good news. When my parents decided to move to Canada, I was angry. I was just 12 years old. We lived in a big house with all of our family around us. I was considered a good student in my school, and I had lots of friends. I was a ping-pong champion and spent weekends playing with friends or competing in tournaments. Suddenly, my parents wanted me to give up the life I loved. Bad news.

I hated my new life. Even though I had studied English in my home country, I felt lost. My accent made it hard for people to understand me, and everyone spoke so fast I could barely understand them. I had to work twice as hard, and I was still not considered a good student. I made it worse by staying by myself; I didn't have any friends. I was a very unhappy person.

Looking back today, I wonder when all the bad news changed to good news. I am now at a prestigious university. I play on a club ping-pong team and have more friends than I have time for. I speak perfect English, and my parents are proud of me. When I graduate, I'll be able to take care of them. The change has done me good, and I'll probably stay where I am.

Comments (2) | Write a Comment | Email to a Friend

PREVIOUS REVIEW   NEXT REVIEW

1. Would you consider a move like the one described here as good news or bad news? Why do you think the writer's feeling about his situation eventually changed?

2. Do you want to live and work in the same city where you were born?

3. Have you always had the same plan for your future career, or has it changed?

LISTENING 1 | The Reindeer People

VOCABULARY

Here are some words from Listening 1. Read the paragraphs. Then write each bold word next to the correct definition. (One definition under each paragraph will not be used.)

Some people feel sorry for groups of **nomads**. They must change environments during different times of the year in order to make sure their animals have enough food. It is not easy for outsiders to understand how these people feel close to their animals, the land, and nature. However, these groups choose not to **settle** in one place, despite government threats to remove any financial **subsidies** they receive that help them continue their lifestyle. With each new cycle of nature, nomadic tribes pack up and move on to a different area to **sustain** their herds of animals—and their way of life.

1. _____ (v.) to make a place your permanent home

2. _____ (n.) money provided to help individuals or groups reduce costs of services or goods

3. _____ (n.) members of a community that moves with its animals from place to place

4. _____ (v.) to provide enough of what somebody or something needs in order to live or exist

5. _____ (v.) to develop or create a close relationship or connection with somebody or something

The 21st century will be a **critical** time for nomads and other indigenous groups. While the **elders** feel an **obligation** to preserve their customs and rituals and keep the beliefs of the culture alive, some members of the younger generation are ready to **embrace** change.

6. _____ (adj.) extremely important because a future situation will be affected by it

7. _____ (n.) something which you must do

8. _____ (n.) stories from ancient times, especially one that was told to explain natural events to describe the early history of a people

9. _____ (n.) older people, usually with a special status

10. _____ (v.) to accept an idea or proposal with enthusiasm

Many of these young people **contemplate** how different life would be if they went away to college or moved to a city to get a job and **make a living**. It's not that they dream of an **elite** lifestyle; they just don't want to **cope** with the hardships their parents endured.

11. _____ (v.) to deal successfully with a difficult matter

12. _____ (v.) to think about whether you should do something, or how you should do it

13. _____ (adj.) unnecessarily expensive; more costly that the value of the object

14. _____ (adj.) powerful, influential; wealthy or of high status

15. _____ (v.) to earn money to buy the things you need

PREVIEW LISTENING 1

The Reindeer People

You are going to listen to a radio documentary, *The Reindeer People*, produced for the nonprofit organization Worlds of Difference. It is about a nomadic group that travels around the regions of Mongolia in order to find food for their animals.

How do you think nomads would react to opportunities to settle down and give up their life as herders? Check (✓) your prediction.

☐ They would welcome the government's help to relocate.

☐ They would fight to maintain their traditional culture.

☐ They would want to keep their nomadic life for themselves, but encourage their children to change.

LISTEN FOR MAIN IDEAS

 CD 3
Track 16

Listen to the report. Write short answers. Then discuss them with a partner.

1. What two worlds do the nomadic reindeer herders feel they are caught between?

   _____

   _____

2. In what ways have the nomads been fighting to preserve their culture?

   _____

   _____

3. Why does the elder Sanjeem not want to settle?

   _____

   _____

LISTEN FOR DETAILS

 CD 3
Track 17

A. Read the sentences in Activity B. Listen again and use the T-chart to take notes on the details.

Traditional mongolian life	Facing changes

B. Use your notes from Activity A to complete the sentences. Compare your answers with a partner.

Traditional mongolian life

1. The reindeer eat _____.

2. There are _____ people living in Sanjeem's group in the Tiga region.

3. Some of the staples, or main foods, in the Tiga diet that reindeer provide are _____, _____, and _____.

4. Uyumbottom went to the government for support for the traditional culture by pleading for _____.

Facing changes

5. With the end of government subsidies, nomadic life was threatened because herders lost free _____ care for their reindeer.

6. Because of _____ and attacks by _____, the size of the reindeer herd is decreasing.

7. The biologist from Colorado works for the NGO called Itgel. In Mongolian, *itgel* means _____.

 WHAT DO YOU THINK?

Discuss the questions in a group.

1. Why do you think some elders in many cultures resist change? Why do you think younger people embrace change?

2. What are some reasons others in Mongolia might think the nomads should settle in permanent homes?

3. Do you think that these Mongolian nomads will be able to survive in the 21st century? Why or why not?

Intonation is a tool speakers can use to indicate their attitude or emotions without stating them directly.

It is useful to recognize common intonation patterns because people do not always express their true attitude or feeling through their words alone. You can use their intonation and tone of voice to make inferences about what they really mean.

Intonation pattern	This can convey . . .
flat mid-pitch, low fall	sadness, regret
varied pitch	excitement, interest, or pleasure
very high, rising pitch	disbelief or surprise
sharp rise with a sharp fall	disagreement or denial

CD 3
Track 18

Listen to the intonation and attitude in these examples.

1. **Sadness or regret**

   The future of the reindeer herders sounds pretty uncertain.

2. **Excitement or interest**

   The female nomads have a lot to say about this issue.

3. **Disbelief or surprise**

   The number of reindeer is decreasing?

4. **Disagreement or denial**

   Personally, I think the herders are going to survive.

CD 3
Track 19 **A.** Listen to the sentences. Check (✓) the box for the attitude you can infer.

Sentence	Sadness	Excitement or interest	Disagreement	Disbelief or surprise
1	☐	☐	☐	☐
2	☐	☐	☐	☐
3	☐	☐	☐	☐
4	☐	☐	☐	☐
5	☐	☐	☐	☐
6	☐	☐	☐	☐
7	☐	☐	☐	☐
8	☐	☐	☐	☐

CD 3
Track 20 **B.** Listen to these statements from Listening 1 and Listening 2. Circle the best inference for each one. With a partner, discuss how you made your choice.

1. a. The speaker feels that the world should respect the life the nomads have chosen, even if others cannot understand their choice to live such a difficult life.

   b. The speaker feels the government should protect the nomads from the forces of nature that are ruining a culture that cannot survive.

   c. The speaker feels that the nomads should settle in one place and adopt a western lifestyle.

2. a. The speaker admires and envies the members of the group he is describing.

   b. The speaker seems surprised and fascinated by this group of frequent travelers.

   c. The speaker criticizes the members of this group for wanting to travel so much.

LISTENING 2 | High-Tech Nomads

VOCABULARY

Here are some words from Listening 2. Read their definitions. Then complete each sentence.

> **accomplish** *(v.)* to succeed in doing or completing something
>
> **attention span** *(n.)* the length of time somebody can stay interested in something
>
> **breakthroughs** *(n.)* important developments that may lead to an agreement or an achievement
>
> **evolved** *(adj.)* advanced; developed from simple early forms
>
> **intrepid** *(adj.)* brave; not afraid of danger or difficulties
>
> **irony** *(n.)* the amusing or strange aspect of a situation that is very different from what you expect
>
> **marginal** *(adj.)* not part of a main or important group or situation
>
> **mundane** *(adj.)* not interesting or exciting; ordinary
>
> **payoff** *(n.)* an advantage or award for something done
>
> **psyche** *(n.)* the mind; deep feelings and attitudes
>
> **roots** *(n.)* the feeling or connections that you have with a place because you have lived there or your family came from there
>
> **stability** *(n.)* a state of being steady and unchanging

1. Labeling people according to their income level, ethnic background, or language risks making them seem like _____ groups and can lead to discrimination.

2. Those who want to investigate their _____ and learn about their culture often go back to the country where their parents were born.

3. Those who have signed up for a trip on a spaceship are certainly _____ travelers.

4. Something about the human _____ makes us need to define our own space.

5. Scientific _____ such as high-tech devices or advanced medical treatments have the potential to improve our lives.

6. The parents felt the children needed more _____ and didn't want to move from one city to another too frequently.

7. He found _____ in the idea that the city dwellers thought they were giving freedom to the nomads by making them move to the city.

8. Once you know what you want to _____, it is easier to plan your actions and set goals.

9. The _____ for working so hard was that she earned enough money to buy a new computer.

10. Some people complain about _____ jobs, but others like having a set, predictable routine, even if it gets boring after a while.

11. Traditional societies that resist change are sometimes considered to be less _____ than those that are more concerned with modern technological advances.

12. People with a short _____ jump from project to project so they don't get bored.

PREVIEW LISTENING 2

High-Tech Nomads

You are going to hear Rudy Maxa, host of the radio show *The Savvy Traveler*, interview reporter Joel Garreau about his research on a special group of businesspeople called *high-tech nomads*.

Check (✓) the descriptions you think would apply to a high-tech nomad.

☐ a self-employed businessperson

☐ a cyberspace traveler, rather than a plane traveler

☐ a worker who changes offices frequently

☐ a computer "geek"

☐ an employee who can't keep one job

☐ a worker who has an email address but no business address

☐ a businessperson who works from home

LISTEN FOR MAIN IDEAS

Listen to the interview. Write short answers. Then discuss them with a partner.

1. How could you summarize Joel Garreau's description of the character of the high-tech nomad in one sentence?

   _____

   _____

2. According to Garreau, why do these business travelers choose this nomadic life?

   _____

   _____

3. What do high-tech nomads give up for their lifestyle?

   _____

   _____

4. Garreau asks, "If these guys are so plugged in, and they can communicate from anywhere, why bother to travel at all?" How does he answer his own question?

   _____

   _____

LISTEN FOR DETAILS

Listen again. Check (✓) the details that are correct. Compare your answers with a partner.

☐ 1. Both men and women are members of this high-tech nomad group.

☐ 2. Some high-tech nomads have million-dollar incomes.

☐ 3. High-tech nomads have common jobs, but just do them in uncommon ways.

☐ 4. One high-tech device that these businesspeople no longer have use for is the cell phone.

5. Even though these nomads like to travel for business, most have one specific home where they spend weekends, do laundry, and get mail.

6. The woman who swims every day does so because she needs exercise after the long plane rides.

7. Garreau says he needs more stability than the high-tech nomads.

8. Some high-tech nomads take their families with them when they travel on business.

9. Garreau states that high-tech nomads have short attention spans.

10. Nomads hope that one day technology will be so advanced that they won't need face-to-face meetings.

WHAT DO YOU THINK?

A. Discuss the questions in a group.

1. What do the speakers seem to think of the high-tech nomads? Do you agree with them? Why or why not?

2. Do you have the type of personality required to be a high-tech nomad? Do you have any interest in that sort of lifestyle? Why or why not?

3. In what ways do you try to be "wired" to the outside world? How much has your use of high-tech devices changed your daily life?

B. Think about both Listening 1 and Listening 2 as you discuss the question.

The reports described changes in the world around us (e.g., a lack of resources; an increase in technology). What other changes in today's world can you think of that could change the way some groups of people live, work, or study?

Phrasal verbs, made up of a verb followed by a **particle**, are a common type of collocation. The particle (usually a preposition or an adverb) following the verb changes the meaning. For example, *take on* does not have the same meaning as *take* or *take over*. Phrasal verbs are listed separately in learners' dictionaries and are marked with a symbol.

> ,take sth/sb↔'on **1** to decide to do something; to agree to be responsible for something or someone: *I can't take on any extra work.* ♦ *We're not taking on any new clients at present.* **2** (of a bus, plane, or ship) to allow someone or something to enter: *The bus stopped to take on more passengers.* ♦ *The ship took on more fuel at Freetown.*

Some phrasal verbs take an object. A phrasal verb is **separable** if the object can be placed between the verb and the particle (*take* something *on*) as well as after it (*take on* something).

> That group **took over** the meeting and discussed their changes to the plan.
> We had contemplated **taking** the new project **on**, but decided not to.
> **Taking** it **on** would have been too much work.

Phrasal verbs are often less formal and more conversational than one-word verbs with a similar meaning.

> We decided to *take on* the new project. = more informal
> We decided to *undertake* the new project. = more formal

Over time, some phrasal verbs join together to become nouns; examples from Listening 2 include *breakthrough* and *payoff*.

All dictionary entries are from the *Oxford Advanced American Dictionary for learners of English* © Oxford University Press 2011.

A. Use a dictionary to complete the phrasal verbs with particles from the box. Then write S if the phrasal verb is separable and I if it is inseparable.

at	in
away	out
away	up
back	up
back	up on
down	up with

_____ 1. give _____: to give something as a gift

_____ 2. give _____: to stop trying to do something

_____ 3. give _____: to return something to its owner

_____ 4. keep _____ (something): to continue working or doing something

_____ 5. keep _____: to avoid going near something or someone

_____ 6. keep _____ _____: to stay in contact with someone; to stay informed about a situation

_____ 7. pick _____: to choose or select something

_____ 8. pick _____: to collect something

_____ 9. pick _____ _____: to return to a point already discussed

_____ 10. turn _____: to return the way you have come

_____ 11. turn _____: to reject or refuse something

_____ 12. turn _____: to go to bed / go to sleep

B. Complete the sentences with a phrasal verb from Activity A. If the verb is separable, rewrite the sentences using a pronoun. If the verb is not separable, put an *X* on the line.

The group submitted an application for a government subsidy, but unfortunately, the government _____turned down_____ the application.

_The government turned it down._____

1. It's important to _____ from the edge of the cliff. You could fall!

   _____

2. I know that it's unhealthy to consume a lot of sugar, so I'm trying to _____ soda.

   _____

3. High-tech nomads have no central place to _____ their mail.

   _____

4. I'm not sure I understand what you mean. Can we _____ the point you raised earlier about subsidies?

   _____

5. It's getting very late. I'm going to _____ soon.

   _____

6. If you receive something you can't use and don't want, I think it's OK to _____ that item _____.

   _____

Grammar | Gerunds and infinitives

Gerunds are formed by verb + *-ing*.

Infinitives are formed by *to* + base form of the verb.

Gerunds and infinitives are both nouns, even though they may look like verbs. They take the same position in a sentence as other nouns, such as subjects, direct objects, and objects of prepositional phrases.

1. Both gerunds and infinitives can be used as sentence subjects; this can make a sentence seem more formal.

2. Both gerunds and infinitives are used as direct objects; whether you use a gerund or an infinitive sometimes depends on the main verb in the sentence.

3. Only gerunds can be used as objects of prepositional phrases.

4. Gerunds are used as objects of verb phrases with *have* + noun.

5. Infinitives are also used in sentences whose subjects are noun phrases with *It* + adjective.

Study the examples in the chart.

	Infinitive	Gerund
1. Subject	**To meet people face-to-face** is important.	**Meeting people face-to-face** is important.
2. Object	High-tech nomads like **to meet people face-to-face.**	High-tech nomads like **meeting people face-to-face.**
3. Object of a prepositional phrase	✗	He is interested in **meeting people face-to-face.**
4. Object of a verb phrase with *have* + noun	✗	He has difficulty **meeting people face-to-face.**
5. Object of a noun phrase with *it* + adjective	It is important **to meet people face-to-face.**	✗

Here are some common verbs and phrases that are followed by gerunds or infinitives.

	Infinitive	Gerund
avoid, dislike, enjoy, finish, mind, practice, quit		✓
agree, decide, expect, force, hope, intend, plan, promise	✓	
continue, hate, like, love, prefer, start	✓	✓
have difficulty/fun/a problem/a hard time/trouble		✓
it is easy/hard/important/necessary	✓	

A. Complete each sentence with the gerund or infinitive form of the verb in parentheses. Check your answers with a partner. In some cases, more than one answer is possible.

1. Many Mongolian nomads would prefer _____ (maintain) their traditional lifestyle.

2. It appears that the Mongolian nomads don't have trouble _____ (move) as the seasons change.

3. Mongolia's geography forces people _____ (embrace) the nomadic life.

4. Still, it is not easy _____ (cope) with so many changes.

5. High-tech nomads avoid _____ (stay) in any one place or job for too long.

6. They don't have a problem _____ (use) an airport as their office.

7. Some of them intend _____ (travel) for just a few years, and others choose it for their entire career.

B. Work with a partner. Discuss the questions. Use verbs and expressions from the chart followed by gerunds and infinitives.

1. Think about your life now and then how it might change in the future. What do you enjoy doing now? What do you dislike doing? What do you intend to change in the future? What are some things you hope to do?

2. Think about a career you are interested in. Do you hope to get a job in that field? How do you plan to prepare or train for that? Will it be easy or difficult to find a job? Could it be necessary to move to another city or country? Would you mind moving?

| Pronunciation | Consonant variations | |

As you learned in Unit 1, vowel sounds may change according to their position in a word and the other sounds around them. **Consonant sounds** may also change. This chart summarizes some of the important variations in English consonant sounds.

 CD 3 Track 23

Listen to and repeat the examples.

Consonant variation	Explanation	Conditions	Examples
Aspiration of /p/, /t/, /k/	add an extra puff of air after the voiceless sounds /p/, /t/, /k/	when /p/, /t/, /k/ come at the beginning of a stressed syllable (except when preceded by *s*)	*poor* *appeal* *tech* *return* *cope* *account*
Flap or tap /ṭ/	use a quick flick or tap /ṭ/ of the tongue on the roof of the mouth for *t* and *d*	when a *t* or *d* comes between a stressed vowel and an unstressed vowel (American English)	*leader* *matter* *subsidy*
Palatalization	pronounce *d* like /dʒ/ and *t* like /tʃ/, creating friction rather than a stop	when *d* or *t* combines with a following /y/ sound	*question* *nature* *situate* *gradual*

A. Listen to these pairs of words and repeat them.

1. Feel the extra puff of air with your hand when you say the second word in each pair.

   open – opinion

   atom – atomic

   intern – turn

2. Feel how the quick tap /ṭ/ is substituted for /t/ or /d/ in the second word in each pair.

   master – matter

   lender – leader

   invitation – invited

3. Feel how your tongue creates friction with the roof of your mouth in the second word instead of just stopping the sound.

   grader – gradual

   native – natural

   captive – capture

CD 3
Track 25 **B.** Circle the three words in each set that have these features. Then listen and check your answers.

1. aspirated /p/
   - a. cope
   - b. expand
   - c. payoff
   - d. policy

2. aspirated /k/
   - a. connection
   - b. crazy
   - c. accomplish
   - d. cycle

3. aspirated /t/
   - a. routine
   - b. elite
   - c. attention
   - d. tourist

4. flap /ṭ/
   - a. critical
   - b. material
   - c. ability
   - d. letter

5. flap /ṭ/
   - a. media
   - b. pleaded
   - c. nomadic
   - d. advisor

6. palatalized /tʃ/
   - a. century
   - b. future
   - c. fifty
   - d. culture

7. palatalized /dʒ/
   - a. gradual
   - b. reindeer
   - c. schedule
   - d. individual

CD 3
Track 26

C. Listen to these sentences and circle the words with an aspirated, flap, or palatalized *t*.

Welcome to the world of the high-tech nomad. Writer Joel Garreau investigated this unique breed of traveler for *The Washington Post*, and he sat down with us recently to tell us what he learned.

| Speaking Skill | Paraphrasing | web |

To **paraphrase** is to repeat an idea in a way that keeps the same meaning but uses different words. Speakers paraphrase for emphasis, or to make a meaning clearer or easier to understand. Sometimes we paraphrase what we have heard a speaker say just to clarify our own understanding.

CD 3
Track 27

Listen to the way the Rudy Maxa paraphrases some of Joel Garreau's words in his interview.

> Garreau: One of the great ironies of this lifestyle is that, you know, you ask yourself, well if these guys are so plugged in, and they can communicate from anywhere, **why bother travel at all**?
>
> Maxa: Exactly. **Why do you even move?**

Here, Maxa shows that he has understood the question that Garreau is asking; also, by repeating it, he emphasizes the question for the listening audience.

Here are some techniques that you can use to paraphrase.

> Original sentence: Discovering the nomads was a surprising experience for us.

Use synonyms

> Paraphrase: The reporter said that finding the nomads was an astonishing experience.

Vary word forms

> Paraphrase: The discovery of the nomadic group surprised them.

Change positive to negative forms

> Paraphrase: The discovery of the nomads was not expected.

When paraphrasing, it is also common to:

Combine sentences and ideas

> Original sentences: We were at least listened to... I'm encouraged by this.
>
> Paraphrase: Uyumbotton said that she felt encouraged because at least the government listened to them.

Break a long idea or sentence into two

> Original sentence: Mongolia's geography, a boundless wilderness with soil that can't sustain agriculture, forces people to embrace the nomadic life.
>
> Paraphrase: The narrator explains that Mongolia has vast lands, but it is impossible to grow food there. As a result, a nomadic life is necessary.

When paraphrasing in a conversation, use expressions such as *in other words, what I'm/you're saying is . . ., so what I/you mean is . . . .*

A. Listen to your partner read a sentence below. Paraphrase the sentence using the techniques in the Speaking Skill box. Ask your partner to confirm that you paraphrased the ideas accurately.

A: These guys tend to have very short attention spans on average.
B: So you mean most high-tech nomads don't have long attention spans?
A: Yes, exactly / Yes, that's right / Indeed.

1. The economic advisor to Mongolia's president did not have encouraging words.

2. And the great irony is that the reason they are nomads is for face-to-face contact.

3. Well it's only been in the last ten years that we've had enough wired technology to make this barely possible.

4. When Mongolia's communist government was toppled by a democratic revolution in the 1990s, his state salary was withdrawn.

B. Work with a partner. Role-play a conversation between one of the people in the recordings and an interviewer who paraphrases the speaker's words.

A: Mr. Garreau, do you believe that high-tech nomads are crazy?

B: No, I couldn't live that nomadic lifestyle, but these people are successful.

A: In other words, even though the life of a nomad isn't for you, their success shows that they aren't crazy.

Possible topics:

Ask Sanjeem what would happen if his people moved closer to the city.

Ask Sanjeem's wife why she went to the capital or what the results of the trip were.

Ask Sanjeem's granddaughter about the songs she sings.

Ask Dyson why she swims every day.

Ask Garreau what he thinks high-tech nomads miss most.

Ask Maxa what he learned from his interview with Garreau.

Unit Assignment | Conduct a personal interview

 In this section, you will interview a classmate to find out whether she or he resists or embraces change and then report on your findings. As you prepare your presentation, think about the Unit Question, "How do people react to change?" and refer to the Self-Assessment checklist on page 196.

For alternative unit assignments, see the *Q: Skills for Success Teacher's Handbook.*

CONSIDER THE IDEAS

The topic of change has fascinated many great thinkers, writers, and leaders. In a group, read and discuss the following quotations about change. Take turns paraphrasing the ideas and explaining your reactions to them. Which ones seem positive? Which are negative?

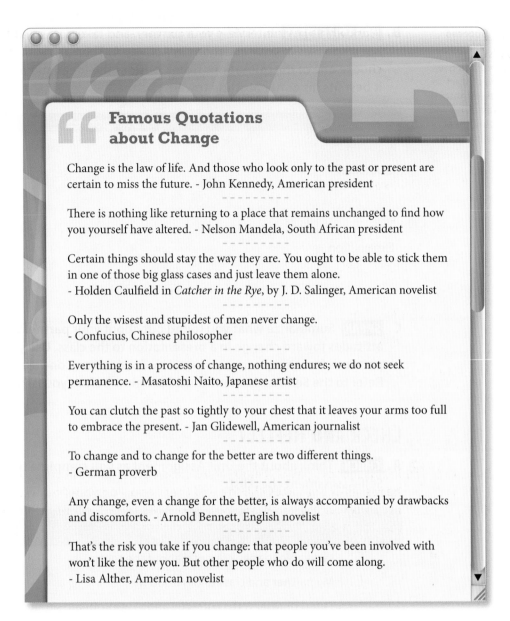

Famous Quotations about Change

Change is the law of life. And those who look only to the past or present are certain to miss the future. - John Kennedy, American president

There is nothing like returning to a place that remains unchanged to find how you yourself have altered. - Nelson Mandela, South African president

Certain things should stay the way they are. You ought to be able to stick them in one of those big glass cases and just leave them alone.
- Holden Caulfield in *Catcher in the Rye*, by J. D. Salinger, American novelist

Only the wisest and stupidest of men never change.
- Confucius, Chinese philosopher

Everything is in a process of change, nothing endures; we do not seek permanence. - Masatoshi Naito, Japanese artist

You can clutch the past so tightly to your chest that it leaves your arms too full to embrace the present. - Jan Glidewell, American journalist

To change and to change for the better are two different things.
- German proverb

Any change, even a change for the better, is always accompanied by drawbacks and discomforts. - Arnold Bennett, English novelist

That's the risk you take if you change: that people you've been involved with won't like the new you. But other people who do will come along.
- Lisa Alther, American novelist

PREPARE AND SPEAK

Tip Critical Thinking

In Activity A, you have to discuss the quotations and **defend** your ideas by giving explanations for your opinions. When you defend your opinions, you use your own personal values and beliefs.

A. **GATHER IDEAS** **Follow these steps to prepare for your interview.**

1. Work with a partner. Discuss the quotations above. Explain why you agree or disagree with them.

2. In your notebook, write seven questions that will help you find out how your partner reacts to change. Your questions can cover different areas including changes in family, school, careers, traditions, or reactions to the people in the recordings.

In a conversation, it is important to have good eye contact so the speaker knows you are listening and interested in what he or she is saying.

B. **ORGANIZE IDEAS** Interview your partner, and take notes on his or her responses to your questions in Activity A. Then ask your partner to choose one of the quotations from Consider the Ideas and explain why it best fits his or her attitude toward change.

	Partner's Responses
Quotation	
Explanation	

C. **SPEAK** Summarize what you found out about your partner's attitudes toward change in a presentation to the class. Use your partner's favorite quotation as an introduction or a conclusion. Refer to the Self-Assessment checklist below before you begin.

CHECK AND REFLECT

A. **CHECK** Think about the Unit Assignment as you complete the Self-Assessment checklist.

SELF-ASSESSMENT		
Yes	No	
☐	☐	I was able to speak fluently about the topic.
☐	☐	My partner and class understood me.
☐	☐	I used phrasal verbs correctly and in appropriate situations.
☐	☐	I used gerunds and infinitives correctly and in a variety of sentence positions.
☐	☐	I pronounced consonants correctly.
☐	☐	I paraphrased to emphasize and to clarify understanding.

B. **REFLECT** Discuss these questions with a partner.

What is something new you learned in this unit?

 Look back at the Unit Question. Is your answer different now than when you started this unit? If yes, how is it different? Why?

Track Your Success

Circle the words and phrases you learned in this unit.

Nouns
attention span
breakthrough
elder
irony
nomad
obligation
payoff
psyche
roots
stability AWL
subsidy AWL

Verbs
accomplish
contemplate

cope 🔑
embrace
evolve
settle 🔑
sustain AWL

Phrasal Verbs
give away 🔑
give back
give up 🔑
keep at
keep away from
keep up with
pick out
pick up 🔑

pick up on
turn back
turn down
turn in

Adjectives
critical 🔑
elite
evolved AWL
intrepid
marginal AWL
mundane

Phrase
make a living

🔑 Oxford 3000™ words
AWL Academic Word List

Check (✓) the skills you learned. If you need more work on a skill, refer to the page(s) in parentheses.

LISTENING	●	I can recognize attitudes. (p. 179)
VOCABULARY	●	I can use phrasal verbs. (p. 185)
GRAMMAR	●	I can use gerunds and infinitives. (pp. 188–189)
PRONUNCIATION	●	I can use consonant variations. (p. 190)
SPEAKING	●	I can paraphrase. (pp. 192–193)
LEARNING OUTCOME	●	I can interview a classmate and report on that person's attitudes concerning change.

LEARNING OUTCOME ●

Participate in a class debate in which you support opinions concerning the future of energy.

Q

? *Unit* QUESTION

Where should the world's energy come from?

PREVIEW THE UNIT

A Discuss these questions with your classmates.

Where does most of the energy in your community come from?

Why do environmentalists care whether energy is non-renewable (in limited supply) or renewable? What new energy sources can solve the world's energy needs?

Look at the photo. What kind of energy plant is shown here? Is this a renewable or non-renewable source?

B Discuss the Unit Question above with your classmates.

⊙) Listen to *The Q Classroom*, **Track 2** on **CD 4**, to hear other answers.

C Work in a group. Label the pictures with the names of the energy sources. Discuss whether the sources are renewable or non-renewable.

1. _____ 2. _____ 3. _____

4. _____ 5. _____ 6. _____

D With your group, choose one energy type from Activity C. Complete the idea map. Then decide if you think this is an appropriate energy source for your community or not.

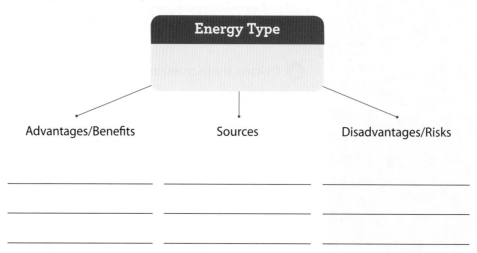

Energy Type

Advantages/Benefits   Sources   Disadvantages/Risks

_____   _____   _____

_____   _____   _____

_____   _____   _____

LISTENING 1 | Nuclear Energy: Is It the Solution?

VOCABULARY

Here are some words and phrases from Listening 1. Read the sentences.
Circle the answer that best matches the meaning of each bold word
or phrase.

1. Choosing which type of energy to finance is so **controversial** that investors
   end up not knowing where to invest their money.
   a. expensive
   b. debatable
   c. confusing

2. Our **reliance** on energy increased during the period when people drove
   cars and began to use electricity to do many things that used to be done
   by hand.
   a. dependence on
   b. atmosphere of
   c. understanding of

3. **Fossil fuels** like gas, coal, and oil are often criticized for putting CO_2
   (carbon dioxide) into the air and contributing to the greenhouse effect.
   a. fuels made in factories
   b. fuels formed over millions of years from animal and plant remains
   c. fuels made from corn and converted to gas

4. One concern with using gas, coal, and oil as fuels is the **emissions**
   they produce, which can cause illnesses in people and animals that
   breathe them.
   a. sticky, greasy substances
   b. liquid leaked into the environment
   c. gases sent out into the air

5. More greenhouse gases that pollute the air are produced as human
   consumption of energy increases.
   a. usage
   b. fear
   c. awareness

6. To save water and energy, it is better to fill the washing machine to **capacity** instead of washing just a few things.
   a. entirely full
   b. entirely dirty
   c. entirely able

7. The rain was only **intermittent** yesterday, so we could still go out for a walk.
   a. stopping and starting
   b. pounding
   c. light

8. The researcher's ideas were **misguided** because they were foolishly based on guesses and not on scientific evidence.
   a. famous
   b. important
   c. incorrect

9. The British invest more money in wave energy research than other countries, so tidal power is a **large-scale** industry in the U.K.
   a. cheap
   b. unusual
   c. widely used

10. If companies could improve the **efficiency** of production, less energy would be used in industry.
    a. no waste of time or money
    b. ability to make a fast recovery
    c. higher sales

11. If people could **conserve** energy by not wasting power or by buying better-designed products, we wouldn't need to use so much oil.
    a. use less of; save up
    b. choose more selectively
    c. manufacture or produce

12. Since each speaker had a different viewpoint, it was a very **thought-provoking** discussion, and I learned a lot of new things.
    a. relaxing
    b. fascinating
    c. typical

PREVIEW LISTENING 1

Nuclear Energy: Is It the Solution?

You are going to listen to part of a city council meeting in which two members explain the science behind opposing views on nuclear energy.

What have you heard or read about nuclear energy? Check (✓) the phrases that you think best describe this type of fuel and then listen to see if the speakers agree with your views.

Nuclear energy:

☐ is safe   ☐ isn't well regulated

☐ is reliable   ☐ is a green energy source

☐ causes less pollution than oil   ☐ is being used around the world

☐ produces radioactive waste   ☐ is expensive

LISTEN FOR MAIN IDEAS

 CD 4
Track 3

Listen to the debate. Circle the correct answers.

1. What do the people of the town have to decide?
    a. Whether to build a nuclear power plant in their city.
    b. Whether to vote for a mayor who is for or against the nuclear power plant.

2. What point do both sides agree on?
    a. The need to reduce reliance on fossil fuels.
    b. The need to increase the production of fossil fuels.

3. What scientific view does Chen present against nuclear energy?
    a. Nuclear energy is less expensive, but it can't produce enough power.
    b. Nuclear plants can produce a lot of energy, but they are not safe or clean enough.

4. Why does Dr. Scott believe that renewable energy alone cannot replace fossil fuels?
    a. Renewable energy technologies are not completely reliable.
    b. Renewable energy technologies are too expensive.

5. What makes renewable energy sources less reliable than nuclear or fossil fuels?

    a. They are not available all of the time, so they do not provide enough power.

    b. They are too expensive to produce, so people do not want to finance them.

6. What idea does Chen seem to end the discussion with?

    a. Candidates for mayor should take a firm stand against nuclear energy.

    b. Candidates for mayor should focus on how to improve efficiency and cut down on consumption.

LISTEN FOR DETAILS

CD 4
Track 4

A. Listen again. Use the T-chart to take notes on the information presented by Regan and Chen. Compare notes with a partner.

For nuclear energy	Against nuclear energy

B. Work with a partner. Use your notes from Activity A to write short answers to the questions.

1. According to Regan, what are three reasons we should reduce our consumption of fossil fuels?

   _____

2. What two arguments has Chen found explaining why nuclear energy is not a safe alternative?

   _____

3. What is the title of the book by Dr. Makhijani that was cited in the presentation against nuclear energy?

   _____

4. What argument does Dr. Moore give in defense of the safety of nuclear energy?

   _____

5. According to Regan's sources, how much of the emission-free electricity in the U.S. is currently produced from nuclear energy?

   _____

6. What are three renewable sources of energy that Chen mentions as ones supported by environmentalists?

   _____

7. What percentage of all energy does Dr. Goldemberg propose that windmills and biofuels could provide by the year 2050?

   _____

8. According to Dr. Scott, what is the problem with renewable energy sources?

   _____

Q WHAT DO YOU THINK?

Discuss the questions in a group.

1. Do you agree with the views of the pro-nuclear or the anti-nuclear group regarding the best sources for future energy? Explain your reasons.

2. Which of the different energy sources discussed by the speakers do you think are the most efficient? Which are the least risky?

3. The speakers warn of three concerns when considering solutions to energy problems: climate change, nuclear accidents, and an energy shortage. Which do you think should be our greatest concern?

Many discussions are based on a presentation of causes and effects. Certain **organizational cues** or **signal words**, as well as some verbs, can indicate a cause-and-effect relationship.

Signal words/phrases for cause	since, because, because of, when, due to, on account of, if
Signal words/phrases for effect	so, as a result, consequently, for this reason, then, therefore, in order to
Signal verbs for cause	cause, bring about, give rise to, contribute to, initiate, trigger, affect, make happen, produce, set off, have an effect on, have an impact on, result in

Usually you will hear the cause in the first clause, followed by the effect. Sometimes, however, the speaker will give the effect in the first clause.

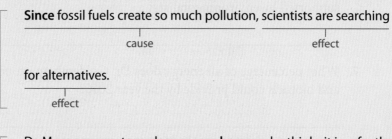

Since fossil fuels create so much pollution, scientists are searching
          cause   effect

for alternatives.
   effect

Dr. Moore supports nuclear energy **because** he thinks it is safer than
           effect   cause

people realize.
  cause

Sometimes the cause is the subject of a verb that shows the relationship to the effect.

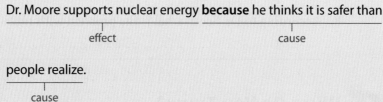

Threats to the environment **have triggered** many concerns.
        cause   effect

A. Complete the chart with causes or effects mentioned in Listening 1.

Cause	Effect
1.	We're forced to import energy from other countries.
2. Emissions from fossil fuels escape into the air.	
3.	Wind and solar power can't provide enough energy.

CD 4 Track 5

B. Listen to the excerpts from news stories about energy. Write down the cause-and-effect relationships expressed by the speakers. Use the key words provided. Compare answers with a partner.

1. ethanol, fuel, fertilizer

    Cause: _____

    Effect: _____

2. electrons, generator, hydrogen

    a. Cause: _____

    Effect: _____

    b. Cause: _____

    Effect: _____

3. chemical reactions, leftovers, tank

    a. Cause: _____

    Effect: _____

    b. Cause: _____

    Effect: _____

    c. Cause: _____

    Effect: _____

    d. Cause: _____

    Effect: _____

VOCABULARY

Here are some words from Listening 2. Read the sentences. Circle the answer that best matches the meaning of each bold word.

1. Engineers want to **harness** the energy from the ocean.
   a. attach a horse to a carriage with a device made of leather
   b. control and use the force of something to produce power
   c. use straps to hold something in place

2. The strong **current** from the ocean brings warm water from other areas.
   a. flow of electricity
   b. of the present time
   c. continuous flow of air or water

3. We need to **tap** the power of the wind by using windmills.
   a. make use of
   b. touch lightly
   c. listen to phone conversations

4. When there is a **free** flow of fast-moving water, the energy from a river could provide electricity for many homes.
   a. not paid for
   b. not controlled
   c. not being used

5. The secretary of the environment has the **power** to limit the use of fossil fuels.
   a. strength or energy
   b. right or authority of a person or group to do something
   c. public supply of electricity

6. New Hampshire residents hope that wind energy will power at least 20 percent of the homes in their **state**.
   a. mental, emotional, or physical condition that a person or thing is in
   b. to formally write or say something, especially in a careful or clear way
   c. a part of the country with its own governmental/political organization

7. Legislators passed a **bill** that provided funds for research into renewable energy.
   a. a plan for a new law
   b. a statement of how much money is owed
   c. the hard part of a bird's mouth

8. The local **commission** on energy conservation found the number of residents using green energy in their homes is on the rise.
   a. an official group of people with the responsibility to control or find out about something
   b. an amount of money paid to someone for selling goods or services, which increases with the amount sold
   c. a piece of work that someone has been asked to do

9. Some critics of tidal and wind energy argue that the power **generation** is intermittent and unreliable.
   a. the next stage of development
   b. the production of something
   c. all the people born around the same time

10. Marine animals such as stripers and lobster are **present** in the cold waters of the New Hampshire seacoast.
    a. a gift
    b. to introduce formally
    c. in a particular place

11. The factories along that **stretch** of the river use coal.
    a. to pull to become longer
    b. an area of land or water
    c. to extend one's arms and legs

12. The engine will have an open **center** that will allow animals to swim through.
    a. building or place used for a particular purpose or activity
    b. middle area of an object
    c. moderate political position between two extremes

PREVIEW LISTENING 2

Tapping the Energy of the Tides

underwater turbine

You are going to listen to a news report. Amy Quinton, a reporter for New Hampshire Public Radio, investigates the possibility of using tidal power (the rise and fall of sea levels) to provide energy to residents in the state of New Hampshire.

What do you think might be some advantages and disadvantages of using tidal energy?

Advantages: _____

Disadvantages: _____

LISTEN FOR MAIN IDEAS

 CD 4
Track 6

Listen to the report. Write short answers. Then compare them with a partner.

1. According to the speakers, what are some of the advantages of tidal power? Write at least two benefits.

   _____

   _____

2. Jack Pare states his support of tidal power by saying, "there's no single magic bullet, [but] this is one pellet of that shotgun to be able to take the top off global warming." What does he mean by this metaphor?

   _____

   _____

3. According to Pare, what effect will tidal power have on the energy available to New Hampshire residents?

   _____

   _____

4. According to the speakers, what are some of the problems that might be caused by trying to develop tidal power in New Hampshire? Write at least two problems.

   _____

   _____

LISTEN FOR DETAILS

 CD 4
Track 7

Read the sentences. Then listen again. Circle the answer that best completes each statement.

1. Tidal power is a (renewable / non-renewable) source of energy.

2. The first speaker says that energy from the tides, currents, and waves could produce (12 / 20) percent of American electricity.

3. New Hampshire state representatives appear to be (supporters / opponents) of pursuing tidal power.

4. According to Representative Tom Fargo, (wind / tidal) power is more reliable.

5. The underwater turbines in the East River resemble (windmills / vehicles).

6. The water in New Hampshire's Piscataqua River presents (more / fewer) problems for technology than the water in New York's East River.

7. (Two / Four) companies hold federal permits to research tidal power in the Piscataqua River.

8. Small fish will (be turned away from / safely pass through) the screens in the turbine engines of the Underwater Electric Kite Company of Maryland.

9. The companies (agree / disagree) on how much power they will be able to produce from the tides.

10. Charles Cooper, one of the technical engineers, says that since the plant will generate 100 megawatts of power at most, it (can / cannot) produce enough energy for the region.

 **WHAT DO YOU THINK?**

A. Discuss the questions in a group.

1. Are you convinced that tidal power is an idea worth pursuing as a solution to our energy problems? Why or why not?

2. Considering the conditions needed for turbine technology to work well, in what countries would tidal power be a good energy source?

3. Do you think tidal power will ever be able to compete with oil as a source of energy?

Tip Critical Thinking

These questions ask you to **interpret** someone else's ideas to decide what he or she might do or think. When you interpret, you are using your own knowledge and opinions to better understand and evaluate ideas.

B. Think about both Listening 1 and Listening 2 as you discuss the questions.

1. Would State Representative Tom Fargo and Dr. Moore and other supporters of nuclear energy agree or disagree about the potential of water as an energy source? What might they say to one another about this issue in a debate?

2. What are some ways in which the human need for energy is in conflict with environmental protection? Who should decide which is more important?

3. What are some ways that governments can encourage people to consume less energy and develop cleaner energy sources? Should these measures be voluntary or required?

A **root** is the part of a word that has the main meaning. We often add prefixes before a root and suffixes at the end to create new words.

Many English words can be traced back to Greek and Latin. Learning Greek and Latin word roots can help you build your vocabulary and figure out unfamiliar words. It can also help you recognize words that are part of the same word family.

Word Root	Meaning	Examples
aero	air	airplane, aerodynamics
bene	good	benefit, benign
bi	two	bicycle, biped
bio	life	biology, biomedical
chron	time	chronological, chronicle
dict	say, speak	dictation, dictionary
geo	earth	geography, geodesic
hydro	water	hydrant, hydroelectric
phon	sound	telephone, phonetics
port	carry	portable, support
proto	first	prototype, protocol

A. Think about the meaning of the example words. Use your knowledge of these words to figure out the meaning of the underlined word root. Circle the correct answer.

1. de<u>flect</u>, re<u>flect</u>ion, <u>flex</u>ible

   flect =   ⓐ bend   b. break

2. <u>di</u>ameter, <u>di</u>oxide, <u>di</u>alog

   di =   a. one   b. two

3. tele<u>vis</u>ion, <u>vis</u>ual, <u>vid</u>eo

   vid/vis =   a. see   b. hear

4. <u>tele</u>phone, <u>tele</u>vision, <u>tele</u>scope

   tele =   a. far   b. near

5. <u>sub</u>way, <u>sub</u>marine, <u>sub</u>terranean

   sub =   a. over   b. under

6. <u>scrib</u>ble, in<u>scrip</u>tion, de<u>scrib</u>e

   scrib =   a. write   b. destroy; undo

7. <u>therm</u>al, <u>therm</u>ometer, geo<u>therm</u>al

   therm =   a. heat   b. weather

B. Work with a partner. Look at the word root, its meaning, and the example. Without using a dictionary, write more words you know that come from that root. Then compare your lists with another pair.

Word Root	Meaning	Examples
1. *auto*	self	automobile,
2. *graph*	write	biography,
3. *meter/metr*	measure	metric,
4. *phys*	body/nature	physician,
5. *sol*	alone	solo,

C. Write two sentences with words from Activity B. Make sure that the meanings of the words are clear in the sentences. Read your sentences aloud to a new partner and ask him/her to identify and define the words that have Greek or Latin roots.

Top athletes work hard to have a perfect physique.

_____

_____

_____

_____

SPEAKING

Grammar | Adverb clauses

Adverb clauses are dependent clauses that modify independent clauses (or main clauses). They can start a sentence or come after the independent clause. Adverb clauses begin with a subordinator, and although they have a subject and verb, they cannot stand alone.

There are several types of adverb clauses; two of them are used to express reasons and concessions.

Adverb clauses that express reasons tell *why* the action in the main clause happens. They start with the subordinators *since, because, as,* or *due to the fact that.*

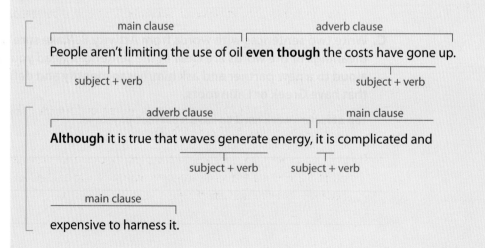

Adverb clauses that show concession acknowledge an idea and show that it is less important than the idea in the main clause. Subordinators for concession include *even though, although, though, despite the fact that,* and *in spite of the fact that.*

Be careful with the subordinators *despite the fact that* and *in spite of the fact that*. They can be confused with *despite* and *in spite of*, which introduce words or phrases, not clauses.

✓ Some people heat their homes with electricity **despite the fact that/ in spite of the fact that** it is so expensive.

✓ Some people heat their homes with electricity **despite/in spite of** the expense.

✗ Some people heat their homes with electricity **despite/in spite of** it is so expensive.

CD 4
Track 8

A. **Listen to the sentences. What relationship do you hear between the two clauses? Circle *reason* or *concession*.**

1. a. reason   b. concession   4. a. reason   b. concession

2. a. reason   b. concession   5. a. reason   b. concession

3. a. reason   b. concession   6. a. reason   b. concession

Tip for Success

When adverbial and other dependent clauses start a sentence, it is important to use a low- to mid-rise in pitch and add a slight pause before the main clause to show the sentence is not finished.

B. **Work with a partner. Circle the correct expressions. Then practice the conversations.**

1. A: (Even though / Because) we need to start consuming less energy, it's difficult for people to change their daily habits.

   B: I agree. We're not making as much progress as we could be (in spite of the fact that / due to the fact that) people stick to their old habits.

2. A: (Even though / Because) hybrid and electric cars are expensive, governments should provide subsidies so people can afford them.

   B: You've got a point, but is that really necessary? In my city, many people are already buying hybrids (in spite of the fact that / since) they cost a little more.

3. A: I'm not sure why wind energy isn't more popular, (as / though) it's a clean, renewable source of power.

   B: I'm not exactly sure either, (although / because) I know some people don't want wind turbines built nearby (in spite of the fact that / because) they're unattractive.

C. With a partner, create two conversations like those in Activity B. Take turns using the expressions in the Skill Box to add an adverb clause before or after one of the main clauses below.

1. . . . investing in solar energy seems unprofitable . . .

2. . . . many people around the world still rely mostly on coal . . .

3. . . . some people object to having wind turbines near their homes . . .

| Pronunciation | Sentence rhythm | web |

Rhythm in language is like rhythm in music, with contrasts between long and short, high and low, and soft and loud notes. In English, rhythm is produced by a combination of elements you've already learned: stress, linking, intonation, reduced forms, thought groups, and alternation of long and short syllables.

Listen to the difference in rhythm between these two sentences.

CD 4
Track 9

> BUY GAS NOW.
> It's too exPENsive to buy the GAS at this STAtion toDAY.

The first sentence has all short stressed words. The second has more rhythm, with multi-syllable words and stressed and unstressed syllables.

To have a natural-sounding rhythm in English, you need to:

- slow down and lengthen the vowels in stressed syllables of **content words** (verbs, nouns, adjectives, and adverbs) and vary your pitch. Listen to this example and repeat.

CD 4
Track 9

> If we WANT to prevent GLObal WARming, we have to CHANGE our
> conSUMPtion of FOssil FUELS.

- reduce and shorten function words (articles, prepositions, pronouns, conjunctions, and auxiliary verbs). Listen to this example and repeat.

CD 4
Track 9

> The BIKE-to-WORK PROgram was deSIGNED to help us SAVE Energy and
> SHOW that we can all aFFECT the PACE of CLImate CHANGE.

A. **Listen to the sentences. Then take turns reading each set of sentences to a partner. Put the most stress on the capitalized syllables.**

1. CARS CAUSE SMOG.

   The CARS in Los ANgeles cause SMOG.

   The OLD cars on the FREEways in Los ANgeles cause TOO much SMOG.

2. WE can TRY.

   We can TRY to SOLVE it.

   We can TRY to SOLVE the PROblem.

   We can TRY to SOLVE the Energy problem with TIdal POwer.

B. **Work with a partner. Circle the stressed syllables. Then listen to the conversation and check your answers. Make any necessary changes. Then practice the conversation with your partner.**

A: Did you see the energy debate on TV last night?

B: No, I should have watched it, but I had to study for a math test. Give me the highlights.

A: Well, it was the big oil companies versus the environmentalists.

B: Which side had the best arguments?

A: Both sides presented good cases. The oil companies had more research, but the environmentalists made more compelling arguments. They convinced me that some of the oil companies' efforts are really misguided and that our reliance on fossil fuels has to end.

B: Was it possible to tell who won the debate?

A: Not really. Because the issues are so controversial, I think it's hard to come to any real resolution. I recorded it, so I'm going to watch it again.

B: There aren't any easy answers; that's for sure. Well, I'd like to watch that recording of the debate with you. It sounds thought-provoking.

A: Sure. And I think it'll be useful for our class discussion next week.

Tip for Success

In a conversation, stress often shifts to new information being provided or requested: Speaker A: *I just bought a CAR.* Speaker B: *Is it a NEW car or a USED one?*

Feeling comfortable **expressing ideas** and **defending opinions** is important in any conversation, and it's even more important in a debate. To keep a conversation going, when the other speaker gives a point, you can show your agreement and then add your own reason or a similar point; or you can disagree and explain why. Even close friends need to be careful about being too negative when presenting their own views, and direct disagreements should always be stated in a polite tone of voice.

Expressions to ...	
Show agreement and add a further reason	**Concede a point and then disagree**
That's just it. I strongly believe that...	*While that is true, it's clear that...*
Exactly. The way I see it, ...	*You have some good points, but...*
I couldn't agree more. The fact of the matter is...	*You raise an important question; however, ...*
I think so, too. As far as I'm concerned...	*Although I agree that..., I have to point out that...*
That's very true. Furthermore, another thing we need to consider is...	*You might be right, but...*
	I see what you're saying; on the other hand, ...

 CD 4 Track 12

A. Listen to this excerpt from Listening 1. Notice how both speakers present their ideas and concede some points while defending a point of view. Complete the sentences with the phrases you hear.

Moderator: Thank you. I'm sure we'll get back to some of those

points later in the discussion. So, on the other side, now, Jack Chen,

would you please present the case against nuclear energy?

Chen: I'd be happy to. _____ with
                                        1

Emily that we need to reduce our consumption of fossil fuels,

_____ that nuclear energy is the
            2

answer. Emily, you mentioned that nuclear energy is cleaner.

_____ if we're only talking about the
            3

consumption of energy, but we have to look at how the energy

is produced and how waste is dealt with.

Regan: _____, but many scientists disagree
₄

with the notion that nuclear energy is somehow dangerous,

_____ that not one single person in North
₅

America has been injured at a nuclear power plant or died because of a

radiation-related accident. My research confirmed that this is a very well-

regulated industry. Right now, nuclear power plants supply 70 percent of the

emission-free electricity in the United States. It has a proven safety record.

Chen: _____ that at the moment, nuclear
₆

energy is providing more power than other non-fossil fuel sources,

_____ that we need to develop our renewable
₇

options, energy that can be replaced naturally. Hydroelectric energy, or the

energy provided by moving water, provides 25 percent of non-fossil fuel

energy at the moment. _____ that we should also
₈

continue to invest in wind and solar energy. These sources are much safer

and cleaner than nuclear energy.

Moderator: Emily, what did you find out about the benefits of these

other sources?

Regan: _____, and scientists and
₉

environmentalists confirm, that renewable sources are safe and clean.

_____ that we're working at capacity in terms
₁₀

of hydroelectric power. More importantly, according to Dr. David Scott,

a professor at the University of Victoria, quote, "We've gotta be very

careful about what renewables can provide."

B. Work with a partner. Complete each conversation with one of the
expressions from the Speaking Skill Box. Are the speakers agreeing or
disagreeing? Then read the conversations with your partner.

1. **A:** I really don't think we are going to run out of energy any time soon.

   B: _____ we are already using more energy than

   we can produce, especially during hot summers.

a city council debate

2. **A:** Students seem to be making an effort to save energy, like turning off their computers when they're not using them and biking to campus instead of driving.

   B: _____ even more people in our generation need to become aware of their energy consumption if we really want to fight global warming.

3. **A:** I'm shocked that people still support nuclear power, and scientists try to convince us it's not risky.

   B: _____; just think about how many people are exposed to radiation from aging nuclear power plants.

4. **A:** Politicians should support researchers working to harness the power of the tides and the wind.

   B: _____ we could never really get enough power from those sources to make it worth the investment.

5. **A:** Fossil fuels should be eliminated as an energy source as they put pollutants into the air and decrease the ozone layer.

   B: _____ banning fossil fuels completely is not a realistic solution.

6. **A:** I believe everyone should drive a hybrid or electric car to reduce harmful emissions.

   B: _____ these types of vehicles are currently too expensive for most people to buy.

C. Role-play the conversations in Activity B. Student B, give your own reactions and opinions.

Unit Assignment	Debate the future of energy

 In this section, you will have a class debate on the future of energy. As you prepare for the debate, think about the Unit Question, "Where should the world's energy come from?" and refer to the Self-Assessment checklist on page 222.

For alternative unit assignments, see the *Q: Skills for Success Teacher's Handbook*.

CONSIDER THE IDEAS

A. Read these posts to an online discussion thread by an instructor and students in an environmental studies class.

KNOW-NOW FORUM

Log in

Post Reply

| Register | FAQ | Calendar | Today's Posts | Search | 🔍 |

Forum > Environment > Thread: Renewable energy

Instructor   Senior member   #1 Posted at 9:28 AM   Posts: 209

Our most common sources of energy are nonrenewable resources, and they will only be able to support the world's growing demand for energy for a limited amount of time. Furthermore, fossil fuels produce large quantities of greenhouse gases. How can you respond to the current debate on ways to provide power to meet the increasing demand, while minimizing the impacts to the environment?

Amal   New member   #2 Posted at 9:43 AM   Posts: 12

There are several "cleaner" sources of energy which have been proposed as alternatives to fossil fuels. However, each alternative has its own negative impacts.

Brian   Junior member   #3 Posted at 9:50 AM   Posts: 89

Exactly. As an example, although it dramatically reduces the emissions of greenhouse gases, nuclear energy creates a problem with dangerous waste.

Song Woo   Senior member   #4 Posted at 10:12 AM   Posts: 160

Brian and Amal make good points. Furthermore, an alternative biofuel like ethanol requires energy to produce, so that's not efficient. In addition, the use of corn for fuel has disadvantages. It reduces the amount available for the food supply and increases its prices.

Marcos   Junior member   #5 Posted at 10:16 AM   Posts: 43

Yes, Song Woo, but I have to disagree. In the U.S., anyway, corn is overproduced. There is more than enough for the food supply, so I do think it's an economical energy solution.

Yushen   Senior member   #6 Posted at 10:31 AM   Posts: 148

As far as I'm concerned, wind and solar are some of the cleanest sources of energy, but require large stretches of land. Not everyone wants a wind turbine or a bunch of solar panels in his or her backyard.

Aziz   Senior member   #7 Posted at 11:02 AM   Posts: 321

Good point, Yushen. Wind and solar sound good, but they aren't perfect. Also, wind energy impacts bird species, as they often collide with the blades of the wind turbines.

B. Discuss the questions in a group.

1. What ideas would you have contributed to this discussion if you were a student in this environmental studies class?

2. Do the students mostly agree with each other or mostly disagree? Do you agree or disagree with any of the posts?

PREPARE AND SPEAK

A. **GATHER IDEAS** **Work in groups of four. Prepare for a debate.**

1. Divide into two teams of two students each.
   - Team 1 will represent energy producers by supporting at least two sources of energy and inform Team 2 of the choices.
   - Team 2 will represent environmentalists by presenting the environmental impacts of those two energy sources and offering alternatives.

2. Share your information. Review details from the unit with your teammate, and take notes on information that might help to support your argument.

3. Plan for arguments. How do you think the other team might respond to your opinions? Write down three arguments your opponents might make. Then decide how you might defend your opinion.

B. **ORGANIZE IDEAS** **Study this format for a simple debate.**

1. The first member of Team 1 and then Team 2 will give an overview of their opinion. (five minutes per team)

2. Team 2 will ask Team 1 questions to check understanding or get further information; then Team 1 will ask Team 2 questions. (five minutes per team)

3. The second member of Team 1 and then Team 2 will respond to the other team's position and then give a conclusion. (six minutes per team)

C. **SPEAK** **Conduct the debate. Refer to the Self-Assessment checklist below before you begin. After the debate, discuss the results.**

CHECK AND REFLECT

A. **CHECK** **Think about the Unit Assignment as you complete the Self-Assessment checklist.**

SELF-ASSESSMENT		
Yes	No	
☐	☐	I was able to speak fluently about the topic.
☐	☐	I used adverb clauses to express my ideas.
☐	☐	I used vocabulary from the unit to express my ideas.
☐	☐	I stressed the correct syllables and words in sentences.
☐	☐	I agreed and disagreed with opinions appropriately and politely.

B. REFLECT **Discuss these questions with a partner.**

What is something new you learned in this unit?

 Look back at the Unit Question. Is your answer different now than when you started this unit? If yes, how is it different? Why?

Track Your Success

Circle the words and phrases you learned in this unit.

Nouns
aerospace
bill 🔑
capacity
center 🔑
commission 🔑 AWL
consumption AWL
current 🔑
efficiency
emission
exporter AWL
fossil fuels
generation 🔑 AWL
hydropower

power 🔑
reliance AWL
root 🔑
state 🔑
stretch 🔑

Verbs
conserve
harness
tap 🔑

Adjectives
beneficial AWL
chronological
conducive

controversial AWL
free 🔑
geothermal
intermittent
misguided
predictable AWL
present 🔑

Phrases
in the scheme of things
large-scale
thought-provoking

🔑 Oxford 3000™ words
AWL Academic Word List

Check (✓) the skills you learned. If you need more work on a skill, refer to the page(s) in parentheses.

LISTENING	●	I can listen for cause and effect. (p. 206)
VOCABULARY	●	I can recognize some Greek and Latin word roots. (p. 212)
GRAMMAR	●	I can use adverb clauses. (pp. 214–215)
PRONUNCIATION	●	I can use a sentence with a natural rhythm. (p. 216)
SPEAKING	●	I can debate opinions. (p. 218)
LEARNING OUTCOME	●	I can participate in a class debate in which I support opinions concerning the future of energy.

UNIT 10

Size and Scale

LISTENING ●	listening for pros and cons
VOCABULARY ●	connotations
GRAMMAR ●	parallel structure
PRONUNCIATION ●	word stress patterns
SPEAKING ●	developing interview skills

Role-play interviews for a job or a school and be prepared to answer a question that is creative or unusual.

Q *Unit* QUESTION

Is bigger always better?

PREVIEW THE UNIT

A Discuss these questions with your classmates.

What can a large business offer its employees that a smaller company cannot? What can smaller businesses offer?

Do you prefer to have a large group of acquaintances or a small group of closer friends? Why?

Look at the photo. Do you prefer to shop in large stores or small stores? Why?

B Discuss the Unit Question above with your classmates.

Listen to *The Q Classroom*, Track 13 on CD 4, to hear other answers.

C Complete the survey. (If you are already in college or if you have finished college, think about how you would have answered in the past.)

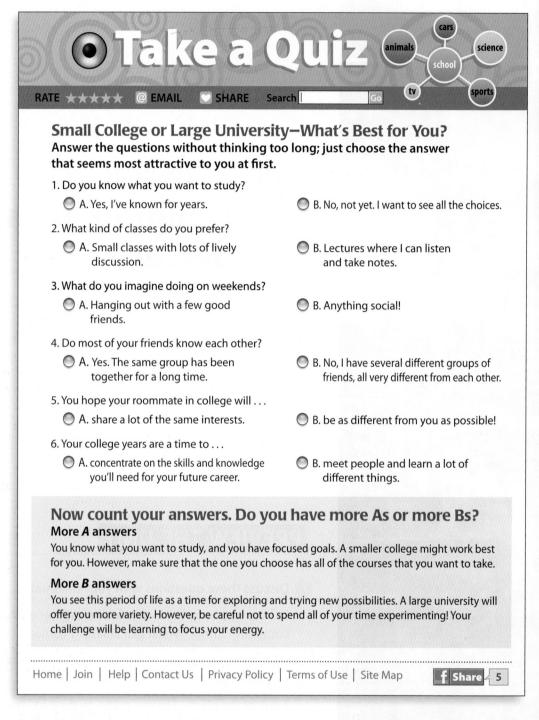

Take a Quiz

cars
animals
science
school
tv
sports

RATE ★★★★★   @ EMAIL   ♥ SHARE   Search [   ] Go

Small College or Large University—What's Best for You?

Answer the questions without thinking too long; just choose the answer that seems most attractive to you at first.

1. Do you know what you want to study?
   - ○ A. Yes, I've known for years.
   - ○ B. No, not yet. I want to see all the choices.

2. What kind of classes do you prefer?
   - ○ A. Small classes with lots of lively discussion.
   - ○ B. Lectures where I can listen and take notes.

3. What do you imagine doing on weekends?
   - ○ A. Hanging out with a few good friends.
   - ○ B. Anything social!

4. Do most of your friends know each other?
   - ○ A. Yes. The same group has been together for a long time.
   - ○ B. No, I have several different groups of friends, all very different from each other.

5. You hope your roommate in college will . . .
   - ○ A. share a lot of the same interests.
   - ○ B. be as different from you as possible!

6. Your college years are a time to . . .
   - ○ A. concentrate on the skills and knowledge you'll need for your future career.
   - ○ B. meet people and learn a lot of different things.

Now count your answers. Do you have more As or more Bs?

More *A* answers

You know what you want to study, and you have focused goals. A smaller college might work best for you. However, make sure that the one you choose has all of the courses that you want to take.

More *B* answers

You see this period of life as a time for exploring and trying new possibilities. A large university will offer you more variety. However, be careful not to spend all of your time experimenting! Your challenge will be learning to focus your energy.

Home | Join | Help | Contact Us | Privacy Policy | Terms of Use | Site Map   **f Share** 5

D Work with a group. Share and discuss your answers to the survey. Do you agree with your results? Why or why not? What are some other reasons students choose small colleges or large universities?

LISTENING 1 | Small Is the New Big

VOCABULARY

Here are some words and a phrase from Listening 1. Circle the correct word or phrase to complete each sentence. Use the context of the sentence to help you.

1. In some large cities, health problems can quickly become **widespread** because of the (*close contact between* / greater distances between) people.

2. In order to **facilitate** the admissions process and decrease the stress for new students, the university set up (*easy online applications* / difficult selective requirements).

3. During finals, even when **simultaneous** exams are being held across campus, students cannot take tests that are (too difficult to pass / *given at the same time*).

4. Because the **motto** of that organization is "The Customer Comes First," the workers try to live up to that (*guiding belief* / overall license) by providing good service.

5. When a company is **audited** due to suspicious activities, outside accountants are called in to (*investigate* / praise) its finances.

6. The company is **collapsing** due to negative changes in the industry; as a result, many workers have been (hired / *fired*).

7. The company does an exhaustive **feasibility** study before any investment is made in a new product. That means they do a study to see (*if the product will succeed* / if the product will be easy to use).

8. When two companies are said to be **in the same league**, they (play the same sport / *have equal qualities or characteristics*).

9. If interviewers ask you to rate your **flexibility**, they probably want to find out about your ability to (*adapt to* / teach about) changes in the workplace.

10. In order to save money, some companies **outsource** their work to (*other organizations or countries* / their own in-house employees).

11. If you (can / ~~can't~~) find a job, you might go to an employment **agency**, which is an organization designed to match businesses with employees.

12. If you want to make an **investment** in your future, you should try to (limit money for / ~~put your money into~~) education and job training.

PREVIEW LISTENING 1

Seth Godin

| Small Is the New Big

Seth Godin has an MBA from Stanford University and writes about business from his position as an entrepreneur—one who takes risks in starting businesses. You are going to listen to him read a chapter from his book *Small Is the New Big*.

What businesses, places, or things do you think Godin might say are better off being small? Check (✓) your guesses.

☐ an airline   ☐ a computer   ☐ a social networking site

☐ a bank   ☐ a law firm   ☐ a television

☐ a university   ☐ a restaurant   ☐ a city government

Why choose a big computer . . .

. . . versus a small computer?

LISTEN FOR MAIN IDEAS

CD 4
Track 14

Listen to the audiobook chapter. Check (✓) the main ideas that represent Godin's point of view.

☐ 1. People used to trust big companies more.

☐ 2. Startup companies used to want to stay small so that they could be more efficient.

3. Organizations that once benefited from being big may now suffer from being too big.

4. One of the overall benefits of newer small operations is the personal contact between owners and the public.

5. "Get Big Fast" is the motto for small companies today.

6. Entrepreneurs have to learn to think small in order to make a small business successful.

LISTEN FOR DETAILS

CD 4
Track 15

Read the questions. Then listen again and write the answers.

1. What are three of the advantages of past big businesses that Godin mentions?

_____

_____

2. Why does Godin feel that "big computers are silly"?

_____

_____

3. When listing smaller products that are better than big ones, what example does Godin give to illustrate the saying "An exception that proves the rule"?

_____

_____

4. According to Godin, what does the example of free WiFi at the skateboard park demonstrate?

_____

_____

5. What can you infer from Godin's statement "Small means you can tell the truth on your blog"?

_____

_____

6. What kinds of jobs might a small company outsource and why?

_____

_____

7. What does Godin mean when he says, "A small venture fund doesn't have to fund big, bad ideas in order to put their capital to work"?

_____

_____

8. Godin asks, "Is it better to be the head of craigslist [the network of online communities, featuring free online ads] or the head of UPS [the worldwide package delivery service]?" How would he answer this question?

_____

_____

 WHAT DO YOU THINK?

Discuss the questions in a group.

1. What does the expression "small is the new big" mean?

2. Do you agree with Godin that small businesses have a large advantage over big businesses today? Why or why not?

3. Which company would you rather work for, a smaller company like craigslist or a larger one like UPS? Why?

Speakers can compare and contrast options by listing the **pros and cons**, or benefits and drawbacks. They may signal their intentions with phrases such as these.

> There are some advantages and disadvantages . . .
> Let's compare . . .
> We'll examine both sides of . . .

When you can predict that a speech, lecture, or program will compare pros and cons, you can divide your paper into a T-chart and note information in the appropriate column.

Small restaurants

Pros	Cons
nice atmosphere	more expensive
owner greets you by name	less variety

Speakers often use transitions to show that they are going to present contrasting information. It is important to note the points being made about each of the sides discussed. Speakers may follow one of these patterns.

- Pros of A. Transition, cons of A.
- Pros of A. Transition, cons of B.
- Cons of A. Transition, pros of B.

Listen for organizational cues such as these:

> on (the) one hand . . . on the other hand   however
> on the other side   yet
> in contrast   though
> but

Listen to the organizational cues in these examples.

CD 4
Track 16

> A large law firm may have many lawyers that specialize in different areas. **However**, smaller firms often hire lawyers who have better training.
>
> **On the one hand**, Craigslist probably has happier employees because it is small. **On the other hand**, it may lose employees who prefer to work for a bigger company.

A. Listen to someone speak about the pros and cons of small-town and big-city life. Complete the chart. Use the organizational cues you hear to help you.

Small town	
Pros	Cons

Big city	
Pros	Cons

B. Listen again. Write the organizational cues the speaker uses to signal pros and cons.

1. _____   3. _____

2. _____   4. _____

LISTENING 2 | Sizing Up Colleges: One Size Does Not Fit All

VOCABULARY

Here are some words from Listening 2. Read the sentences. Circle the answer that best matches the meaning of each bold word or phrase.

1. "How Trade Influences Economics" is too broad a topic for your research paper; you'll need to **narrow** it to something more specific.

   a. expand   b. limit   c. double

2. **Countless** students have passed through the halls of this famous university since the college opened in 1821.

   a. numerous   b. uneducated   c. not enough

3. The terrible cold and pouring rain didn't seem to affect the **passion** of the sports fans at all; the stadium was packed full with cheering spectators.

   a. enthusiasm   b. understanding   c. hatred

4. The university liked to tell prospective students about the many **distinguished** graduates who had contributed to politics, business, and the arts.
   a. modest; shy
   b. unpopular; controversial
   c. successful; admired

5. The scientists finally received permission to **conduct** the sensitive and important experiment they needed to complete their research.
   a. perform
   b. cancel
   c. shorten

6. Traveling to a new city in a country where you don't speak the language can be **intimidating** until you get used to it and find your way around.
   a. inviting
   b. scary
   c. impossible

7. Many companies give **priority** to job applicants' work experience instead of their grades in college, which makes it difficult for new graduates to find work.
   a. moderate consideration
   b. top importance
   c. unfavorable attention

8. Do you think it's better for university students to concentrate on just one or two subjects or to study a **diversified** range of different subjects?
   a. specialized
   b. simplified
   c. varied

9. A careful **analysis** of the causes of the problem is necessary before anyone can propose a useful solution.
   a. study; examination
   b. result; outcome
   c. rejection; dismissal

10. More scholarships would **enable** students from low-income families to study at this expensive private school.
    a. prevent
    b. inspire
    c. allow

11. Before I book a room in a hotel, I like to check online to see if it has the **facilities** I enjoy, such as a good restaurant, a gym, and parking.
    a. rooms
    b. abilities
    c. features

12. In addition to looking at high school grades, college admissions officers look at applicants' participation in **extracurricular** activities such as sports and school clubs.
    a. academic
    b. supplementary
    c. required

PREVIEW LISTENING 2

Sizing Up Colleges: One Size Does Not Fit All

You are going to listen to a podcast about some pros and cons of attending big universities versus small colleges.

How common are the following features in small private colleges, large public universities, or both? Write the features into the Venn diagram. Discuss your ideas in a group before you listen to see if your ideas are correct.

competitive sports teams   dormitories   high tuition

large lectures   personal advisers   teaching assistants

medical schools   small classes   social clubs

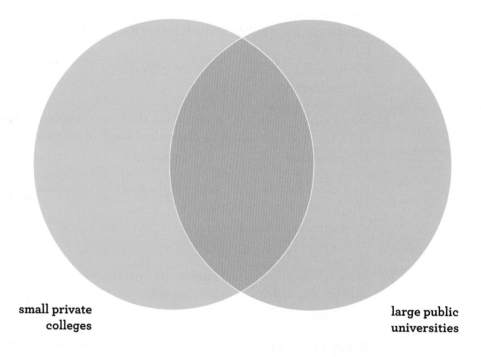

small private
colleges

large public
universities

LISTEN FOR MAIN IDEAS

CD 4
Track 18

Read the questions. Then listen to the podcast. Write short answers.

1. What is the main purpose of this recording?

   _____

2. According to the first speaker, what should students think about when evaluating colleges?

   _____

3. What are the areas the speakers emphasize to highlight the differences between big universities and small colleges?

   _____

4. The subtitle of this podcast is "One Size Does Not Fit All." What do you think that means, and how do the speakers show this point?

   _____

LISTEN FOR DETAILS

CD 4
Track 19

A. Read the T-chart. Listen again to Part 1 of the podcast. Complete the chart.

Big schools: pros & cons

Pros	Cons
• more sports and other school activities	• courses taught by _____ , not professors
• endless options and countless _____ programs	• professors focused on _____ rather than teaching
• access to _____ facilities	• more red tape and administrative procedures
• ability to work with graduate students	• introductory classes with _____ of students
• _____ professors	• problem of being unnoticed

CD 4
Track 19
B. **Read the T-chart. Listen again to Part 2 of the podcast. Complete the chart.**

Small schools: pros & cons

Pros	Cons
• hands-on learning opportunities _____ class sizes	• _____ research facilities
• classes taught by _____	• no _____ students to interact with
• opportunities to create your own major and curriculum and explore areas outside your field of study	• limited sporting events and other _____ activities
• strong sense of community	• difficulty moving in and out of social groups
• high level of _____ interaction	

 WHAT DO YOU THINK?

A. Discuss the questions in a group.

1. What do you think is the most important advice the podcast gives to students deciding on a college?

2. How much thought did you put into choosing the school you are studying at now? What factors influenced your decision? At this point, do you think you made the right choice?

Tip Critical Thinking

In Activity B, you will **incorporate** information from different sources in your answers. Incorporating ideas from different sources is a way of synthesizing information.

B. Think about both Listening 1 and Listening 2 as you discuss the questions.

1. In what ways do the two Listenings help you answer the question "Is bigger always better?"

2. Do the two recordings give a balanced view of the pros and cons of big (and small) businesses or schools, or do the speakers present a biased view? Explain your reasons.

Words have **denotations**, or literal dictionary meanings, as well as **connotations**, which are the emotional or cultural associations the word evokes. We often characterize connotations as neutral, positive, or negative. For example, there are several words that refer to a person who weighs less than average. The word *thin* has a relatively neutral connotation, whereas *skinny* or *gaunt* are more negative, and *slender* is more positive. Understanding the connotation of words can help you understand and convey ideas more clearly.

A. Work with a partner. For each pair of words, indicate which word has the more positive (+) connotation and which has the more negative (–) connotation. Use a dictionary to check your ideas.

1. ____ passion ____ obsession
2. ____ economical ____ cheap
3. ____ fire (*v.*) ____ downsize
4. ____ assertive ____ pushy
5. ____ smile ____ smirk
6. ____ nerdy ____ studious
7. ____ notorious ____ distinguished
8. ____ gossip ____ talk
9. ____ lazy ____ relaxed
10. ____ persistence ____ stubbornness

B. Complete each sentence with one of the words from Activity A. With a partner, discuss the reasons some sentences sound more negative.

1. I think I need a new roommate—the one I have now is so

   _____ that she won't even buy her own toothpaste.

2. One of Jim's best qualities is his _____. He stays with a task

   until it is completed.

3. Two of my co-workers _____ all the time, and I can't

   concentrate on my work.

4. I really like working in a(n) _____ atmosphere. As long

   as everything gets done, I don't think the work environment needs to

   be stressful.

5. That actress is _____ for her wild lifestyle. She's always in

   the news for some problem or another.

6. When I arrived, Tom kept looking at me with a funny

   _____ on his face. I wondered what he was hiding.

7. I am so sorry to inform you that we have to _____ staff.

   We just don't need all the employees we have now.

8. It's important to be _____ when someone is intimidating

   you. You need to stand up for yourself.

Grammar   Parallel structure

When listing two or more things, it is important to maintain **parallel structure**. This means that your list should have the same pattern of words, phrases, or clauses. Parallel structure helps your listener understand that the ideas are connected and have the same level of importance. The words *or* and *and* usually come before the last item in a list.

Mixing words, phrases, and clauses will cause a break in the parallelism. If you read your sentences out loud, you can often hear that the rhythm has been broken when the items are not parallel.

> ✓ The small planes weren't in the same league as the larger ones that were **fast**, **efficient**, and **economical**. (parallel structure: adjectives)
>
> ✗ The small planes weren't in the same league as the larger ones that were fast, had efficiency, and economical. (non-parallel structure: mix of words and phrases)

> ✓ Students need to **attend class**, **complete assignments**, and **pass tests**. (parallel structure: verb + noun phrases)
>
> ✗ Students need to attend class, completion of assignments, and pass tests. (non-parallel structure: different types of phrases)

> ✓ I am a good candidate for the job because **I attended a good college**, **I have experience**, and **I am a hard worker**. (parallel structure: clauses)
>
> ✗ I am a good candidate because I attended a good college, my strong experience, and I am a hard worker. (non-parallel structure: mix of clauses and phrases)

Tip for Success

You can reduce clauses in a list to phrases by deleting a subject that is repeated in each: *He is distinguished because he is rich, owns a company, and has a good education.*

If you are listing three single items, remember that your voice pitch will rise at the end of the first two items and then fall at the end of the last one.

If you are listing three phrases, your voice pitch will rise on the last content word of each of the first two phrases and then fall at the end of the last content word in the final phrase. Notice the intonation of the following example:

CD 4
Track 20

> My adviser told me that I needed to **concentrate on my major**,
> _____
> phrase
>
> **find an internship**, and **do some research**.
> _____   _____
> phrase   phrase

CD 4
Track 21

A. Listen to the sentences and complete the chart by indicating whether the sentences are parallel or not parallel. Use intonation as a clue.

	Parallel	Not parallel
1	☐	☐
2	☐	☐
3	☐	☐
4	☐	☐
5	☐	☐
6	☐	☐
7	☐	☐
8	☐	☐
9	☐	☐
10	☐	☐

B. Work with a partner. Take turns using the prompts below to ask questions about businesses and schools. Include a list of at least three items in each answer.

A: *Can you give me three characteristics of a good company to work for?*

B: *A good company should pay employees well, have friendly bosses, and provide clean working conditions.*

Ask about:

1. Three reasons you don't want to work for a big or small company

2. Three places you would like to work

3. Three reasons why you prefer a big city or a small town

4. Three reasons why you do or do not want to go to school in a different country

5. Three reasons that young children should go to a large or small school

Words in English have different **stress patterns**. Using the correct pattern ensures that your listener will be able to understand what you are saying.

For example, many nouns in English fall into the 2-1 pattern: a two-syllable word with stress on the first syllable (*WIN-dow, COL-lege, OF-fice*). The first number represents the number of syllables. The second number indicates the number of the syllable that is stressed.

Remember that:

- stressed syllables have a longer beat and a higher pitch than unstressed syllables.
- unstressed vowels may be reduced to /ə/.
- suffixes often change the stress in a word.

CD 4
Track 22

Listen to and repeat the examples.

2-syllable words	
2-1	**2-2**
founder	expand
passion	diverse
drawback	pursue

3-syllable words		
3-1	**3-2**	**3-3**
motivate	location	employee
agency	distinguish	volunteer
company	enable	reinforce

4-syllable words		
4-1	**4-2**	**4-3**
secretary	environment	academic
relatively	analysis	application
accurately	intimidate	independent

When learning a new vocabulary word, it is helpful to make a note of the syllable-stress pattern so you can make sure to pronounce it correctly.

CD 4
Track 23

A. Listen to the following words and circle the syllable you hear the speaker stress. Then label each word stress pattern (for example, as 2-1 or 4-3).

1. conducted _____
2. fortune _____
3. overwhelming _____
4. facilities _____
5. assistant _____
6. correct _____

7. corporation _____
8. socially _____
9. investment _____
10. audit _____
11. graduate _____
12. televised _____

Tip for Success

Organizing lists of academic words and terms in your field according to their stress patterns and reading the lists provide an efficient way to practice correct word stress and rhythm.

B. Work with a partner. Read the list of words you might use to describe yourself during an interview. Put each word in the correct column, based on the number of syllables and stress.

clever	efficient	independent	passionate
confident	energetic	intelligent	reliable
conscientious	experienced	mature	sociable
creative	gifted	motivated	talented
dependable	honest	organized	unique

2-1	2-2
	mature

3-1	3-2	3-3

4-1	4-2	4-3
motivated		

C. Role-play an interview with a partner. Student A will choose some adjectives from the chart on page 242 and ask Student B if those adjectives describe him or her. Student B will respond and expand on one of the adjectives. Listen for correct word stress.

A: Are you dependable and organized?

B: I am very dependable, but I'm not always organized when I'm under pressure.

Speaking Skill | Developing interview skills

Interviews can be stressful speaking situations. You can ease the stress by knowing what to expect and preparing for the questions. Practice responding to the interview questions in advance so that you will be relaxed and confident during the actual interview.

Before the interview:

- **Prepare:** Find out about the college or company so you know how to answer and ask questions.
- **Predict:** Develop a list of potential questions the interviewers might ask.
- **Practice:** Have a friend act as an interviewer and practice responding to the questions.

During the interview:

- Maintain good eye contact and don't be afraid to smile.
- Use a formal speaking style and avoid slang.
- Emphasize key words to show interest and enthusiasm.
- Avoid long pauses before responding. When necessary, ask for clarification.

> Do you mean, would I be comfortable living in a dormitory?
>
> Are you asking if I have taken any classes in statistics?
>
> Since you are asking if I feel prepared to work in such a large organization, let me say that . . .

- Use expressions to fill in the gap while you are thinking of a response.

> That's a good question.
>
> Let me think about that for a minute.

- Leave on a positive note by thanking the interviewers and saying you look forward to hearing from them.

A. Listen to three interviews. Which person would you hire? What advice would you give the other candidates? Discuss the pros and cons of the candidates in a group.

B. Work in pairs. Choose a job or college interview situation and practice your interview skills. Use the questions in the chart and/or some of your own. Take turns being the interviewer and the applicant.

Questions for college applicants	Questions for job applicants
What about our college attracted you to apply here?	How did you hear about our company?
What do you know about our campus and student body?	What job experiences have you had that make you qualified for this job?
Do you have a passion for any particular career?	What do you expect to learn by working for us?
Why do you think this small/big college is right for you?	What special skills would you bring to the table?
What do you like most about your current school?	What is your long-term career goal?
Have you decided on a major yet, and if so, why did you choose it?	Do you think you would be happy working for such a large/small organization?
	Have you ever been fired from a previous position?

Unit Assignment | **Role-play interviews for a job or a school**

In this section, you are going to role-play interviews for a workplace or a school. As you prepare for your interview, think about the Unit Question, "Is bigger always better?" and refer to the Self-Assessment checklist on page 246.

For alternative unit assignments, see the *Q: Skills for Success Teacher's Handbook*.

CONSIDER THE IDEAS

A. Sometimes employers ask unexpected or unusual questions at an interview. Often there are no right or wrong answers; employers may be more interested in how candidates respond than what candidates say. They may be looking for creativity, clarity, confidence, and even a sense of humor. Read these examples of unusual interview questions and think about how you might respond to them.

1. What are you reading these days?
2. What are your weaknesses?
3. If you were a character in a book, who would you be?
4. If you were a car, what type of car would you be?
5. If you won ten million dollars, what would you do with the money?
6. If you could have dinner with anyone from history, who would it be?
7. If you had six months left to live, what would you do with your time?
8. What is the most stressful situation you have handled? How did you deal with it?
9. Describe a time when you worked with a difficult person.

B. What do you think an interviewer would hope to learn by asking these questions? How would you answer each one? Discuss your possible responses in a group.

PREPARE AND SPEAK

A. GATHER IDEAS Work in a group. Follow these steps to gather ideas.

1. Decide if your group will conduct a business interview (with a committee of employers and staff interviewing candidates applying for a job) or an academic interview (with college admissions staff members interviewing applicants to the school).

2. Discuss the type of position or program that you are interviewing candidates for. What qualities would the ideal candidate have? List adjectives to describe the position or the candidate.

B. ORGANIZE IDEAS Break into two smaller groups: interview committee members and candidates.

Interview committee members: Choose five questions to ask each candidate. At least one should be creative or unusual. Write the questions below. Then divide the questions among the committee members.

1. _____

2. _____

3. _____

4. _____

5. _____

Candidates: List five questions you predict the interviewers might ask you and note ideas for possible responses.

	Possible questions	Possible responses
1.		
2.		
3.		
4.		
5.		

C. **SPEAK** Role-play your interviews. Refer to the Self-Assessment checklist below before you begin.

1. Interview committees: Write each candidate's name and ask the questions. Take notes on the pros and cons for each candidate. Interview candidates: Use your notes for possible questions and responses to help you answer the questions.

2. When the interviews are over, committees will briefly confer with each other, choose the best candidate, and tell the candidates who was selected and why.

3. As a group, discuss which questions were the most difficult to answer and which questions gave the most important information about the candidates.

CHECK AND REFLECT

A. **CHECK** Think about the Unit Assignment as you complete the Self-Assessment checklist.

SELF-ASSESSMENT		
Yes	**No**	
☐	☐	I was able to speak fluently in the interview.
☐	☐	My group understood me.
☐	☐	I used vocabulary with the appropriate connotations.
☐	☐	I used parallel structure when listing three or more ideas.
☐	☐	I stressed 2-, 3-, and 4-syllable words correctly.
☐	☐	I anticipated interview questions and practiced my answers to sound relaxed and natural.

B. **REFLECT** **Discuss these questions with a partner.**

What is something new you learned in this unit?

 Look back at the Unit Question. Is your answer different now than when you started this unit? If yes, how is it different? Why?

Track Your Success

Circle the words and phrase you learned in this unit.

Nouns	Verbs	Adjectives
agency 🔑	audit	countless
analysis 🔑 AWL	collapse 🔑 AWL	distinguished
facilities 🔑 AWL	conduct 🔑 AWL	diversified AWL
feasibility	enable 🔑 AWL	extracurricular
flexibility AWL	facilitate AWL	intimidating
investment 🔑 AWL	narrow 🔑	simultaneous
motto	outsource	widespread AWL
passion 🔑		
priority 🔑 AWL		**Phrase**
		in the same league

🔑 Oxford 3000™ words

AWL Academic Word List

Check (✓) the skills you learned. If you need more work on a skill, refer to the page(s) in parentheses.

LISTENING	●	I can listen for pros and cons. (p. 231)
VOCABULARY	●	I can use connotations. (p. 237)
GRAMMAR	●	I can use parallel structure. (p. 239)
PRONUNCIATION	●	I can speak with word stress patterns. (p. 241)
SPEAKING	●	I can develop interview skills. (p. 243)
LEARNING OUTCOME	●	I can role-play interviews for a job or a school and be prepared to answer a question that is creative or unusual.

Audio Scripts

Unit 1 New Media

The Q Classroom Page 3

Teacher: Today we're beginning Unit 1. Every unit in Q starts with a question. As we go through the unit, we'll continue to discuss this question. Our answers may change as we explore the topic. [pause] The question for Unit 1 is: "How do people get the news today?" So, how about it, Yuna? Where do you get your news?

Yuna: Online mostly.

Teacher: Where online? Do you watch news videos? Read blogs or magazines?

Yuna: I read the headlines. Sometimes I click on a story. Sometimes I watch the video.

Teacher: What about you, Felix? Where do you get your news?

Felix: I'm very interested in the news, so I get it from a lot of different places. I read a couple of blogs that cover topics I'm interested in; I check the main Spanish and English news sites. When something important is happening, I also watch the news on TV.

Teacher: Wow! You really do keep up! Marcus, how would you compare the news we get today to the news our parents and grandparents got? Could Felix's father have been as well informed when he was Felix's age?

Marcus: Well, of course he didn't have access to online news sites. He probably got a lot of it from the newspaper—

Felix: —Oh, I pick up a newspaper once in a while, too.

Teacher: [laughs] Of course you do. Go on, Marcus.

Marcus: I was going to say that one benefit of a newspaper, whether it's online or in print, is that a big organization like a newspaper company has a reputation to protect. They try to give accurate, well-researched news reports.

Teacher: What do you say, Sophy? How do people get the news today?

Sophy: When something important is happening, a lot of people get their news through social networks. The information may not be as accurate or well researched as it would be from a big news organization, but you can really get a sense of how the events are affecting the people involved.

Teacher: Good discussion, class. Throughout this unit, we'll keep looking at how people get the news today, and you can continue to share your opinions.

LISTENING 1 Citizen Journalism
Pages 6–7

Host: Robin Hamman, from Headshift, which is an agency that advises organizations and governments on blogging and other aspects of social media and he's a visiting fellow in the College of Journalism at City University in London. And yes, even his two toddler children have a blog of their own. And, uh, I began by asking him to define what *citizen journalism* is.

Robin Hamman: Well, citizen media is ordinary people. Sometimes they're people who have been trained as journalists, other times they have no journalistic training whatsoever. But they're people who become interested in a story or an idea, and they go out and they start reporting on it and telling the world about it. Sometimes they'll do that in the same way as, as one would hope journalists would do, which is you know, gather the facts, make sure everything has been checked two or three times, and then run the story. Other times it's full of opinion and, and personal **viewpoints** that haven't been checked, that may or may not have any kind of **foundation** in truth.

Host: You've been in, sort of involved in watching citizen media and social **networking** sites for a long time. How have they changed over the years?

Hamman: On one hand, it's become a lot easier to do. People are now, for the most part, used to doing things like taking a digital photograph and uploading it to the Internet or emailing it to a friend. Uh, creating a document on their computer, maybe printing it, emailing it. So, people are used to kind of the basic tools of home computing. And actually you don't need to know a whole lot more to set up a blog, or to post a photograph to a photo-sharing website, or indeed to take a video on your camera phone, upload it to the Internet, and show it to millions of people on YouTube.

Host: Are there times when citizen journalism has really sort of taken to the forefront of, of news gathering?

Hamman: Well, it kind of depends on how you define "citizen journalism." Because a lot of times people who fall into the buckets of citizen journalism are actually people who just happen to witness something, happen to have a **unique** viewpoint, or unique access at the moment the story broke. And all they did was try to tell their friends what they saw. So, for example, we had the guy who took a photograph of the plane, uh, sinking in the Hudson River last year, um from, from a ferry. And all he was trying to do when he uploaded that photo was to tell his friends, "Whoa, I'm on a ferry and I've just seen a plane crash in the water, and there's people swimming out of it—this is crazy!" So, he wasn't trying to become a journalist; he wasn't trying to report to the world what he saw. He was just trying to tell his friends and people that he knew this crazy and bizarre scene that was **unfolding** in front of him. There are many, many examples of citizen journalists, or um, **accidental** citizen journalists out there. Um, many of them are, uh, great examples of, of, you know, people just trying to tell a story. Occasionally, the flip side of the coin happens, which is people with a particular viewpoint, um, you know, really trying to press that viewpoint home. They do have a **bias**; they do have an opinion. Uh, and there's lots of good examples of that out there too.

Host: It seems that one of the criticisms of citizen journalism is, uh, that they're not as **accountable** as branded corporate journalists are. Because in the most, most of the time blogs haven't been around long enough, some of them are **anonymous**—how are they dealing with that concern?

Hamman: Well, one of the interesting things about blogging and citizen journalists is that, for a long time now, most people who are doing it, um, have been quite concerned about openness and honesty and transparency about any biases that they might have. So, unlike a typical, traditional, uh, media outlet where if a journalist happens to, you know, have some particular bias, and tends not to tell that to the audience, tends not to expose that to the audience because they don't want to think that they might be biased. Um, in the instance of most citizen journalists and bloggers, they're actually pretty **upfront** about that sort of thing.

Host: What's the next step in the evolution of, of journalism and citizen journalism?

Hamman: I think one of the reasons why citizen journalism is becoming so interesting to a lot of people at the moment is this idea that the person who does the story usually tells people, you know, their background—any biases they might have, uh, any opinions that they may have before they started covering the story or indeed formed as the story came out. That's something that's missing from mainstream media, but I hope we start to see a lot more of it. I don't see any reason why a journalist who has a particular bias, who has a particular opinion, shouldn't tell the audience that upfront so that they can make their own mind up about how that bias might or might not have affected their coverage of the story. So I think that's one change that we're going to see where citizen journalism and blogging is actually going to affect the, the future of journalism. I also think, and have witnessed lots of journalists using social media tools—blogging, Facebook, Twitter, as a way of reaching out—not only to potential **sources** of information, but also to new audiences. So, as they're creating a story, they'll oftentimes—these days, say, "Here's what I'm working on; here's what I'm researching. Do you, the audience, know anything about it? Can you help me?" These are **techniques** that have come from the world of blogging and social media and that journalists are starting to pick up. Um, so, I think, you know, accidental citizen journalism—definitely we'll see a lot of it in the future. Citizen journalism—I think we aren't going to see a big explosion of it as such, um, but, you know, I may be proven wrong.

Host: Well that was Robin Hamman who, uh, spoke to me earlier. He works for Headshift, an agency that advises organizations and governments on blogging and other aspects of social media.

LISTENING SKILL Identifying main ideas
C. Pages 10–11

1. People are now, for the most part, used to doing things like taking a digital photograph and uploading it to the Internet or emailing it to a friend. Uh, creating a document on their computer, maybe printing it, emailing it.

2. So, for example, we had the guy who took a photograph of the plane, uh, sinking in the Hudson River last year, um from, from a ferry. And all he was trying to do when he uploaded that photo was to tell his friends, "Whoa, I'm on a ferry, and I've just seen a plane crash in the water, and there's people swimming out of it—this is crazy!"

3. I don't see any reason why a journalist who has a particular bias, who has a particular opinion, shouldn't tell the audience that upfront so that they can make their own mind up about how that bias might or might not have affected their coverage of the story.

4. I also think, and have witnessed lots of journalists using social media tools—blogging, Facebook, Twitter, as a way of reaching out—not only to potential sources of information, but also to new audiences. So, as they're creating a story, they'll oftentimes—these days, say, "Here's what I'm working on; here's what I'm researching. Do you, the audience, know anything about it? Can you help me?"

LISTENING 2 Pod-Ready: Podcasting for the Developing World
Pages 13–14

Host: Podcasts are taking off as a way that anyone, anywhere, can get their voice heard on the Internet. Access to information and communication technology (ICTs) in developing countries is growing day by day. With recognition from decision makers that ICTs are a key **component** in development, podcasting could play a role in the new communication order. But in the areas that don't have electricity, never mind the Internet, how can podcasting and other forms of audio communication succeed? Podcasts are digital audio files that are automatically downloaded from the Internet onto a computer, with the further option of transferring them to a portable audio player like the Apple iPod. Podcasting started in about 2004, as a way to give a voice to the voiceless, or at least those who didn't have access to large media organizations. Today, people all over the world are producing podcasts about topics ranging from astrophysics to knitting, and media organizations and institutions are spending time and effort to get "pod-ready." An appealing quality of podcasts is their **on-demand** nature. Ian James is a presenter from BBC's *Digital Planet* radio program and podcast.

Ian James: It's attractive for people because they can control when to listen. There's something quite **liberating** about unlocking the content of your computer and carrying it around with you.

Host: And according to Charlotte Moore, *Nature* magazine's podcast editor, audio is a great way to communicate complex ideas.

Charlotte Moore: Voice is more **compelling** to listen to. Listening to a conversation between two people feels more immediate than reading on a page.

Host: Podcasting's function in giving people a voice could play a large role in its uptake in developing countries. The **medium** clearly has roots and retains links with traditional radio. The importance of radio in developing countries, particularly in rural areas, is well-documented. But it is a one-way medium and doesn't necessarily offer opportunities for local people to get involved. Ben McChesney is head of the International New Technologies Programme at the U.K.-based technology charity Practical Action.

Ben McChesney: Radio seems a bit too distant, too formal. Radio stations also have a structured and **finite** broadcasting schedule, allowing little flexibility and limited capacity.

At Practical Action, we found that local enthusiasm for their podcasting is such that the local people asked to be taught how to make audio files, indicating that they felt the podcasts were valuable and that they wanted to use their own voices to communicate.

Host: But how **feasible** is access to podcasting equipment for the rural poor?

McChesney: One aspect that makes podcasting more attractive than radio is its relative low cost and **logistical** ease. You need a license to broadcast over the radio waves for example, and there are considerable capital costs in equipping a station, however basic. When setting up podcasting projects, we used open-source software entirely so any computer loaded with the—extremely low-cost—software, a microphone and some way of recording and saving the information was all we needed.

Host: Practical Action has been working on podcasts for the Cajamarca region of northern Peru since 2006. A poor, rural area, most of the people there rely on agriculture for their livelihoods. The project was part of another Practical Action **initiative**, which set up and maintains eight local telecenters in the region. These consisted of a telephone and a solar-powered computer providing two hours of satellite-derived Internet access a day. On one visit, McChesney saw that the telephone was much more popular than the computer. He realized that it was audio—voice and stories—that people used to communicate and share information, rather than text, particularly on a computer. Practical Action's local office in Peru surveyed local people about the type of information they needed to support their livelihoods—advice on grape cultivation or raising cattle for example. This information was then gathered from experts and recorded as digital audio files that could be sent to each of the telecenters via the Internet. For McChesney, it's about using the appropriate technology to get information to people in specific circumstances.

McChesney: Strictly speaking, this isn't a podcast, but it's a blend of some new technology—**transmitting** voice files from central points out to local telecenters—with old technology.

Host: The Kothmale Community Radio project in Sri Lanka is another example of communication evolving to suit the environment, bringing the benefits of ICTs to **isolated** rural communities in hilly central Sri Lanka. The project doesn't just use radio. Members of the team use a *tuk tuk*—a motorized three-wheeled vehicle—loaded with a laptop computer, wireless Internet, generator, printer, camera, telephone, and scanner. This mobile broadcasting unit, dubbed an "e-tuk tuk," allows the team to transmit audio information in two ways—using loudspeakers mounted on the vehicle's roof and broadcasting over the radio via the telephone line. Historically, news in Sri Lanka was distributed by people who would beat out messages and news as they moved from village to village. Kenneth Dale, coordinator of the project, describes the e-tuk tuk as a modern-day, Internet-connected drum, beating out news and information as it travels. While the Practical Action and e-tuk tuk initiatives and others like them can provide benefits on a community level, it remains to be seen whether podcasting can have a wider impact in the developing world. In the developed world, iPods and other digital audio players have raised the popularity of podcasts. But electricity is the main barrier to audio players penetrating remote areas, McChesney says. McChesney points to Zimbabwe, where Practical Action groups are carrying out research into audio access.

McChesney: We're beginning to explore different ways of getting information over to different groups of people—not just people responsible for livelihoods but for education as well. Girls are often kept away from school because they're doing other things for the family such as collecting water and feeding cattle. They're walking—what if their lessons are transmitted to them using some audio **device** so that they can learn while they walk?

Host: And this wouldn't necessarily have to be done using the Internet. Where Web access is simply not possible, audio files could be delivered physically with other goods. The image of a podcast trundling its way down a road towards a remote village is a million miles from downloads coasting along the information superhighway. But this is no surprise to David Benning, head of the common knowledge program at development charity Christian Aid.

David Benning: Technology often finds different uses and formats in developing countries. Podcasting in developing countries will not look like it does here, but that doesn't mean it won't happen.

Unit 2 Language

The Q Classroom Page 29

Teacher: Class, the Unit 2 question is: "How does language affect who we are?" So maybe we can start by talking about ourselves. How about you, Marcus? Do you think you would be a different person if you had a different first language?

Marcus: Yes, in some ways I would be.

Teacher: Why?

Marcus: Our language is part of our culture. The way we express ourselves reflects the things we care about. Sometimes there are things that I feel just can't be said as well in English.

Sophy: I don't think that's true, though. I think you can say anything in any language. You just feel more comfortable with how to say it in your native language.

Teacher: What do you think, Felix? How does language affect who we are?

Felix: I agree with Marcus. I think some things are easier to express in some languages than in others. Take showing respect, for example. In my native language, there are certain verb forms that you can use when you're talking to an older person that help you show respect, but in English that's difficult to do. You speak the same way to everyone. It made me uncomfortable when I first started speaking English.

Sophy: But you can show respect in English, just not with verb forms. You use more formal language, you don't contract as much, and that kind of thing. It's just different.

Teacher: Interesting. Would you like to add something, Yuna? How would you say language affects who we are?

Yuna: I think that for all people their language is very important to who they are. In Korea, our spoken language and our writing system are important parts of our culture.

LISTENING 1 My Stroke of Insight: A Brain Scientist's Personal Journey
Pages 32–33

David Inge, Host: Good morning. Welcome to the second hour of *Focus 580*. This is our morning talk program; my name's David Inge . . . . In this hour of *Focus 580* we'll be talking with Jill Bolte Taylor; she is a neuroanatomist. She's affiliated with the Indiana University School of Medicine in Indianapolis. And back in 1996, she was teaching and doing research at the Harvard Medical School when she had a stroke, a very serious and severe stroke. On that day, as she writes in her book *My Stroke of **Insight***, on that day she woke up with a sharp pain behind one eye. She tried to get on with her usual morning activities, but clearly she knew something was very wrong. She wasn't sure what. Uh, instead of finding answers or information, she writes she "met with a growing sense of peace." She writes that she felt "enfolded by a blanket of **tranquil** euphoria."

We should talk a little bit more about the, the **structure** of the brain, and, and I think that probably people have an idea in, in their head of what the brain looks like. And that I think the thing that people think about as being the brain is in fact the cortex, the cerebral—

Jill Bolte Taylor: Right.

Inge: —cortex, which is that part of the brain that sets us apart from a lot of other living things and in fact maybe sets us apart in degree from other mammals as well. Uh, and maybe also

people are used to the idea that it has two halves, right and left, and that the two halves are different. So, talk a little bit about that, the structure of the brain at that level, and the two halves, the right and the left, and what makes them different.

Taylor: Well, they process information in, in different kinds of ways, um, but of course they're always both working all at the same time. So as you look out into the world right now, whatever your **perception** is, you, you have choices. You can look first at the big picture of the room and not really focus in on any of the details. And the right hemisphere looks at things for the big picture. It blends the, softens the **boundaries** between things so that you take in the bigger picture of the room. Is this a really lovely room? Is this a great room? Um, and you just have the **overall** perception. If you're at the beach, um, you look out over the, the, um, horizon and you look out over the water, and, and you, you allow yourself to feel expansive, and that's the bigger picture of everything. The left hemisphere, then, is going to—and it's all in the present moment. The right hemisphere is all about right here, right now. And then the left hemisphere is going to take that big picture and it's going to start picking out the details. So if you're at the beach, now it's going to start looking at the kinds of clouds, and it's going to label them and it's going to look at the whitecaps and label them, and it's going to look at the kinds of grains in the sand and label them. And everything now starts working into language and the details that we can then communicate with, so it's looking—and, and, and in order to do that, it's going to compare things to things that we've learned in the past, and it's going to project images into the future. The right hemisphere thinks the big picture in pictures. The left hemisphere thinks the details using language, so the two hemispheres work together constantly for us to have a normal perspective.

And, and on the morning of my hemorrhage, I lost the left hemisphere, which lost my language, it lost my ability to associate or relate anything to the **external** world or to communicate either creating language or understanding other people's language. But what I gained was this experience of the present moment and the expansiveness, so, so they're, they're very different ways of perceiving the world. And most of us, you know, I think we can identify that there are these two very different parts of ourselves and that we use them together. I just had the opportunity to lose the detail of the left hemisphere so that I could really just experience the right hemisphere untethered to the left hemisphere.

Inge: Our guest on this hour of *Focus 580*, Jill Bolte Taylor; she's a neuroanatomist. And of course questions are welcome. [L]ine 1. Hello.

Caller: Hello.

Inge: Yes.

Caller: I find this **fascinating**. I'm, I'm an experimental psychologist, retired. And, um, there's an old, uh, out of the behavioristic tradition, you know, they believed that **consciousness** was intrinsically tied to language. And it sounds like that's out the window now because you evidently didn't lose consciousness and, uh, because you—but you did lose your language. But what I'm interested in, is did you lose the concept of future and past? It sounds like you were living entirely in the present. Is that true or not?

Inge: All right.

Taylor: Thank you. Yeah. No, that's a great question. I did lose my perception of past and future when I had that hemorrhage in the left hemisphere, and I lost all of the consciousness of the language center. I lost the portion of my brain that said, "I am an individual. I am Jill Bolte Taylor. These are all the data connected to me." These are all the memories associated with who I had been and when that person went offline, which is the best way for me to explain it, I lost all of her likes and dislikes, and I didn't—but I was still completely conscious. And in the process of **recovery**, I essentially had to say that woman died that day, and I was now an infant in a woman's body. And this new consciousness was going to **regain** the **function** of the left hemisphere, but I was not going to regain being whom I had been before. So, um, uh, I love your perspective on it. At the, at the same time I, I see it as, as, just as far as language is concerned, picture yourself as a, a purely English-speaking person and then you wake up one day and you're in the heart of China where nobody speaks any English whatsoever, so you're no longer dependent on the language. You're dependent on having a heightening of your other experiences, the inflection of voice and facial expression, and, and you're, you're really in the present moment, then, in order to gain information about what, where, where you're at and what you have to do. So we do function; there's a whole part of us that is non-language, and once that language goes off, I was still a whole human being, even though I didn't have my language center and the rest of my left hemisphere was, was swimming in a pool of blood. I still had the experience that I was perfect and whole and beautiful just the way that I was even though I only had part of my, my mind functioning.

LISTENING SKILL Making inferences

A. Page 35

1. The thing that people think about as being the brain is in fact the cortex, the cerebral cortex, which is that part of the brain that sets us apart from a lot of other living things . . .

2. The right hemisphere thinks the big picture in pictures. The left hemisphere thinks the details using language, so the two hemispheres work together constantly for us to have a normal perspective.

3. I just had the opportunity to lose the detail of the left hemisphere so that I could really just experience the right hemisphere untethered to the left hemisphere.

4. At the same time I, I see it as, as, just as far as language is concerned, picture yourself as a purely English-speaking person and then you wake up one day and you're in the heart of China where nobody speaks any English whatsoever, so you're no longer dependent on the language. You're dependent on having a heightening of your other

experiences, the inflection of voice and facial expression, and, and you're, you're really in the present moment, then, in order to gain information about what, where, where you're at and what you have to do.

LISTENING 2 The Story of My Life
Pages 38–39

Helen Keller: I cannot recall what happened during the first months after my illness. I only know that I sat in my mother's lap or clung to her dress as she went about her household duties. My hands felt every object and observed every motion, and in this way I learned to know many things. Soon I felt the need of some communication with others and began to make crude signs. A shake of the head meant "No" and a nod, "Yes." A pull meant "Come" and a push, "Go." Was it bread that I wanted? Then I would **imitate** the acts of cutting the slices and buttering them. If I wanted my mother to make ice cream for dinner, I made the sign for working the freezer and shivered, indicating cold. My mother, moreover, succeeded in making me understand a good deal. I always knew when she wished me to bring her something, and I would run upstairs or anywhere else she indicated. Indeed, I owe to her loving wisdom all that was bright and good in my long night. . . .

I do not remember when I first realized that I was different from other people, but I knew it before my teacher came to me. I had noticed that my mother and my friends did not use signs as I did when they wanted anything done, but talked with their mouths. Sometimes I stood between two persons who were conversing and touched their lips. I could not understand and was vexed. I moved my lips and **gesticulated** frantically without result. This made me so angry at times that I kicked and screamed until I was exhausted. . . .

Many **incidents** of those early years are fixed in my memory, isolated, but clear and distinct, making the sense of that silent, aimless, day-less life all the more **intense**. . . .

Meanwhile, the desire to express myself grew. The few signs I used became less and less **adequate**, and my failures to make myself understood were **invariably** followed by **outbursts** of passion. I felt as if invisible hands were holding me, and I made frantic efforts to free myself. I struggled—not that struggling helped matters, but the spirit of resistance was strong within me; I generally broke down in tears and physical exhaustion. If my mother happened to be near, I crept into her arms, too miserable even to remember the cause of the tempest. After a while, the need of some means of communication became so urgent that these outbursts occurred daily, sometimes hourly. . . .

The most important day I remember in all my life is the one on which my teacher, Anne Mansfield Sullivan, came to me. I am filled with wonder when I consider the immeasurable contrasts between the two lives which it connects. It was the third of March, 1887, three months before I was seven years old.

On the afternoon of that eventful day, I stood on the porch, dumb, expectant. I guessed vaguely from my mother's signs and from the hurrying to and fro in the house that something unusual was about to happen, so I went to the door and waited on the steps. The afternoon sun penetrated the mass of honeysuckle that covered the porch, and fell on my upturned face. My fingers lingered almost unconsciously on the familiar leaves and blossoms which had just come forth to greet the sweet southern spring. I did not know what the future held of marvel or surprise for me. Anger and bitterness had preyed upon me continually for weeks, and a deep languor had succeeded this passionate struggle.

Have you ever been at sea in a dense fog, when it seemed as if a **tangible** white darkness shut you in, and the great ship, tense and anxious, groped her way toward the shore with plummet and sounding-line, and you waited with beating heart for something to happen? I was like that ship before my education began, only I was without compass or sounding line, and had no way of knowing how near the harbor was. "Light! Give me light!" was the wordless cry of my soul, and the light of love shone on me in that very hour.

I felt approaching footsteps, I stretched out my hand as I supposed to my mother. Some one took it, and I was caught up and held close in the arms of her who had come to **reveal** all things to me, and more than all things else, to love me.

The morning after my teacher came she led me into her room and gave me a doll. The little blind children at the Perkins Institution had sent it . . . but I did not know this until afterward. When I had played with it a little while, Miss Sullivan slowly spelled into my hand the word "d-o-l-l." I was at once interested in this finger play and tried to imitate it. When I finally succeeded in making the letters correctly I was flushed with childish pleasure and pride. Running downstairs to my mother, I held up my hand and made the letters for *doll*. I did not know that I was spelling a word or even that words existed; I was simply making my fingers go in monkey-like imitation. In the days that followed I learned to spell in this uncomprehending way a great many words, among them *pin*, *hat*, *cup* and a few verbs like *sit*, *stand*, and *walk*. But my teacher had been with me several weeks before I understood that everything has a name. . . .

Miss Sullivan had tried to impress it upon me that "m-u-g" is mug and that "w-a-t-e-r" is water, but I **persisted** in confounding the two. In despair, she had dropped the subject for the time, only to renew it at the first opportunity. I became impatient at her repeated attempts, and seizing the new doll, I dashed it upon the floor. I was keenly delighted when I felt the **fragments** of the broken doll at my feet. Neither sorrow nor regret followed my passionate outburst. I had not loved the doll. In the still, dark world in which I lived, there was no strong **sentiment** or tenderness. I felt my teacher sweep the fragments to one side of the hearth, and I had a sense of satisfaction that the cause of my discomfort was removed. She brought me my hat, and I knew I was going out into the warm sunshine. This thought, if a wordless sensation may be called a thought, made me hop and skip with pleasure.

We walked down the path to the well-house, attracted by the fragrance of the honeysuckle with which it was covered. Someone was drawing water, and my teacher placed my hand under the spout. As the cool stream gushed over one hand, she spelled into the other the word *water*, first slowly, then rapidly. I stood still, my whole attention fixed upon the motions of her fingers.

Suddenly I felt a misty consciousness as of something forgotten—a thrill of returning thought—and somehow the mystery of language was revealed to me. I knew then that "w-a-t-e-r" meant the wonderful cool something that was flowing over my hand. That living word awakened my soul; gave it light, hope, joy; set it free! There were barriers still, it is true, but barriers that could in time be swept away.

I left the well-house eager to learn. Everything had a name, and each name gave birth to a new thought. . . .

I learned a great many new words that day. I do not remember what they all were; but I do know that *mother, father, sister, teacher* were among them—words that were to make the world blossom for me, "like Aaron's rod, with flowers." It would have been difficult to find a happier child than I was as I lay in my crib at the close of that eventful day and lived over the joys it had brought me and for the first time longed for a new day to come. . . .

I recall many incidents of the summer of 1887 that followed my soul's sudden awakening. I did nothing but explore with my hands and learn the name of every object that I touched and the more I handled things and learned their names and uses, the more joyous and confident grew my sense of kinship with the rest of the world.

Unit 3 Work and Fun

The Q Classroom Page 53

Teacher: It's time for us to start talking about the Unit 3 question, which is: "Where can work, education, and fun overlap? First of all, can they overlap? What do you think, Yuna?

Yuna: Yes. When I enjoy my work, it's fun. And usually I only enjoy my work if I'm learning something.

Teacher: What do you think, Sophy? Where can work, education, and fun overlap?

Sophy: They can overlap at school. For example, if you take a field trip, it's fun, and you're learning, and you're also preparing the report or whatever other work you have to do for it.

Teacher: Felix?

Felix: I agree with Yuna, that work is fun when you're learning, but I think fun can be educational as well. To me, fun is more fun when I'm learning something. When I go on vacations, I love to learn all about the places I visit. I'm one of those tourists who reads all of the brochure information. That's not work, I guess, but it's definitely fun and learning.

Teacher: OK. We've talked about fun at school and learning on vacations—what about fun at work? When is work fun? Marcus?

Marcus: I think work is fun when you're doing something out of your normal routine, and especially if you're working on something in a group. At my job, we needed to change some of our procedures, and the manager wanted us all to be a part of the change, so she set up informal meetings for us to discuss how we wanted to change things. We got a chance to talk to each other in a way we usually don't, we got some good planning done, it was a learning experience because none of us had done anything like that before, and it was a break from our routine. It was actually a lot of fun. Plus there were donuts!

Teacher: Sounds like you have a smart manager. Well, we've covered a lot of bases in this discussion: work, education, and fun can clearly overlap at school, on vacation, and in the workplace. We'll keep discussing this idea as we go through the unit.

LISTENING 1 Voluntourism
Pages 56–57

Chris Christensen, Host: [music] *Amateur Traveler*, Episode 125. Today we talk about volunteer travel, or voluntourism. Find out what kind of person is doing this kind of travel, what they're doing when they get there, and just who it is they're meeting. On today's *Amateur Traveler*.

Welcome to the *Amateur Traveler*; I'm your host, Chris Christensen. I'd like to welcome to the show Linda Stuart. Linda is the executive director of the Global Citizens Network. Linda, welcome to the show, first.

Linda Stuart: Thank you Chris. Glad to be here.

Christensen: What is the Global Citizens Network?

Stuart: Global Citizens Network is a nonprofit organization based out of St. Paul, Minnesota, that's in its 16th year. We've been providing cross-cultural **expeditions** to **indigenous** communities around the world.

Christensen: OK, and so what we're talking about on this show is volunteer travel, or voluntourism is the other phrase that's been used. Let's start with the why. Why after I've been working so hard for the whole year would I want to go and work someplace else?

Stuart: Yeah, that's a great question. We've seen an increase over the last couple of years in individuals, families, groups, couples that are interested in an experience where they feel like they're able to contribute, or give back, and so while going to see new lands, meet new people is still very **enticing**, there is something to be said about going and doing good, and that is an opportunity that Global Citizens provides with its cross-cultural trips and the service aspect on the trip. And there's an opportunity to meet others, meet friends, see new places and new lands, taste new foods, but then in addition, there's an opportunity to work on a service project that will make a contribution to the community where we're partnering.

Christensen: Before we get into specifically what you guys are doing, can you tell us a little bit more about what are the **ranges** of opportunities when we talk about volunteer travel?

Stuart: Everywhere you turn around now, you'll see volunteer opportunities. Voluntourism is on the rise. And one thing that our organization has maintained over the last 16 years is the opportunity to travel and volunteer together as a team. And so we do solicit intact teams, but also individuals are welcome to come and join us on any group trip. There is a wide range of opportunities. Others include individual placement; some are in rural areas versus urban areas. Others may be more of a tutoring or English teaching placement—

Christensen: Mm-hmm.

Stuart: —others may be in orphanages. Our organization partners with indigenous communities and works with them on small-scale development projects of their choice and so it often focuses on physical labor, construction of health clinics, schools, community centers, etc. But other projects may include, for example, in a village in Guatemala, in Cantel, we're partnering with the Mayan Peace Center on youth empowerment projects. And that is, again, of the community's choice and by their initiation and direction. So in Cantel, there's the center where the youth come and they learn about Mayan weaving, medicinal medicines, traditional dance, etc., and our presence there is really to also kind of **validate** the culture and the **preservation** of the culture. So that's a really significant project that we feel like we're working on. So there's a wide variety of opportunities for people if they feel like they want to go together as a team, if they want to go as an individual, if they want to go 50s and older, there's also an opportunity for baby boomers and senior citizens to be together. And one thing about GCN is that we are an age-**diverse** organization so families, children eight and up are welcome on our program.

Christensen: Can you describe your volunteers? Can you give us a couple of examples of people who volunteer for you?

Stuart: Well, two-thirds of our volunteers are women.

Christensen: Interesting.

Stuart: The other **demographics** of our volunteers would include, as I just mentioned some sort of family combination. But I would say that the majority of the people that travel with us do range between probably 30 and 55 years old. And then the second group after that would be the youth, because the one area I guess that we don't see as many is the kind of the university-aged individuals, and that's because I think oftentimes they're looking for credit or possibly more of a longer-term program and our programs are short-term.

Christensen: Mm hm.

Stuart: They're one to three weeks long and so . . .

There are many motivating reasons for this kind of experience, in addition to giving back and contributing. Another one is the camaraderie and sharing that meaningful experience with a family or, like as you mentioned, allowing children to have that kind of eye-opening experience and seeing not it's us versus them, but it's us all together.

We do stress that there's always something for everyone, and so while maybe the construction on a health center, sometimes it can be as simple as hauling some sand, assisting in sand— the project usually occurs in the morning, followed by a community lunch and in the afternoon there's opportunity for interacting with the community members in weavings and classes and lessons, learning, educational forms at the clinics. I mean, there's always such a wide variety because the goal is to really **immerse yourself in** the daily lives of the village people and to see how they live.

Christensen: So what was your personal experience with how you got so involved in volunteer travel?

Stuart: Well, as a youth I was fortunate enough to have an experience to go on an alternative project when I was in high school. It was very eye-opening for me. It was an **ecological** project in Dominica in the Caribbean. And it was my first taste of what alternative travel is, and everyone is pretty aware of a lot of what the mass tourism opportunities are, but I was really touched by that experience and very moved that at that time, someone was **raising my awareness** and my realization and my conscientiousness about supporting the local economy . . . versus buying all the souvenirs that you would buy on a cruise ship per se. And so there was something that really resonated with that experience for me. And then just kind of **prompted** a lifetime of seeking those kinds of experiences, learning a second language, doing research and study abroad in college, and just one experience led up to another, so . . .

Christensen: And then if you could get a little more specific in terms of what we would expect if we actually went someplace with GCN, what countries are you in, first of all?

Stuart: We partner here in the United States, with several Native American reservations—

Christensen: OK.

Stuart: —as well, first nations in Canada. We are in Mexico, Ecuador, Peru, Guatemala. We're in Africa, Asia, Kenya and Tanzania specifically, and Nepal and Thailand.

Christensen: And what's the average group size?

Stuart: Our groups are small. They range anywhere from 4 to 12.

Christensen: OK. And then what kind of cost, I know it's going to vary depending on whether we're going to Arizona or Tibet.

Stuart: Our program fees range anywhere from $900 to $2400, depending, yeah, on where you go and for how long. If it's a week to three weeks long.

Christensen: And that's not counting airfare, I assume?

Stuart: Airfare is in addition to that as well as any visa costs or any immunizations that would be needed.

Christensen: OK.

Stuart: But the program fee does cover your lodging, transportation, food, and a portion of it goes to the project.

Christensen: Well, I thank you so much for coming on the show and telling us a little bit about this different kind of, uh, opportunity for travel and just appreciate you sharing your experience with us.

Stuart: Great. Thank you.

LISTENING SKILL Listening for examples
A. Page 59

1. **Stuart:** Our organization partners with indigenous communities and works with them on small-scale development projects of their choice and so it often focuses on physical labor, construction of health clinics, schools, community centers, etc.

2. **Stuart:** There are many motivating reasons for this kind of experience, in addition to giving back and contributing. Another one is the camaraderie and sharing that meaningful experience with a family or, like as you mentioned, allowing children to have that kind of eye-opening experience and seeing not it's us versus them, but it's us all together.

3. **Christensen:** And then if you could get a little more specific in terms of what we would expect if we actually went someplace with GCN, what countries are you in, first of all?

   Stuart: We partner here in the United States, with several Native American reservations—

   Christensen: OK.

   Stuart: —as well, first nations in Canada. We are in Mexico, Ecuador, Peru, Guatemala. We're in Africa, Asia, Kenya and Tanzania specifically, and Nepal and Thailand.

LISTENING 2 Science Fairs and Nature Reserves
Pages 61–63

Narrator: The climax of many **outreach** programs run by the University of Cambridge occurs in March each year with a science festival. Sober university buildings take on a carnival **atmosphere** in a week-long celebration of science.

Nicola Buckley: It's a unique chance for all the scientific, mathematical, engineering departments to get together and put on this amazing week of activities for kids and adults. And you've never seen anything like it with all of these quite staid university buildings being sort of overrun by children that week, and it's just a chance to open the doors and interest people in science, really. The science festival is a very large event at the university. It's the largest public event we run each year. We record over 45,000 visits to all of the events. The atmosphere on the Science on Saturday is absolutely fantastic.

Narrator: This experiment is part of a project called "crash-bang-squelch." By mixing corn flour and water, you get a material that can both be a liquid and a solid at the same time. It's strange, and fun to play with, but there is a serious point. It might cause a child to begin to think differently about the materials of everyday life. In the week before the festival, Sebastian Watt and his fellow volunteers from the Earth Science department climb into their time truck and tour many of the local schools.

Buckley: Which is packed with **interactive exhibits** about geology, volcanoes, and these sorts of things, little demonstrations. The aims of the festival are to enthuse the general public about science, especially children, young people, to encourage them to be the next generation of scientists. And that's why the science festival is so important. It breaks down barriers between scientists and the wider community and the university and the wider world. And we think that's a benefit to both. Of course, we want to encourage children and young people to study science at this and other universities, but above all, we want children and parents to understand how wonderful science is and how important a part it plays in all our lives.

[music]

Speaker: In this report on the Sedgwick Nature Reserve, you will near a narrator and two speakers: Dr. Michael Williams, the reserve director, and Professor Jennifer Thorsch of the University of California, Santa Barbara.

Narrator: The University of California Natural Reserve system provides a testing ground for developing innovative solutions to California's tough environmental and educational challenges. With more than 30 **sites** dedicated to teaching, research, and public outreach, NRS Reserves can be found throughout the state. The Sedgwick reserve, near UC Santa Barbara, provides a perfect example of the kinds of activities that go on throughout the system. Here UC faculty and staff are exploring ways to preserve the state's disappearing oak woodlands and **restore** native grasslands, delving deep into the earth to understand the microorganisms that support California's ecosystems, and **pioneering** new ways to serve the state's diverse student population.

Community support is essential to the success of the reserve. Many people in the area volunteer to serve as docents at the reserve, leading public tours and conducting educational programs for school groups.

Dr. Michael Williams is the reserve director.

Michael Williams: Without an outreach program, you can't get people excited about a site. And the outreach also is a, it fits into the mission of NRS for public service. And to actually show people, in a very controlled setting—we don't allow open use of the reserve, but with trained docents, um, we can have classes come out here and see research happening. The nice thing about outreach, for me, for me personally, is I like to see kids get excited about science, to see it in action.

The special programs we have that are under, um, the oversight of the outreach **coordinator** is one program in particular called "Kids in Nature," where we bring low-income, uh, poor-performing school district kids from throughout, currently Santa Barbara county, but that will be expanding into other adjoining counties this next year. Uh, we bring them in for almost, um, a whole year of interaction. And that includes a number of field trips here to work on a restoration project, and to work on the biology of the plants they're using in the restoration project, and to understand the communities under which the restoration project is taking place. And it just keeps multiplying itself out. Then they go on campus and they actually learn about plant anatomy. And they look at the anatomy of the very plants they're planting out here. And then they've got computer games that they can take back with them to the classroom that are developed specifically of plants at Sedgwick. They come back out here and they start asking more questions that they've learned or that's been generated by the game.

Narrator: The Kids in Nature program draws on the **resources** of both the reserve and the campus. Professor Jennifer Thorsch and her students at UC Santa Barbara played a key role in creating and running the program.

Jennifer Thorsch: My concept was to bring botany to K through 12 students and bring them to the university for experiences in the laboratory and also at our natural area sites on campus. Sedgwick Reserve was running their own schools program. We learned about each other's program, so we met, and a **collaboration** was born, and Kids in Nature was the result.

I think the **impact** that Kids in Nature is having is probably more far-reaching than we will even begin to understand. Not only are they introduced to the university environment—many of these children have never, ever been on a university campus, and the concept of going to college is not in their realm. The visits to the university **familiarize** them with what a university is, and we all try and be extremely positive when these students are on campus and show them that they can come here too.

Williams: I think that's a wonderful use of a natural reserve site. Again, it's very controlled, research sites are protected, uh, the kids are, get to meet a lot of the researchers doing these programs.

Thorsch: And I think often, especially young girls, at the ages between the 4th grade and 6th grade, begin to believe that they cannot be scientists or that it's not a cool thing to do. And so we try and show them that you can be anything you want to be. And also, I think science is really interesting, and by and large, it's not taught in a really hands-on, "teaching by doing" rather than "teaching by telling." And so, this program not only has them doing experiments in the labs at UCSB, but they're out here in this beautiful environment.

Unit 4 Deception

The Q Classroom Page 77

Teacher: Unit 4 is about deception, and the Unit Question is: "Can the eyes deceive the mind?" Let's start with our own experience. What are some common examples of the eyes deceiving the mind?

Sophy: The first things that come to my mind are those pictures with a hidden image in them. When you first look at them, your eyes tell you that it's just a repetitive pattern, but there are actually differences in the pattern that show up as a hidden image when you look at it for a while.

Marcus: Those things drive me crazy! I can never see the picture. But to answer the question, I'd say that 3D movies are a very common example of the eyes deceiving the mind. What looks like 3D is really just the same image being shown from different angles.

Teacher: Good point. What are some other examples of the eyes deceiving the mind? Felix?

Felix: Well, to take off from what Marcus said, we use visual deception all the time. For example, we put mirrors in rooms to make them look bigger, or we wear vertical stripes to make ourselves look thinner. Even animal camouflage is an example of the eyes deceiving the mind—the animal is there, but you don't see it because its patterns and colors match the background.

Teacher: That's true. Are there other examples of the eyes deceiving the mind? Does it happen in ways we don't plan? What do you think, Yuna?

Yuna: When people are in the desert, they sometimes see pools of water. I forgot what that's called . . .

Teacher: A mirage. Yes, people often see mirages in the heat, on highways, too.

Yuna: And on the ocean.

Teacher: That's right. People think they see land when there is no land there at all. So we have lots of examples of the eyes deceiving the mind, and we'll see more as we continue with this unit.

LISTENING 1 Wild Survivors
Page 81

Narrator: In the ruthless world of **survival**, the battle for life and death takes on **infinite** forms. The endless struggle to eat and avoid being eaten has created weapon and defense systems that are continuously changing. The balance of power in nature is continually shifting. Sometimes it favors the hunter and sometimes the hunted. Those that are best at the game escape from the very jaws of death.

Adapting is necessary for survival. As conditions change—availability of food and water, temperatures, the presence of predators both animal and human—animals must change to meet the challenges or die.

Both weather and landscape play a part in how animals **adapt**. Those that live must be well suited to the demands of the environment. For example, the brown feathers of the ptarmigan, a bird about the size of a pigeon that lives in Europe and North America, make it almost invisible to **predators**. But the feathers serve another purpose as well—they protect the bird from the extreme cold by keeping its body heat next to its body, as well as keeping the cold air out.

The ptarmigan also grows long white feathers on its feet for the winter, which act like built-in snowshoes. Undoubtedly, the feathers also provide effective **camouflage**, a disguise that helps the ptarmigan hide from predators by matching the color of its environment. When the snow disappears, so too do the white winter feathers of the ptarmigan. Its summer outfit, speckled grey and brown feathers, is well designed to suit the environment that is now free of snow. The young ptarmigans are in special need of good camouflage, since they cannot fly as well as the adults. They must protect themselves from predators by crouching and hiding among the rocks, moss, and wildflowers. Camouflage is **virtually** all the protection they have in the rocky landscape of the Pacific Northwest.

An even more **elaborate** survival system is found among the leaves of the oak tree, home to a variety of birds and a small, unimpressive-looking moth. In the springtime, the moth lays its eggs on the underside of the leaves, where they are less likely to be found by any hungry passersby. When the caterpillars hatch, they begin a dangerous journey. Those that survive make straight for the oak trees' flowers. As they feed hungrily upon the flowers, they absorb the chemicals within them. This triggers a startling transformation. Quite literally, the caterpillar is what it eats. It can **mimic** the flowers superbly, even imitating the movement of the flowers in the spring breeze.

Camouflage allows many of the caterpillars to **mature** safe from predatory birds. But the story doesn't stop there. In the summer, another set of caterpillars is hatched. By now, the flowers have fallen, and the caterpillars feed on the leaves instead. But there are different chemicals within the leaves now that set off a completely different reaction. This time, the caterpillars take on the appearance of the oak twigs, rather than the flowers. To its great advantage, the same species has shown a striking capacity for variation.

Adaptations can be remarkably specific to the environment. A praying mantis looks dangerously out of place on the forest floor, easy pickings for any nearby predators. But a disappearing act takes place when the mantis reaches the flowers of the Asian orchid. So closely does it **resemble** its surroundings that the other insects sometimes search for nectar on its body. Those that do may pay for their mistake with their lives.

The unbroken reaches of the desert seem to offer little in the way of protection or places to hide. Even here, though, natural selection has resulted in some very effective adaptations. The desert snake can transform itself from **obvious** to almost invisible in the sand, where it then hides in wait for potential **prey**. A lizard is no match at all for the deception of the snake.

The sandy bottom of the ocean floor can also hide its inhabitants. The Caribbean flounder, a fish whose flat body is the color of the ocean floor, makes good use of the seabed to hide from view. Only its eyes are left exposed to sight a likely meal. Its looks may be unusual, but they work superbly in these surroundings.

The pressure of natural selection, or survival of the fittest, is an irresistible force shaping all of nature. Those individuals who live to reproduce pass on their useful traits to succeeding generations. This is the essence of adaptation. As a general rule, the more closely you match your environment, the better your chances are of surviving. The genetic combinations that result in camouflage like this, as well as the behaviors passed on from parents to offspring by example, are the product of an unknowable number of hits and misses. Successful techniques and features live on in future generations, and unsuccessful ones necessarily pass away. It is one of the true miracles of nature.

LISTENING SKILL Recognizing appositives that explain
Page 83

1. Adapting is necessary for survival. As conditions change—availability of food and water, temperatures, the presence of predators both animal and human—animals must change to meet the challenges or die.

2. Both weather and landscape play a part in how animals adapt. Those that live must be well suited to the demands of the environment. For example, the brown feathers of the ptarmigan, a bird about the size of a pigeon that lives in Europe and North America, make it almost invisible to predators.

3. The ptarmigan also grows long white feathers on its feet for the winter, which act like built-in snowshoes. Undoubtedly, the feathers also provide effective camouflage, a disguise that helps the ptarmigan hide from predators by matching the color of its environment.

4. When the snow disappears, so too do the white winter feathers of the ptarmigan. Its summer outfit, speckled grey and brown feathers, is well designed to suit the environment that is now free of snow.

5. The sandy bottom of the ocean floor can also hide its inhabitants. The Caribbean flounder, a fish whose flat body is the color of the ocean floor, makes good use of the seabed to hide from view.

LISTENING 2 Magic and the Mind
Pages 85–86

Marco Werman: Magic is one of the oldest art forms around, and it's based on fooling the human mind, which is why some scientists in Britain and Canada are interested in magic. They wrote an article about it for the journal *Trends in **Cognitive** Sciences*. In it, they say that by studying the tricks used by magicians, scientists could gain a deeper understanding of human perception.

Gustav Kuhn is one of the co-authors; he's a psychologist and a practicing magician, and he's at the University of Durham in England.

Now, in your study, you argue that the time has come to create a science of magic. What exactly do you mean by that?

Gustav Kuhn: Most of you will have experienced magicians, for example, making objects magically disappear. Now, these kinds of tricks don't rely on **supernatural** powers. What the magician is really doing is **utilizing** a fairly wide range of techniques to **manipulate** your perception. Now, as you mentioned in your introduction, magic is a very old art form, and magicians have, through generations of practicing this art, have accumulated vast amounts of experience and knowledge about how these principles work. Now many of these principles are very similar to the kind of **phenomenon** that are typically studied by psychologists. And what we've been trying to do is kind of to find this **link** between magic and science. In other words, what we're trying to do is sort of try to **tap into** some of this experience by the magicians and sort of try to understand the scientific foundation of some of these techniques. And hopefully this will actually then lead toward a sort of science of magic.

Werman: Right, and what specific techniques of the magic trade are you talking about?

Kuhn: Um, there's a wide variety. In this paper, we've been looking at three different techniques: namely, misdirection, **illusions**, and forcing.

Werman: Maybe you can kind of just quickly explain what each of those means.

Kuhn: So, misdirection relates to the magician's ability to prevent you from seeing certain things happen. Now, magicians will typically **distract** your attention so that you don't see what's happening. And, uh, work in visual sciences has shown that even though when you are looking around the room around you, you feel that you are aware of everything that's going on. However, our representation of this world is much more limited. Now what it basically means is that unless you really specifically attend to an object or an event, you don't necessarily see it. Now, whilst this has taken the scientific community by surprise, magicians have been aware of this for a long time, and this is how they can use misdirection to basically distract your attention away from what they want to hide, and so that means you don't see it.

Then there's illusions. Now, uh, much of what we actually perceive is related to how we believe the world to be, and is based on our expectations about the world, rather than what's actually really out there. So that means our perception of the world is actually fairly **subjective**. Now again, magicians, they can manipulate your expectations so as to make you perceive things that have not necessarily taken place.

Werman: And then finally there's forcing. What is forcing?

Kuhn: In everyday life, we sort of—usually we feel that most of the decisions that we make are sort of fairly free, we sort of feel we've got free will. However, again, magicians have sort of developed techniques that can actually influence your choice. And, um, often you're not actually aware of how your choice has been influenced. And that's known as forcing.

Werman: Now, your study shows that cognitive science and psychology can learn a lot from, uh, what magicians do, but can magicians go out and buy a psychology book and kind of become better magicians?

Kuhn: I think so. I mean, I guess this is sort of what we are hoping to do, as well, so whilst I think scientists can learn a lot from magicians, magicians also have, sort of, can learn quite a bit. Um . . .

Werman: And yet, and yet successful magic also depends on secrecy, so suddenly you're giving away all these secrets.

Kuhn: Well, we sort of try to make a bigger point that we're not actually giving away any of the secrets, so our aim is make use of the techniques, rather than the secrets. And even though you know that these techniques are in place, when you're actually seeing a magic performance, this will probably not help you **work out** how the trick is actually done.

Werman: Gustav Kuhn is a psychologist and a practicing magician. He's part of a research team from Durham University and the University of British Columbia that has studied the science of magic. Thanks very much for your time.

Kuhn: Thank you.

Werman: You'll find examples of some of the tricks that Gustav Kuhn used in his research at theworld.org.

GRAMMAR Relative clauses
A. Page 92

1. Mixing up the knives that cut the boxes during a magic show is dangerous.

2. A magician from France whom we saw perform last week astonished us with every trick in the book.

3. The elephant that walked across the stage was not even noticed by the audience.

4. The sounds of nature that we thought we heard were really radios.

5. The performer pulled out a rabbit whose ears were bigger than the hat.

6. Many magic tricks are actually pretty easy for a beginner to learn, which surprised me.

Unit 5 Global Cooperation

The Q Classroom Page 101

Teacher: It's time again for us to talk about the Unit Question. For Unit 5, it's: "What does it mean to be a global citizen?" Marcus, why don't you start us off today?

Marcus: Hmm. Global citizens are people who see themselves as citizens of the world, not just of their own country or community.

Teacher: I think that's a good definition. So what are some examples of seeing yourself as a citizen of the world? How does that affect your behavior? Sophy?

Sophy: One thing a global citizen does is protect the environment. The energy we waste, the trash we produce, and the pollution we cause can affect people in far-off places. If you're a global citizen, you're concerned about that, and you try not to be wasteful.

Teacher: OK. Yuna, what do you think? What does it mean to be a global citizen?

Yuna: It means we have to care about what happens to people in less fortunate countries. We do things to help them.

Teacher: Can you give me an example?

Yuna: Mostly by sending money, but some people join volunteer corps and go to other countries to help out.

Teacher: That's true. What do you say, Felix. What does it mean to be a global citizen?

Felix: I think we are all global citizens, whether we want to be or not. As Sophy said, how we live affects other people in other places—not just in terms of how we take care of the environment, but also in terms of how we do business. Many corporations these days manufacture things all over the world, and we need to make sure they're acting responsibly no matter where they are. It's easier to just buy cheap stuff without thinking about it, but we should really pay attention to who we do business with. That's one way to be a better global citizen.

LISTENING 1 The Campaign to Humanize the Coffee Trade
Page 105

Deborah Amos: Be honest: When you drop by your local coffeehouse . . .

Barista: Hi, how are you?

Amos: . . . do you ever think about the farmers who grew that coffee, thousands of miles away?

Customer: I need two, let's see, two vente mocha frappuccinos with whipped cream.

Amos: When you pay the bill . . .

Barista: Eight twenty-nine!

Amos: . . . do you ever wonder, How much of this money will the coffee farmers and their families actually get?

Barista: What can I get for you?

Amos: An international network of **activists** wants you to start thinking about it, because they say they've figured out a simple way that you can affect the global economy and **transform** the lives of farmers: Look for coffee with the special label marked "Fair Trade."

With Part 3 in our special report, here's American RadioWorks correspondent Daniel Zwerdling.

Daniel Zwerdling: Let's go right to coffee country. Let's head to the mountains of Guatemala. They grow some of the best coffee you can drink. It's late afternoon, the sun's already sinking behind a peak, and farmers are shuffling back down the slopes after a whole day picking beans. [horse whinnies] Some lead pack horses. They're mangy animals; you can count every single rib. The farmers tie the reins to trees next to the village warehouse, and they unload their burlap sacks.

A lot of farmers can't **afford** a horse. One man's staggering down the dirt path. He's lugging more than 50 pounds of coffee on his own back. My interpreter translates.

[Spanish]

Interpreter: Sometimes we do 100 pounds or more. Uh, you come here sweating, really sweating.

Zwerdling: You don't have to be an economist to see that growing coffee here doesn't buy much of a life. Picture the farmers' homes on the hillsides. They're shacks. The floors are bare dirt. There's no running water or electricity. The outside walls are thin wooden planks—and it gets cold here up in the mountains.

The world's coffee prices go up and down, depending partly on supply and demand and **speculation** by big investors. But these farmers are stuck in poverty. They sell their beans to local businessmen whom they derisively call "coyotes," and the coyotes pay them less than 50 cents per pound. At that price, the farmers can barely make a few hundred dollars a year.

[Spanish]

Interpreter: I mean, to produce coffee, it's, it's expensive. It's a lot of work, and sometimes we can't even cover our costs.

Zwerdling: Can I ask all of you something? Do you know how much somebody like me pays for your coffee when I go to my local coffee shop in Washington, D.C.?

[Spanish]

Interpreter: No, we don't know.

Zwerdling: So I tell them that foreign stores typically sell Guatemalan coffee for at least $9 per pound—compared to the 50 cents they get for growing it—and the farmers just stand there, looking puzzled. Then one of them pulls a calculator out of his pocket that's so dirty and scratched, you can hardly see through the screen, and the interpreter helps him convert dollars into local quetzales.

The farmers gasp when they hear the price.

Interpreter: They're just amazed at how much, how much a consumer pays for it, and they keep just saying, "Six thousand, six hundred-something-something quetzales!"—it's like they're repeating it over and over again. It's an enormous difference from what they actually get. It's a huge amount of money.

Zwerdling: These farmers are the poorest and most powerless part of the global coffee trade. And it's a **massive** industry: The world trades more coffee than any **commodity** except petroleum (and illegal drugs). But the farmers say they don't know what happens to their beans once they sell them to the coyote. They don't realize that he sells them to a **processor**; then the processor might sell them to an exporter. The exporter ships the beans to an importer in another country, like the United States. The importer sells them to a roaster. The roaster sells them to a coffee shop, which sells the coffee to you, and everybody makes a healthy profit along the way—except the small farmers who grow it.

[horse hooves/whinnies] Now activists have **devised** a cure that they call the "Fair Trade system." They say it can help farmers make more money than ever before and flex some power over their lives.

[truck sounds] On a recent morning, we joined one of the system's organizers, a man named Guillermo Denaux. He's heading to a meeting with some Fair Trade farmers to see how things are going. And that means that his four-wheel-drive car is straining to climb an insane path next to a cliff, way up in Guatemala's mountains.

Guillermo Denaux: It's the end of the world. There is no more village further away. It's impossible.

Zwerdling: A group of European activists founded Fair Trade in the late 1980s. The program spread to the United States a few years ago. And here's how it works:

First, they've signed up **roughly** 300 groups of coffee farmers from Indonesia to Peru. They'll only sign up small, family farmers who market their coffee together in community **co-ops**—no corporate plantations allowed.

Second, they've figured out how much money a typical farmer needs to support a family of five: decent food, clothes, kids in school, health care. And then the system basically **guarantees** that the farmers can sell their coffee for enough money per pound to achieve that.

How? Well, the companies that sell Fair Trade coffee to you at your local café buy it almost directly from the farmers who grow it. Denaux says the network cuts out the middlemen who traditionally siphon off farmers' profits.

Denaux: Their whole lives, they depended on the, on the **intermediaries**. So once you can be, become independent of those intermediaries, for them it's very important.

Zwerdling: Still, the Fair Trade network can't raise all the money that farmers need just by cutting out middlemen. Consumers have to help, too. You pay at least 10 percent extra for Fair Trade brands.

LISTENING SKILL   Organizing notes with a T-chart
Page 107

Zwerdling: These farmers are the poorest and most powerless part of the global coffee trade. And it's a massive industry: The world trades more coffee than any commodity except petroleum (and illegal drugs). But the farmers say they don't know what happens to their beans once they sell them to the coyote. They don't realize that he sells them to a processor; then the processor might sell them to an exporter. The exporter ships the beans to an importer in another country, like the United States. The importer sells them to a roaster. The roaster sells them to a coffee shop, which sells the coffee to you, and everybody makes a healthy profit along the way—except the small farmers who grow it.

[horse hooves/whinnies]

Now activists have devised a cure that they call the "Fair Trade system." They say it can help farmers make more money than ever before and flex some power over their lives.

A. Page 108

1.

A: The program on Fair Trade coffee shows how activists can help transform an industry. I wonder if there are any other Fair Trade products that can make a difference and help people out of poverty?

B: Sure. Check out this website for the Global Exchange. They say that if people want to help, they can buy Fair Trade jewelry, clothing, tea, and chocolate.

A: That's great. If consumers buy more Fair Trade products, farmers and local artisans can be guaranteed fair wages and find sustainable ways to produce their products.

2.

A: I watched a TV program last night about the water crisis in Africa.

B: Oh, I wanted to see that. It's unbelievable that water is such a precious commodity in so many parts of the world. And why don't more people care about this problem?

A: The program talked about that. It explained how one group, the World Water Organization, is gathering professionals to explore ways to protect water around the world. Together, they're finding ways to solve the crisis.

3.

A: Hey, have any movie stars started organizations to address global concerns?

B: Yes, actually. The actor Leonardo DiCaprio started the Leonardo DiCaprio Foundation.

A: What does it do?

B: They're working to expand public awareness of environmental issues.

A: Has the organization really had an impact on any problems such as pollution?

B: They've worked a lot on the pollution problem. They're contributing to a grassroots campaign, an effort by ordinary people to end the use of plastic bags around the world. And their website suggests a lot of ways we can reduce our plastic bag consumption.

4.

A: Hi. I'm collecting money for an organization called the Disaster Relief Group. Do you want to make a donation?

B: I don't know. I've never heard of that organization. I don't usually give money to relief organizations because I'm never sure if my money is really going to make a difference.

A: Yeah, that's been a problem for this organization. They're pretty new and they're small, so a lot of people don't know about them or trust them yet. Believe me, it's been a challenge raising money for them. But they're trying to improve their outreach and communications through their website.

B: Oh, really?

A: Yes. If you go to DisasterReliefGroup.org, you'll see newsletters, blogs from volunteers, and pictures of all the work they're doing all over the world. You'll also see exactly how much money they've raised for victims of natural disasters and where that money goes.

LISTENING 2   The UN Global Compact
Pages 111–112

Narrator: In 1989, the *Exxon Valdez* sank off the coast of Alaska, spilling 11 million gallons, or 125 Olympic swimming pools' worth, of crude oil into the water. Polluting 1,300 miles of coastline, the disaster which incurred the world's biggest ever corporate fine of five billion U.S. dollars has become a byword in the media for corporate irresponsibility.

Since then, business has gone global as never before, with foreign direct investment tripling to more than a trillion dollars. But as companies extend their reach particularly into **emerging economies** with weaker regulations, the need for responsible business practice is greater than ever before.

Despite increasing scrutiny from consumers and NGOs, companies are still regularly accused of human rights abuses, poor working practices, and environmental crimes. In 2000, the United Nations offered a solution to this growing problem, the UN Global Compact, which asked businesses to take direct responsibility for their actions. Participating companies follow the Global Compact's ten principles, which broadly safeguard human rights, **labor standards**, the environment, and fight corruption, in what could be described as a United Nations of companies.

Georg Kell: Initially we started off, uh, with a moral core. Increasingly over the last couple of years, the business case for engagement has become clearer.

Narrator: By acting responsibly, companies can gain the **confidence of investors**, who are increasingly backing businesses that successfully manage their environmental and social impact. It's said that reputation and **intangible assets** determine up to 70 percent of the company's market value.

Woman/Spokesperson: Today Andrew Fastow, the chief financial officer of Enron, has pled guilty, has admitted his responsibility—his role in this collapse of Enron.

Narrator: When Enron's irregular **accounting practices** were revealed in 2001, its share price plummeted from more than 90 dollars to less than 50 cents. Enron's tattered reputation eventually bankrupted the company.

On the flip side, a good reputation can increase sales. A 2007 report showed that **household expenditure** on **ethical goods** and services in the U.K. had almost doubled in five years. Business is waking up to the fact that the commercial potential of a responsible business can be exploited.

Kell: Business leaders recognize that being **proactive** on this issue has a premium. It allows them to attract skilled people. They also recognize new opportunities because if you are better connected on the social agenda, you spot market needs much better.

Narrator: And attitudes do seem to be changing. A 2007 McKinsey survey found that 90 percent of CEOs said they were doing more now to incorporate environmental, social, and political issues into **core strategies** than they had done five years ago. The Global Compact started with 38 companies in 13 countries. Today it has 4,000 members in 120 countries.

[Background voice: The UN has put its own reputation . . .]

However, the UN remains undaunted in its ambition to gather more companies under the Global Compact umbrella and to see them working together to tackle issues such as climate change. Progress so far has been significant, but this is only the beginning.

Ban Ki-Moon: Together we can achieve a new face of globalization, one that creates inclusive and **sustainable markets**, builds development, and enhances international cooperation.

Unit 6 Personal Space

The Q Classroom Page 125

Teacher: The Unit 6 question is: "How do you make a space your own?" Think about your room right now and your old room at home. What have you done to personalize those spaces? How about you, Yuna?

Yuna: Pictures! I have pictures of my friends and family all over my room. I even have a big collage of pictures of good times with my high school friends. I like to have the faces of the people I love all around me.

Teacher: I can certainly understand that. How about you, Felix? How do you make a space your own?

Felix: Music is very important to me, so any space of mine reflects that. Right now I have my guitar hanging on the wall over my bed where it's easy to reach; I also have a couple of

posters of bands that I like. I have an amplifier and a decent stereo. At home, I have a big collection of CDs and even some records and a turntable to play them on.

Teacher: I haven't seen one of those for a while! What about you, Sophy?

Sophy: I think that for me the important thing about making a space my own is having things in it from home that I find comforting. For example, I have a wonderful soft quilt from my grandmother and a jewelry box that my dad made for me. I have a teddy bear on my bed that I've had since I was little. I guess I would say that I make a space my own by keeping my old things there.

Teacher: What about you, Marcus? How do you make a space your own?

Marcus: Hmm. I'm not much of a decorator. I guess mostly I make a space my own by having a bunch of books there. I really like to read, and I never seem to have enough space for my books, so they're always lying all over the place. It drives my mom crazy when I'm at home.

Teacher: I bet.

Marcus: But I think it makes me feel at home, having my books all around me.

LISTENING 1 Environmental Psychology
Pages 129–131

Professor: Welcome to Lesson 15, Module 1, of Environmental Psychology.

This week I'll be introducing you to the field of environmental psychology, which is an area that studies the interrelationship between human behavior and environments. *Environment* refers to the natural environment such as parks, natural resources, and outdoor settings and built environments, or those structures and spaces which are constructed rather than those that occur naturally. Today, we'll be concentrating on characteristics of behavior and our connection to the space around us, focusing on **gender**, eye contact, and our need for privacy.

We know that our need for space and our reactions to perceived invasion of our space are different for men and women. Males often object to face-to-face invasion. Sitting directly across from a male is often more offensive to them than sitting next to him. However, females often object to **adjacent** invasion. This has to do with competition versus affiliation goals. Males are expected to compete and women to affiliate.

It's not necessary to **affiliate with** someone who is sitting across from you, but if someone sits next to you, it's often felt that you should **engage in** some affiliative behavior, if you're a female. If you're a male, on the other hand, an adjacent invasion is not as important as a face-to-face, or across from you, invasion.

When males and females try to approach one another, this can often lead to miscommunication. Females will often sit next to men in an adjacent seat, trying to make contact, but males do not even see this as approaching them because they're used to face-to-face invasion for people who matter. They typically ignore those who sit adjacent. Females have exactly the opposite view.

What we know is that, because these gender differences exist, you can also look at where people put their **belongings**. Belongings are often placed to avoid invasion. Females will often place their books or belongings to the side of them in a vacant seat in order to force people to have to make another kind of invasion. Males, on the other hand, will often put things across from them to indicate that they are taking up the space in front of them to prevent face-to-face invasion.

In addition, we mark our territory with our belongings, for example, putting your jacket on the chair next to you, or putting your book on the table in the space that you feel belongs to you. In fact, 83 percent of students sit in the same seat all semester during a large lecture course. This is quite **remarkable**. There's nothing really about that seat specifically that makes it theirs, but we have this very territorial behavior **ingrained in** us.

Equally important, we know that when males mark their territory, these markers are taken very seriously. If you look at desks, office space, and seating, you'll find that you behave in a very different way depending on to whom the office belongs. If you enter an office and you believe that a male is in that office, you will respect the desk and office space and seating arrangement. However, females' offices tend to be **invaded** and manipulated; that is, people will move things on the desk, play with objects on the desk, take up their office space, choose a different seat, move the chairs, and so on. In short, the gender of the owner affects our reaction to his or her territory.

Another study that shows this reaction to how seriously we respect people's territories is called the jacket study. In this study, researchers put a clearly feminine or clearly masculine jacket on a chair when no one else was around. They then measured who would sit where and why. If it was a male jacket, people kept their distance; they sat several chairs away. However, if it was a female jacket, people often would move the jacket or turn it in to lost and found. They didn't see it as a marker.

We know that people engage in territorial behavior, and males have larger territories than females. This begins when they are children. If you ask young children, who perhaps have just received a bike and have begun to explore the neighborhood using the sidewalks, you will find that the male children are often able to map out a much larger area of the place in which they play than females. Females typically draw perhaps their block or the houses across the street, but not much beyond that, whereas males will often draw three or four blocks, sometimes even a six-block **radius** around their own home.

You can also look at yourself in terms of whether or not you are territorial. Often when you go to a restaurant and the server puts your plate in front of you, you can't help but touch it. This is why they always warn you the plate is hot, because they know your instinct is to touch the plate. The next time you eat out, try very hard not to touch the plate. It's very difficult to **refrain from** doing so, and now that I've made you aware, maybe you'll see just how territorial you really are.

Eye contact is also an indicator of how we feel about personal space. One study of eye contact was conducted in post offices in three environments. Researchers looked in Parksford (a rural community), Bryn Mawr (a **suburban** town), and Philadelphia (a big city) and found that males and females within each community typically engage in eye contact at the same level. However, both genders were less likely to make eye contact in the city, **moderately** likely to do so in Bryn Mawr, and most likely to do so in Parksford. That is, in Parksford at the post office, you're expected to look at everyone, say hello even. However, in Philadelphia, you should not make very much eye contact, and only about 10 percent of people did.

This is a way of maintaining space. In a rural area such as Parksford, you often feel that you have enough space and you aren't being threatened, so there's no need to be territorial. There is also no reason to feel like you might be invading someone else's territory. However, in Philadelphia, you can maintain a sense of privacy by not making eye contact with others. It's even considered polite, and when people do make eye contact, it's often thought to be strange, weird, or cause for concern.

Another form of visual intrusion is the ability to see or be seen. This is usually seen as stressful. Restaurants or offices have been made to give a sense of privacy. However, even though they add barriers or other clear panels, this does not decrease visual intrusion or give anyone a sense of privacy. What we know about college students is that those who drop out are more likely to be students who had to live in dorms with roommates and use communal bathrooms and showers. So, if you need an argument for getting your own apartment, this could be it.

LISTENING SKILL Recognizing organizational cues
A. Page 133

In addition, we mark our territory with our belongings, for example, putting your jacket on the chair next to you, or putting your book on the table in the space that you feel belongs to you. In fact, 83 percent of students sit in the same seat all semester during a large lecture course. This is quite remarkable. There's nothing really about that seat specifically that makes it theirs, but we have this very territorial behavior ingrained in us.

Equally important, we know that when males mark their territory, these markers are taken very seriously. If you look at desks, office space, and seating, you'll find that you behave in a very different way depending on to whom the office belongs. If you enter an office and you believe that a male is in that office, you will respect the desk and office space and seating arrangement. However, females' offices tend to be invaded and manipulated; that is, people will move things on the desk, play with objects on the desk, take up their office space, choose a different seat, move the chairs, and so on. In short, the gender of the owner affects our reaction to his or her territory.

B. Page 133

1. Students who decorate their dorm rooms tend to be happier at school. More importantly . . .

2. We found teenagers who put a lot of surprising information on Facebook. Actually . . .

3. There's a stereotype that men like to wash their cars every weekend. In addition . . .

4. What kind of car we buy might reveal only a part of our personality. That is . . .

5. So it is clear that gender plays a role in territorial behavior. Moving on . . .

6. Eye contact, visual intrusion, and territorial behavior are all evidence of ways humans interact with their surroundings. In conclusion, . . .

LISTENING 2 What Your Stuff Says About You
Pages 135–136

Neal Conan, Host: This is *Talk of the Nation*. I'm Neal Conan in Washington. The framed items on the wall of my office include my FCC third-class radio telephone operator's license from 1973 and the *New York Times* crossword puzzle from the day my name was used as a clue. There's a baseball on my desk, not signed or anything, just a baseball. Some toys sit on top of the speaker: a beach chair with a life preserver, a double-decker London bus, and a corkboard has family pictures, John F. Kennedy behind the wheel of a PT-109, and a postcard of Giants Stadium in New Jersey. Sam Gosling, are those few things enough to tell you anything about what kind of person I am?

Sam Gosling: Yeah, they certainly could tell us a lot. There's a lot of information, a lot of it not so obvious, but there's a lot of information in places like people's personal spaces, their offices or their living spaces.

Conan: And not just what they are, but the way they're arranged. For example, if the family pictures look out to the guest in the office or, um, or inward to, uh, to the person who occupies it.

Gosling: Yeah. It's really **crucial** to combine not only what they are, but how they've been placed. Because how they've been placed gives us good information on the psychological function that they serve. So if we have photos of, say, our family and our beautiful spouse facing us, that shows us, it's for our own benefit. Um, it's what you might call a social snack, something we can snack on to make ourselves feel better over the day. If it's turned the other way, then it's more for the benefit of others, which doesn't mean it's disingenuous. It may not be trying to pull the wool over people's eyes, but it, uh, informs the function that the photo serves.

Conan: Sam Gosling studies personality by looking at stuff. Stuff in offices, bedrooms, cars, and bathrooms. What's there

and how it's arranged can provide **clues** about who we are and what's important to us. So we want you to call or email us and describe the room or the car you're in right now. What's on the wall or the desk, the videos and the CDs, the bumper stickers, your radio presets. Our phone number is 800-989-8255. Email us, talk@npr.org. You can also join the conversation on our blog at npr.org/blogofthenation. Later on in the show, the romance and monotony involved in real archeology. But first, Sam Gosling. He's an associate professor of psychology at the University of Texas in Austin. His new book is called *Snoop: What Your Stuff Says About You*, and he joins us today from the studios of member station KUT in Austin. Thanks very much for coming in.

Gosling: Pleasure.

Conan: And your book is called *Snoop*, because that's what you **propose** to teach us what to do.

Gosling: Yeah. Snooping around people's, uh, places, and I should say that I construe, uh, "places" very broadly. Not only our physical environments but our oral environments, too, such as our music collections, our virtual environments like our, our personal home pages or our Facebook **profile**. So if people, if people who want to call in want to talk more broadly about spaces, that would be fun, too.

Conan: And of course, to figure out what personality type—what stuff tells you about you, you have to know what personality types are to begin with. **Introvert**, **extrovert**, are two that I guess everybody knows about.

Gosling: That's right. And there are a number of ways of thinking about personality. And, uh, you can think about personality **traits**, which is what most research has done on it, and within that **domain** there's, uh, the, uh, system known as the "Big Five," or the "five-factor **framework**," which talks about these different traits. As you say, introversion-extroversion is the main one, but there are other important ones, too.

Conan: And how did you get interested in this? Are you a natural-born snoop?

Gosling: Well, I think we're all natural-born snoops. And, I mean, some of us are more curious than others. Some of us will open the medicine cabinet when we go to a party, and some of us won't. But I think we all do because it's crucial. If you think, who, who are the people who are—what is the element of the environment that's most important to us in terms of, of how well we get on in terms of professional lives and personal lives? It's other people. So I think we're naturally attuned to picking up on whatever information is out there, and there is a lot of information out there in people's spaces. So I think we all do it.

Conan: And so we size people up as soon as we see them, as soon as we shake their hand, for example.

Gosling: Yeah, as soon as we shake their hand. And there's a—you know, the handshaking has been a part of etiquette books for years and years and years, but it was only recently that it was really subjected to a really rigorous study. And there was a study done by Bill Chaplin in 2000 which looked at exactly that. It looked at what can you learn about someone from a handshake.

Conan: And sometimes, it's, it's interesting, uh, you can learn something about it but you can also come to a conclusion that's, easily wrong.

Gosling: Right. That's the point, yes. For example, taking the example of handshaking, if somebody, uh, grips your hand firmly and looks you in the eye, uh, and smiles as they're doing it, then we form an overall positive impression of them. We, we form all kinds of positive things. Yet it turns out that the handshaking, uh, firmness is only a clue to some traits. So we are going beyond the evidence. And so, it's really important to know which are valid clues and which ones are misleading.

Conan: And in the clip of tape that we heard at the beginning of the program and, uh, throughout your book, you use the example of Agatha Christie's great detective, Hercule Poirot.

Gosling: That's right, because it's really important—you know, if I had one wish, one wish in the world, it would be that one clue told you something about a person. If you had a stuffed teddy on your bed, it meant something, you know. But the world is more complicated than that. So unfortunately, it doesn't work like that because there are many reasons why we might have, say, a stuffed animal on our bed or something like that. And so really, you can't use a codebook approach where *x* means *y*. What you have to do is you have to build up a picture piece by piece, and sometimes you only have a very little piece and you have to hold your view very **tentatively**. But that will, that will guide your search for more information.

Conan: So that postcard of Giants Stadium, well, it could tell you that I'm a Giants fan, which is true, but it could also tell you I grew up in New Jersey.

Gosling: It could, or it could tell you—it might have sentimental meaning. Who is it from? Is it from somebody important? And so in order to resolve that, what we would do is we would look for other clues. So the baseball there would begin to help us resolve the meaning of the, of the, um, uh, the postcard itself. We might also see, well, these other items, the crossword puzzle, these other things which, which might **modify** the meaning that, which helps us resolve— OK, so maybe recognition is important. We learn that you're somewhat sentimental. And that helps us **clarify** the meaning of each clue.

UNIT ASSIGNMENT Consider the Ideas
Page 145

Host: Our special guest today is Dr. Hill, a psychologist. She's going to help people resolve conflicts that arise around issues of personal space. First, she'll be talking with Dan and Jason, two roommates from the University of Texas who share an on-campus apartment. Welcome, Dr. Hill, and welcome, Dan and Jason.

Dr. Hill: Thank you for having me.

Dan: Yeah, thanks.

Jason: Hi. Thanks.

Dr. Hill: So, Dan and Jason, you two have been friends a long time?

Dan: Yeah, we've been friends since middle school. Since we both got accepted at UT, we decided to room together.

Jason: That was our first mistake.

Dr. Hill: That's a pretty strong reaction. Why don't you tell us about the problem?

Jason: Well, even though we were friends, we'd never lived together, so I didn't realize that Dan would consider the whole apartment his domain. I mean, I knew he was kind of an extrovert, but I didn't think he'd have people over all the time, parties every night. There's always somebody coming over to the apartment. I don't have time to study or, or just to think, you know?

Dr. Hill: So are you saying that if you had known that, you wouldn't have roomed with him?

Jason: Yeah, that sounds about right.

Dr. Hill: Dan, do you have anything to add?

Dan: Right, well, I didn't come to college just to study. I came to meet people. Besides, I'm not just some party animal. Sometimes I have study groups over, and we just want to stay up all night talking about the stuff we learn in class.

Jason: If you want Dr. Hill to help us resolve the problem, maybe you should mention that while you are "studying," you're also listening to music and making a lot of noise.

Dan: OK, if you weren't hiding in your room studying all the time, you could come out and join the conversation.

Dr. Hill: Yikes. OK. Well, obviously it's a good thing the two of you decided to seek help since this kind of situation can not only cause living problems but might also ruin your long friendship if they are not solved. Now let's turn to the solutions. Have you thought about . . .

Unit 7 Alternative Thinking

The Q Classroom Page 149

Teacher: In Unit 7, we're going to be talking about alternative thinking. The Unit 7 Question is: "Where do new ideas come from?" So think about yourselves for a moment. If you're working on a problem, and you're stuck, how do you come up with a new idea?

Marcus: For me the key is taking my mind off the problem for a while. Let's say I'm stuck for an idea on an essay or something—that means I need to get out and do something physical. I go out and take a walk, and when I come back, I seem to have a whole new set of ideas.

Teacher: What do you think, Yuna? Where do your new ideas come from?

Yuna: I have the same experience as Marcus. Taking a break is important. I also think it's good to talk to people.

Felix: Yes, I second that. Sometimes when two people who can't solve a problem on their own start talking, the answer just seems to come up between them. That has happened to me many times. My friend says something that gives me part of an idea, and then my part of an idea gives him even more of an idea, and so on. It's really great to talk to people when you need ideas.

Teacher: Sophy, how would you answer the question? Where do new ideas come from?

Sophy: Sometimes people have new ideas because they look at the problem in a completely different way. I guess that's why talking to friends and taking breaks helps you solve problems—because they cause you to look at them in new ways. But I think some people just have the ability to do that naturally. People like Albert Einstein and Thomas Edison saw the same world everyone else did, but somehow they were able to look at it in a new way; this helped them get really creative ideas.

Teacher: That's true. It would be interesting to talk to one of them about how they got their ideas, wouldn't it?

LISTENING 1 Alternative Ideas in Medicine (two reports)
Pages 153–154

Report 1: "Doc-in-a-Box?"

Narrator: In this country, when we get sick we usually get to see a doctor or a nurse. But in most developing countries, there's a huge **shortage of** both. Pulitzer Prize–winning science writer Laurie Garrett was thinking about this problem and flipping through an architectural magazine when she came up with a novel idea.

Laurie Garrett: There was a description of a place called "**Container** City" in London in which shipping containers, painted in primary colors, had been stacked in unusual ways to create apartment buildings. And I, I simply thought of it at that moment and a little sort of "bingo" light bulb went off in my head. This might be the way to solve a lot of our global health problems—by **converting** these abandoned shipping containers into frontline medical clinics.

Narrator: A so-called Doc-in-a-Box could be transported to remote villages, far from health-care centers.

Garrett: Instead of having to trek enormous distances spanning a day or two just in travel to get to a health clinic, you would be able to squeeze this into your daily routine to come in and be tested for a wide array of infectious diseases and have your kids immunized as a matter of routine.

Narrator: Garrett says there are empty shipping containers in almost every port in the world; each one could be converted into a "Doc-in-a-Box."

Garrett: Ministries of Health, or nongovernmental organizations, would be operating these networks of Doc-in-a-Boxes. And that they would have selected paramedics from the very villages that they serve. Uh, the most obvious reservoir is midwives, who already, uh, operate as paramedics all over the world.

Narrator: The idea for the Doc-in-a-Box is still in its early stages. A **prototype** clinic was developed in Haiti earlier this year. While it cost about $5,000 to put together, Garrett says that cost could be even less.

Garrett: We see no reason why, if retrofitting is done on a mass scale and if the retrofitting is done in a developing country port, such as in Durban, South Africa, these containers couldn't come in for well under $1,500 apiece—including the delivery cost.

Narrator: Laurie Garrett, who now works with the Council on Foreign Relations, hopes governments and aid organizations will take her idea and run with it. She believes the container clinics, ultimately, could make portable medicine a reality for people in countries that need it most.

Report 2: "Bee Sting Therapy"

Host: Of the many alternative medical therapies gaining popularity, one is getting a lot of buzz. Some folks claim honeybees and all their products are useful for everything from cancer prevention to pain treatment. It's an ancient alternative therapy that's coming back into use. Practitioners and enthusiasts for all things apiary met in the Triangle recently. Rose Hoban reports.

Rose Hoban: Frederique Keller always makes sure she's got bees with her. But it can be tricky to travel with them, especially on a plane. So when she left her home on Long Island recently to come to North Carolina, she had several hundred honeybees mailed to her here. They arrived in little wooden boxes with perforated plastic tops, each about the size of a Snickers bar. Inside each box wiggled 40 honeybees that amazingly didn't try to get away when the box was opened. Keller is a beekeeper and an acupuncturist. She combines her two trades.

Frederique Keller: You sting a person with a live honeybee in specific places on the body where people have pain or discomfort.

Hoban: Keller calls her practice apipuncture: acupuncture using bee stings instead of needles. *Apis* is the Latin word for bee, so *apitherapy* becomes the word to describe medical therapies using products from the beehive.

Keller: Honey, pollen, propolis, royal jelly, beeswax, and bee venom, of course.

Hoban: Keller was here for the annual meeting of the American Apitherapy Society in Durham a couple of weeks ago. She demonstrated bee venom therapy during a session for about a dozen people who practically buzzed with excitement as they waited to get stung.

Keller: There you go. There's a beautiful sting there.

Hoban: Keller is also the vice president of the AAS. The organization is dedicated to research and application of bee-based therapies for a variety of ailments, from cancer to digestive problems to autoimmune diseases such as multiple sclerosis. There isn't a lot of research on some of these areas, and mainstream doctors are **reluctant** to talk about apitherapy. But Andrew Cokin is a pain management doctor who practices outside of Los Angeles and frequently uses bee venom to treat pain. He says it works most of the time, although he's unsure of how it works. He says there are several theories.

Andrew Cokin: One of the mechanisms is that bee venom causes the release of cortisol, which is the body's own natural anti-inflammatory, from the adrenal gland. And that's been shown in some animal experiments but hasn't really been **verified** in humans yet.

Hoban: Cokin says another theory holds that some **compounds** in bee venom might affect how the body transmits pain signals to the brain, but it's hard to know for sure. Cokin's been trying for years to do formal research in the U.S., but recently had a study **protocol denied** by the FDA. Researchers studying the use of bee venom are mostly in Asia and in some Eastern European countries where use of bee products has a strong tradition.

Cokin: Bee venom has been used as a treatment since the time of the Greeks and for at least 2,000, 3,000 years in Chinese medicine.

Hoban: Cokin says there's lots of **anecdotal evidence**.

Cokin: People find out about this by themselves. I've had patients in the last 20 years who told me that relatives of theirs, older relatives working in the garden, had accidently got stung on their hands by a bee, and their arthritis got better. And so they would go out **periodically** and get stung by a bee to keep their arthritis under control.

Hoban: One of the biggest boosters of apitherapy in North Carolina is Fountain Odom, who invited the Apitherapy Society to come here. He's a lawyer, a former state legislator, and a beekeeper. He says the state's 10,000 beekeepers should embrace apitherapy.

Fountain Odom: We believe that there are tremendous opportunities for the beekeepers of this state to develop some of the ancient modalities for medical treatment of pain and other uses. These are some alternatives that are very, very inexpensive.

Hoban: Odom started getting stung to treat the arthritis he has in his foot and knee. He says it took his family and friends a little bit of time to get used to the idea.

Odom: They might look at you askance or say, "Uh, you know, you're kind of flaky, aren't you? I mean, why would you want to be stung by a bee?"

Hoban: But now Odom's a true believer. He says getting stung is the only thing that helps him with his pain. He's also **convinced** his wife, and that's a big deal, since she's the state secretary for Health and Human Services. Carmen Hooker Odom says she's seen apitherapy work out well for her husband, but the state's probably not going to start reimbursing for apitherapy anytime soon. Rose Hoban, North Carolina Public Radio, WUNC.

LISTENING SKILL Distinguishing between facts and opinions

A. Page 156

1. I think using dogs to detect cancer is unreliable.
2. You can find many hypnotists advertising online.
3. The first Doc-in-a-Box was developed in Haiti and cost $5,000.
4. Even though the first container cost a lot, Garrett believes future costs could be less.
5. The state's 10,000 beekeepers should embrace apitherapy.
6. Cokin reports that bee venom works most of the time for his patients.
7. Apipuncture is based on acupuncture, a traditional Chinese remedy.
8. These alternative ideas are so inexpensive they probably don't work.
9. The best solutions are based on past protocols.
10. Anecdotal evidence is sometimes used in scientific research.

B. Page 156

Speaker: Have you noticed that your legs get tired in the middle of the day? Do you wish you could keep going when your body wants you to sit down? Do you have trouble keeping up with other people—or with life in general? Our amazing product, Go-Cream, is the answer you've been looking for. It offers the absolute best solution for tired legs and low energy. After just one application of this energizing leg cream, you should be convinced. Made from the oils of the Brazil nut and sand from the beaches of Hawaii, Go-Cream soothes and energizes at the same time. Thousands of people suffer from tired legs, but now there is relief. Listen to what some of our satisfied customers have to say.

Customer 1: I'm a busy of mother of four, and I've been using this product for two years. I've tried vitamins and other alternative therapies, but nothing worked—until Go-Cream. It's definitely the most effective product out there and a deal at only $9.99 a jar.

Customer 2: I believe Go-Cream is for people of all ages. My friends and I are students, and we're always on the go. We've all tried Go-Cream and noticed a big difference in our energy. And it probably even helps make your skin smoother and healthier, too.

Speaker: Don't get left behind. Order your Go-Cream today!

LISTENING 2 Boulder Bike-to-School Program Goes International

Pages 159–160

Ryan Warner: You're tuned to *Colorado Matters*, from KCFR news. I'm Ryan Warner. These days, kids are far more likely to get to school in their parents' car than by biking or walking. Well, a program in Boulder is designed to change that, and it's catching on in schools across the country and in Canada. But it didn't start out with that lofty goal. No, it started when two parents were trying to get their kids to bike to school. The kids weren't wild about the idea, and so their parents created punch cards, like the kind you get at a coffee shop or sub place. And when the cards were all punched, meaning the kids had biked **consistently**, there was a reward. Well, the frequent biker, or "Freiker" concept, caught on. Tim Carlin is one of the two dads who started this. He's now Freiker's executive director. And he told me how this grew from a handful of kids at Crestview Elementary School in Boulder into an international program.

Tim Carlin: The way it got started was, he and I were doing punch cards for our kids. And then, we saw some other kids who were riding, and we told them "oh, well we could do a punch card for you." And then some other kids started riding, and then we had punch cards for them. And pretty soon we had 25, 30 kids every morning arriving at the bike racks taking part in this totally **impromptu** punch card system.

Warner: And what did punched cards get you? What was the reward?

Carlin: OK, we had a variety of **incentives**, sort of ranging from things as simple as a pencil to water bottles and to other trinkets that he would bring to school in a, uh, duffel bag. And then the kids would have the opportunity, ah, when they had ten punches, to reach into that bag and grab whatever interested them.

Warner: Excitement of a grab bag!

Carlin: Exactly.

Warner: And, and um, the program has gotten more sophisticated, suffice it to say.

Carlin: Yes. As we moved past 25, 30 kids, it became really complicated—

Warner: Yeah.

Carlin: —to keep track of punching cards, and who had a punch card. And of course, we're talking about young kids, so they have a, had a tendency to lose their punch cards. So, we wrapped up that school year, that was the spring of 2004, ah, with a punch card system, and for the fall of 2005 we came out with a **bar code** system. And, so what we did is we bar-coded every kid's bike. And when the kids rode, ah, the bikes would be parked at the bike rack, and one of, ah, us would walk through all the bikes and scan them and then upload that data to the Internet.

Warner: Now, Tim, that's a leap. I mean, that's a technological advancement, suffice it to say.

Carlin: OK, so, me and the other guy are both from the high-tech industry.

Warner: OK.

Carlin: And so it sort of came natural to us to think of a technology solution.

Warner: So, as the technology got more sophisticated, did the rewards?

Carlin: Ah, the rewards did get more sophisticated. So, once we felt that we had a really good day-to-day tracking system, we, um, well, Rob, the guy who, ah, really started the program, decided that, um, "Why don't we shoot for the moon and offer a crazy incentive?" And, ah, his crazy incentive was an iPod. And so the deal was if you rode over 90 percent of the days to school, you could win an iPod.

Warner: And, so it wasn't just one iPod—

Carlin: Oh, no—

Warner: Anyone who did this—

Carlin: Exactly.

Warner: OK.

Carlin: Yeah, and so, ah, you know, that was upwards of um, ah, 30 kids a year riding over 160 days a year to school. So it was pretty, pretty **substantial** commitment on the kids' part and a pretty **outrageous** incentive.

Warner: So at Crestview, where this program began, how many kids participate, you know, on a regular basis?

Carlin: Yeah, we're seeing, um, roughly about 100 to 120 kids participating every day in the program. And that's out of a community of about 250 kids who could get themselves to school every day. So that's pretty neat; about half the kids at the school who can are getting themselves to school every day.

Warner: And, uh, Freiker has grown well beyond Crestview.

Carlin: That's right. Ah, we've grown into quite a few states now. We have, ah, units installed at McFarland, Wisconsin; Platteville, Wisconsin; Eugene, Oregon; Los Altos, California. And a couple systems actually up in Canada now, which we're very excited about. And I might also add that we also include walkers now, um, as part of the program since the, since the original days.

Warner: That is, a way of getting to school that uses your own energy.

Carlin: Yeah, we call it—

Warner: Is that, is that the idea?

Carlin: Yeah, the **buzzword** is "active transportation."

Warner: OK.

Carlin: And the idea is that it's an inclusive term that includes skateboarding, um, bikes, walking, anything a kid uses to **propel** themselves to school on their own power.

Warner: You're listening to *Colorado Matters*. I'm Ryan Warner and Tim Carlin is our guest. He's executive director of Freiker. It's a frequent biker program. Born in Boulder and spreading not only across the country, but beyond, beyond the borders. Ah, I imagine you'll have to change the name if you keep encouraging walking and, and—

Carlin: That's right, so we're in the process of, uh, coming up with a new name because obviously, uh, we've grown beyond our original, uh, beginning name.

Warner: I gather that there has to be some **infrastructure** in place at a school to make this possible.

Carlin: Yeah. As I described earlier, we started out with punch cards; then we went to bar codes. We now have a very high-tech solution. Um, a device that is out in the, um, bike rack area, um, that we call the "freikometer."

Warner: OK.

Carlin: And this is a solar-powered, Internet-enabled RFID reader. And RFID stands for radio frequency ID. And, um, they're very common these days in products you buy at stores like Walmart. They're actually embedded in the product; CDs have 'em, books have 'em. Basically everything you buy, ah, not only has a bar code on the back, but also has an RFID, ah, chip in it, which identifies the product, ah, through radio instead of through optical scanning.

Warner: And, and what that means is that the kid really doesn't have to do much but park his or her bike.

Carlin: That's exactly right. So, using the bar code system, we had to have a volunteer there every day of the week, scanning each individual bike. Now the kid simply rides by the freikometer, and it automatically records and uploads their data. That relieves the program from having to have a volunteer out there every day. And now that same parent volunteer who would have been out there doing punch cards or scanning bikes, that person can be inside helping kids learn how to read, or focusing their, uh, efforts on some other activity.

Warner: So who's paying for this? I mean is it, is it the school, or, you know, how does it work?

Carlin: Well, there are, there are a variety of ways that this program's being funded. Um, again, there's a federal program called Safe Routes to School. Local communities can, um, **submit grant** requests to get a Freiker system as part of safe routes to school. But in some places a local bike store has funded it. In Los Altos, California, they have a community group called "Green Town Los Altos." And Freiker is one of the four programs that that community group is focusing on. And so they're using their fund-raising dollars to buy more systems and **implement** it at all the elementary and middle schools in town.

Warner: Well, Tim, thank you so much for sharing this story with us.

Carlin: Oh, you're welcome. Thank you for having me.

Warner: Tim Carlin is executive director of Boulder-based Freiker, or Frequent Biker Program.

VOCABULARY SKILL Idioms and informal expressions
B. Page 162

1. **Rose Hoban:** But now Odom's a true believer. He says getting stung is the only thing that helps him with his pain. He's also convinced his wife, and that's a big deal, since she's the state secretary for Health and Human Services.

2. **Rose Hoban:** Keller was here for the annual meeting of the American Apitherapy Society in Durham a couple of weeks ago. She demonstrated bee venom therapy during a session for about a dozen people who practically buzzed with excitement as they waited to get stung.

3. **Fountain Odom:** They might look at you askance or say, "Uh, you know, you're kind of flaky, aren't you? I mean, why would you want to be stung by a bee?"

4. **Laurie Garrett:** There was a description of a place called "Container City" in London in which shipping containers, painted in primary colors, had been stacked in unusual ways to create apartment buildings. And I, I simply thought of it at that moment and a little sort of "bingo" light bulb went off in my head.

5. **Narrator:** Laurie Garrett, who now works with the Council on Foreign Relations, hopes governments and aid organizations will take her idea and run with it. She believes the container clinics, ultimately, could make portable medicine a reality for people in countries that need it most.

6. **Tim Carlin:** So, once we felt that we had a really good day-to-day tracking system, we, um, well Rob, the guy who, ah, really started the program, decided that, um "Why don't we shoot for the moon and offer a crazy incentive?" And, ah, his crazy incentive was an iPod.

PRONUNCIATION Conditional modals: affirmative and negative
A. Page 166

1. He couldn't have known who she was.
2. You should have tried to call me!
3. The program would have been a success.
4. My boss wouldn't have supported such an innovative idea.
5. The medical clinic shouldn't have closed.
6. You shouldn't have given up on that problem so soon.
7. I still think he could have tried to work with me.
8. Even a grant wouldn't have made any difference.

UNIT ASSIGNMENT Consider the Ideas
A. Page 168

Speaker: Ladies and gentlemen, a group of talented young engineers at the MIT Media Lab have designed an innovative product, the latest advance in personal security: the Vibrating Wallet. We all know that credit card loss, which can often lead to identity theft, is on the rise. Statistics reveal that 10 percent of credit card users have left their cards behind in a store or dropped them while traveling, at least once. The Vibrating

Wallet integrates the vibration of a cell phone with a standard wallet. The signal is activated whenever a credit card leaves the wallet and is only deactivated upon replacement. The reminder signal is transmitted until a credit card is replaced in the holder. We believe this product is light-years ahead of other personal security devices that are currently on the market, and we believe it will quickly catch on. We need some help financing this product in order to get it off the ground, and we urge you to consider investing in the future of personal security.

Speaker: OK, guys, here's the deal. We've all had the experience of losing a credit card. You know, we're getting ready to pay for our date, and we grab our wallet, and then— uh-oh, we find out the card's gone! You freak out, right? OK, so maybe it like turns up later at some store, or on the floor of your car, or whatever. Or maybe it doesn't. Maybe someone's already out buying stuff with it, charging it up. Now we're talking major panic mode, right? So check this out. The Vibrating Wallet. It's an awesome product, designed by a bunch of engineering students at the MIT Media Lab. Whenever you take your credit card out of your wallet, the microchip alarm inside turns on and goes like this. And hey, that buzzing sound won't stop 'til you put it back! It's the ultimate in credit card safety and protection against identity theft. Go online and order yours now.

Unit 8 Change

The Q Classroom   Page 173

Teacher: Class, the Unit 8 question is: "How do people react to change?" What about you, Felix? How do you react to change?

Felix: Badly. [laughs] I'm kidding. But it does take me a while to adjust when I move or go to a new school or get a new job. I like the feeling when I know where everything is and when I know the people around me, so I'm happiest when I get settled into a place. I tend to be kind of uncomfortable at first after a big change.

Marcus: Not me. To me, change is exciting. I love it when I'm starting something new and have new people to meet and new places to explore. I kind of get bored if everything stays the same.

Teacher: What about people in general? How do most people react to change? Are they like Felix or like Marcus? What do you think, Sophy?

Sophy: My guess is that more people are like Felix—they find it hard to change. And when they get older, it gets even more difficult. My parents wouldn't want to move even if they had a good opportunity in a different area. They're too comfortable where they are.

Teacher: What do you think, Yuna? How do people react to change?

Yuna: I agree with Sophy. I think most people don't like change. At my job, they put in a new computer program. It was really good, but a lot of people hated it for a long time because it was different.

Felix: Well, I can accept change perfectly well if it's for a good reason. I don't think I would be like Yuna's co-workers, complaining about something good just because it's new. However, I do think change for its own sake can be overrated these days. Look at Sophy's parents—why should they ever want to move? They probably have neighbors they like and a shopping market they like and a home they're comfortable in. What someone on the outside might see as a good opportunity might not really be a good deal for them.

Teacher: Well put, Felix! We'll talk about this issue more as we go through Unit 8.

LISTENING 1   The Reindeer People
Page 177

Narrator: We were all once **nomads**; but in the central Asian nation of Mongolia, many of the people still are. Herders are constantly on the move, finding fresh grasses for their animals. Mongolia's geography, a boundless wilderness with soil that can't **sustain** agriculture, forces people to **embrace** the nomadic life. Sanjeem is a nomadic reindeer herder. He and his people are caught between two worlds. Theirs, and one in which Mongolia's urban **elite** calls on nomads to **settle**. Sanjeem sits, mounted on one reindeer, and drives about 50 others with coats of white and mottled charcoal up a rock-strewn grassy slope.

Sanjeem (via interpreter): Our ancestors have herded reindeer here in mountains of Mongolia for generations. We keep our animals here, and we actually follow our reindeer where they want to go because the environment and the climate are perfectly suited to our reindeer. This is the basis of our culture.

Narrator: Sanjeem's an **elder** within a group of 207 people, 44 families. Every few weeks he moves camp in the Tiga, a vast expanse of mountains, forest, and ice straddling Mongolia's border with Siberia. Today, though, Sanjeem is worried. When Mongolia's communist government was toppled by a democratic revolution in the 1990s, his state salary was withdrawn.

Sanjeem (via interpreter): Under communism, there was a policy of taking care of everyone. There was less poverty there. Personally, I prefer democracy, but we are a young democracy, and some of us are not managing to **make a living**.

Narrator: Herders and their families are trying to **cope**. With the end of state **subsidies**, free veterinary care ended. A reindeer is milked on a flat patch of frozen ground beside a teepee. Reindeer milk, cheese, and yogurt are staples of the Tiga diet. With the end of regular veterinary care, the herd dwindled.

Beside his teepee made of canvas slung over a wood-pole frame, Sanjeem's granddaughter sings of the sweet kiss of a short Mongolian summer. In another teepee, a couple is thinking about giving up the nomadic life. Smoke from a wood stove escapes through the open top of the tent. The sweet aroma of juniper incense fuses with the smell of musky canvas. Yudoon, a wind-burned reindeer herder in his mid-30s, watches the fire. He and his wife, Uyumbottom, have a decision to make.

Yudoon (via interpreter): Honestly, I'm not sure our reindeer and our reindeer culture will continue to exist. I really don't know what will happen to us. The number of families trying to leave the Tiga is increasing. While the size of our reindeer herd is decreasing, due to disease and attacks by wolves. So I'm not sure we can expand our herd to the point it would support the families.

Narrator: But Yudoon's wife, Uyumbottom, isn't willing to give up. She's just returned from the capital, Ulaanbaatar. She went to parliament and met government bureaucrats. She pleaded for financial and veterinary support.

The economic advisor to Mongolia's president did not have encouraging words.

Uyumbottom received nothing of substance. Only a pledge that the government will hold a seminar on herders' issues at some time in the future. Still, she called the trip a success.

Uyumbottom (via interpreter): We were at least listened to. We were able to speak for ourselves in our own voice. I'm encouraged by this.

Narrator: There are Mongolians working to help the herders. Marnagansarma is a government veterinarian who's made the trek—three days by jeep then eight hours by horse—from the capital to visit Sanjeem and his herd. She's here on vacation, working with two American NGOs.

Biologist Morgan Kay of Colorado heads the NGO Itgel, the Mongolian word for hope.

Morgan Kay: Modernity has many faces, and if we learn nothing from encountering these people, at least let us remember that the way we choose to live in the West is only one way, and it's still possible for people even in the 21st century to be living a subsistence, balanced lifestyle that leaves them at the mercy of natural forces that we've become totally separate from.

Narrator: Herder Sanjeem still has hope.

Sanjeem (via interpreter): As long as we can continue earning our living by ways of reindeer, our culture will survive. Myself and other elders always tell the young people how to herd the reindeer properly. That is the **obligation** the older generation must fulfill to the younger generation.

Narrator: Herders know they're at a **critical** moment. They can settle. But Sanjeem says that would be the end of who they are as a people, and that's a thought he can't even **contemplate**.

LISTENING SKILL Recognizing attitudes

A. Page 180

1. He's not going to lose his job if he doesn't agree to move.

2. My routine is the same every day: get up, go to work, come home, go to bed.

3. They don't have time to adjust to the new situation.

4. She really thinks she can just move to a new city and find a job in one day.

5. Those who can't cope with the lack of permanence are just not cut out for the life of a nomad.

6. We're moving today.

7. You're moving today?

8. My sister and I are traveling to Mongolia this summer, and we're going to stay with some nomads.

B. Page 180

1. **Morgan Kay:** At least let us remember that the way we choose to live in the West is only one way, and it's still possible for people even in the 21st century to be living a subsistence, balanced lifestyle that leaves them at the mercy of natural forces that we've become totally separate from.

2. **Garreau:** Well, you know, I thought I traveled a lot, but then I discovered that there were some people who were traveling way, way past anything that I had ever dreamed possible. They basically didn't have homes anymore.

LISTENING 2 High-Tech Nomads
Page 183

Rudy Maxa: [music] Like that **intrepid** group of American tourists, most of us choose to travel because we want to. We've come a long way from times when we had to wander through different lands without homes living as nomads. Or have we? Even today when we can easily interact with someone by picking up a phone or logging onto a computer, some people still make their living constantly traveling from place to place. Their only addresses exist as email or cell phone numbers. Welcome to the world of the high-tech nomad. Writer Joel Garreau investigated this unique breed of traveler for *The Washington Post*, and he sat down with us recently to tell us what he learned.

Joel Garreau: Well, you know, I thought I traveled a lot, but then I discovered that there were some people who were traveling way, way past anything that I had ever dreamed possible. They basically didn't have homes anymore. The road was their home.

Maxa: Tell me, what are the characteristics of a high-tech nomad? Do they generally have one kind of occupation? Are they generally men or women?

Garreau: I was surprised at how many women I found. I thought it would have been an awful lot of cranky males. The **breakthrough** is that these nomads are not **marginal** by any means. They're making 6- and 7- and 8- and 9-digit incomes.

These are people who have to be completely wired to the global economy all the time. They're like nomads of 10,000 years ago in that they're kind of browsing the savannahs of the Fortune 500.

Maxa: And they do what for a living?

Garreau: These guys have jobs that we don't really have names for yet. There's, uh, one guy who's kind of a one-man multimedia mini-conglomerate with a social conscience. He has one place in Barcelona and another in Boston and the film he just finished was in Burundi. Um, there are some of these guys who do have apartments in five or six different places, but when you talk to them, you realize that they're basically cargo dumps with a view.

Maxa: What other high-tech, besides the obvious laptop and your PalmPilot, are there any other high-tech devices these folks carry?

Garreau: Well, it's only been in the last ten years that we've had enough wired technology to make this barely possible. It just drives them nuts how many cell phones they have to carry. And of course, this is their lifeline. They're always looking for somebody to talk to in a different time zone. [laughter]

Maxa: How do these high-tech nomads **accomplish** the **mundane** things of life like laundry and picking up mail, and where do they keep all the stuff I can't even find a place in my apartment to keep? You know, receipts and family photos and tax returns and love letters. Where do they keep all this stuff?

Garreau: Oh, it's a huge problem. I mean, like, what do you do with your shirts, you know, if you're never in a place for two nights? How do you get your laundry done? One guy I talked to says that he has his shirts Federal-Expressed to his next location. Where do you get your, your Visa bill? Well it turns out that these guys have all of their affairs mailed to their lawyer or to their accountant or something. But still, you need some kind of rootedness even if it's inside yourself. Esther Dyson, for example, who's an investor and a kind of a technology pundit, has a ritual every morning. No matter how crazy the day is, she swims with her eyes closed for an hour, no matter what city she's in, because that is her time for herself and that's how she stays connected to her own brain.

Maxa: Most people need some sense of **stability** and connection and a sense of routine. What is it about the **psyche** of a high-tech nomad that seems to allow him or her to put that in abeyance?

Garreau: That's where I part company with these guys. I mean, I do need a base and some **roots**, and they don't have that, and I was wondering just how crazy that makes you.

Maxa: Give me an example of a specific high-tech nomad and what his or her life might be like in an average week or so.

Garreau: Well, for example, there's this one venture capitalist named Jim Woodhill, and he's got a wife and an 18-month-old son, and that 18-month-old has got elite frequent flyer status.

Maxa: Which means he's flown over 25–50,000 miles—

Garreau: Just all the time.

Maxa: —in a year.

Garreau: He's got apartments in St. Louis, Houston, San Diego, San Francisco, New York, and Washington, and he moves his entire entourage: his family, his in-laws—[laughter]

Maxa: What is the **payoff**? Is there a thrill? Is it being a world citizen?

Garreau: Well, the thrill is really the idea of feeling completely plugged in. These guys tend to have very short **attention spans** on average. And their payoff is that it's the idea of never being bored. One of the great **ironies** of this lifestyle is that, you know, you ask yourself, well if these guys are so plugged in, and they can communicate from anywhere, why bother travel at all?

Maxa: Exactly. Why do you even move?

Garreau: And the great irony is that the reason they are nomads is for face-to-face contact. They feel that there's something that we get as a result of being face-to-face that is absolutely un-reproducible no matter how **evolved** the technology is ever going to be. And that's why they're nomads.

Maxa: Joel, thank you so much for joining.

Garreau: It's fun, Rudy.

Unit 9 Energy

The Q Classroom Page 199

Teacher: Today we're going to discuss the Unit 9 question, "Where should the world's energy come from?" Maybe we should look at the different kinds of energy one by one. Sophy, what do you think about solar energy?

Sophy: I think they should use as much of it as possible, and that the more it is used, the cheaper it will be. Of course, in some places it may not be practical because the sun doesn't shine enough. But not only will it get cheaper if we use it more, but the technology for storing the energy will improve. I think it has to be combined with other forms of energy, though.

Teacher: How about nuclear energy? What are the advantages of nuclear energy?

Marcus: The good thing about nuclear energy is that you can make it anywhere—you don't need any special resources like oil or lots of sunshine. You can make a lot of energy with one nuclear power plant. And it doesn't emit greenhouse gases.

Felix: Of course, there's the huge problem of nuclear waste.

Marcus: That's true; they haven't solved that yet. So, as Sophy said about solar energy, it needs to be combined with other kinds of energy.

Teacher: Felix, it sounds like you don't approve of nuclear energy. Where do you think the world's energy should come from?

Felix: First of all, I think we should use less of it. We need to drive more efficient cars and run more efficient factories so we don't need to use so much energy. And then we should use a lot of renewable energy sources like solar and wind power.

Teacher: Yuna, what do you think?

Yuna: It sounds good to say, "Use solar energy," but I think we still need fossil fuels. The whole world is set up for them.

Teacher: Well, we have lots of different opinions! We'll see if any of you change your minds as we go through the unit.

LISTENING 1 Nuclear Energy: Is It the Solution?
Pages 203–204

Moderator: Good evening. Welcome to the first in a series of discussions our community plans to have on the issue of nuclear power. As you know, the candidates in the upcoming election for mayor are on opposite sides in the **controversial** issue of building a nuclear power plant in our region. The citizens have been asking for more information on the reliability and safety of nuclear energy and on the possibility that a power plant could provide much needed jobs in our area so they can decide who to vote for. We've invited two city council members to present some research on energy tonight so we can begin to address some of the issues such a plant might raise for the community. First of all, let me introduce Jack Chen, a local energy consultant and environmentalist. We also have Emily Regan, a chemistry instructor at one of our local high schools who teaches a class on environmental science. Let's welcome both of our speakers.

[applause]

First, I'd like to ask our speakers to make a statement; then I'll guide the discussion a bit before we open to questions from the audience. Ms. Regan, would you please present the case supporting the development of more nuclear power plants?

Emily Regan: Sure. I think we can all agree that we need to reduce our **reliance** on **fossil fuels**. As you know, the use of fossil fuels such as coal and oil is problematic. Because we can't provide enough ourselves, we're forced to import from other countries. We need to be more independent in providing for our energy needs. Also, **emissions** from fossil fuels pollute the environment and contribute to global warming and climate change. So it is extremely important to move away from fossil fuels towards other sources of energy. In the opinion of many experts I've read, nuclear energy is cleaner, safer, and more reliable. Harmful CO_2 emissions are minimal, and the costs remain steady.

Moderator: Thank you. I'm sure we'll get back to some of those points later in the discussion. So, on the other side, now, Jack Chen, would you please present the case against nuclear energy?

Jack Chen: I'd be happy to. Although I agree with Emily that we need to reduce our **consumption** of fossil fuels, many scientists disagree that nuclear energy is the answer. Emily, you mentioned that nuclear energy is cleaner. That's true if we're only talking about the consumption of energy, but we have to look at how the energy is produced and how waste

is dealt with. To quote Dr. Arjun Makhijani, president of the Institute for Energy and Environmental Research and author of *Carbon-Free and Nuclear-Free*, "I don't see how you can call nuclear power the safest of energy sources when there are so many risks." Data shows that the typical nuclear power plant could produce 20 metric tons per year of used nuclear fuel, which is highly reactive. And as we saw with, uh, Chernobyl, in 1986, nuclear accidents can happen.

Regan: You raise an important point, but many scientists disagree with the notion that nuclear energy is somehow dangerous or that it produces carbon emissions. In a podcast debate I listened to, Dr. Patrick Moore, chair of the Canadian firm Green Spirit Strategies, disagreed with Dr. Makhijani. He pointed out that the fact of the matter is that not one single person in North America has been injured at a nuclear power plant or died because of a radiation-related accident. My research confirmed that this is a very well-regulated industry. Right now, nuclear power plants supply 70 percent of the emission-free electricity in the United States. It has a proven safety record.

Chen: While I also found that at the moment, nuclear energy is providing more power than other non-fossil fuel sources, most experts argue that we need to develop our renewable options, energy that can be replaced naturally. Hydroelectric energy, or the energy provided by moving water, provides 25 percent of non-fossil fuel energy at the moment. Environmentalists believe that we should also continue to invest in wind and solar energy. These sources are much safer and cleaner than nuclear energy. In a recent article on energy in the *Guardian*, Jose Goldemberg, professor of physical science at the University of Sao Paolo, Brazil, predicted that energy from windmills and biofuels could provide up to 50 percent of all energy by 2050.

Moderator: Emily, what did you find out about the benefits of these other sources?

Regan: I'd certainly agree, and scientists and environmentalists confirm, that renewable sources are safe and clean. However, many would argue that we're working at **capacity** in terms of hydroelectric power. More importantly, according to Dr. David Scott, a professor at the University of Victoria, quote, "We've gotta be very careful about what renewables can provide. All renewable resources are characteristically **intermittent**." What he means is that solar energy can only be harnessed when the sun is shining, for example. His research confirms that nuclear power is just more reliable than these other options.

Moderator: Jack?

Chen: That's true. I didn't find evidence to confirm that these sources can provide enough energy today. And I'm not suggesting we abandon the idea of a power plant. However, I did find that the cost of building solar power or wind power plants is much lower than the cost of building another nuclear power plant. Many plans for power plants have been held up for lack of funds.

Regan: I see what you're saying. In the end, the question each of us has to decide here is whether nuclear is safe and whether relying on alternative sources of power is just **misguided**. If the experts are correct that solar and wind power are only available about a third of the time, how are we going to keep our hospitals running, our homes heated, our power grid on? These sources are just not **large-scale** enough. On the other hand, if we elect a mayor who supports the new nuclear power plant, we might face another real danger, even if we solve the energy shortage.

Chen: You are right there. Maybe the candidates need to approach this from a different angle—raising awareness through community education. They should focus on the need to improve **efficiency** as one way of reducing energy use, and we need to **conserve** where possible. If we could reduce the amount of energy we use, perhaps hydroelectric, solar, and wind sources could meet most of our needs, and we wouldn't have to worry about a nuclear power plant.

Moderator: Let's stop there. The debate so far has been very **thought-provoking**. Let's take a few questions from the audience. Yes, the woman in the front row?

Woman: I'd like to get back to the issue of safety. I've got young children. How much of a risk does a nuclear power plant present to their health?

LISTENING SKILL Listening for cause and effect
B. Page 207

1. **Reporter:** Ethanol is a fuel produced from corn. However, corn production requires a lot of water and fertilizer. For this reason, scientists and farmers are working to develop new crops called "energy crops" that produce energy on a large scale with less impact on the environment.

2. **Reporter:** Everyone is worried about the high price of gasoline, so a company in Japan has come up with the new idea of using water as fuel. If hydrogen can be separated from the water, then a generator can use the hydrogen electrons to produce electric power.

3. **Reporter:** The tremendous amount of garbage produced by restaurants in the San Francisco Bay area has given rise to a research project at the University of California at Davis. One of the professors there explains that gas production begins when the food leftovers are placed in a large tank. This chemical reaction in the lab's tanks can result in enough electricity to power about 80 homes a day. Not only will this project produce energy, but it will also help decrease the amount of garbage in the city.

LISTENING 2 Tapping the Energy of the Tides
Page 210

Speaker: Concerns over global warming have scientists and engineers looking for cleaner alternative sources of energy. One of those alternatives gaining momentum involves **harnessing** the energy of the ocean. Renewable energy experts say in theory, energy from tides, **currents**, and waves could double the hydropower output in the U.S., producing 20 percent of the nation's electricity. But the technology to capture this renewable energy is in its infancy.

NHPR's Amy Quinton reports on the effort in New Hampshire's seacoast to **tap** the **power** of the tides.

Jack Pare: Coming in it hits this shore pretty heavy; going out it hits the Newington shore pretty heavy. Uh, it is a dramatic roar. It really is.

Amy Quinton: Jack Pare, a retired aerospace systems engineer, points to the water under the General Sullivan and Little Bay Bridge in Dover. He says the tides here in the Piscataqua River move quickly, almost nine feet per second at its maximum. [nature sounds, water] Pare says engineers know how to capture that **free**-flowing energy, and it would be a completely renewable source of **power** for the **state**.

Pare: It's just one of many things that you have to do, uh, if you want to, quote, "save the planet" or otherwise cut down our carbon emissions. There's no single magic bullet; this is, if you will . . . There's no rifle shot, it's a shotgun effect. So this is one pellet of that shotgun effect to be able to take the top off the global warming.

Quinton: Some state representatives believe it's an idea worth pursuing. State legislators passed a **bill** that establishes a **commission** to study tidal power **generation** here under the bridge. Representative Tom Fargo of Dover, the bill's sponsor, says unlike wind power, the benefit of tidal power is its reliability.

Tom Fargo: The tide will flow until the earth rotates no more. It's, it's, it's available; we know when it's coming; we know from, from day to day and even hour to hour how much energy you're going to be able to get from it; it's very predictable.

Quinton: And water is more than 800 times denser than air, making it much more powerful. But almost all the various technologies used to capture tidal power are expensive and experimental. Only one company so far is producing it in the United States. A little known startup called Verdant Power has six underwater turbines, resembling windmills, in the East River in New York. So far, Verdant Power founder Trey Taylor says the turbines power the lights in a supermarket and a parking garage on Roosevelt Island.

Trey Taylor: But also, uh, inside that garage there are electric vehicles. There's, there's hybrid electric buses, but also there's little electric vehicles that go up and down Roosevelt Island, something a little bit bigger than golf carts, and those are all being plugged into our tidal power, which I think is a pretty cool story in and of itself.

Quinton: But Taylor has much bigger hopes. He foresees a time when 300 of these underwater turbines will power about 8,000 homes in New York. But Jack Pare points out the turbine technology that works well in New York's East River may not be appropriate for the Piscataqua.

Pare: Uh, we have deep-water shipping, we have harbor seals, and we have stripers and we have lobsters, none of which are **present** on that other site. And so there's a little bit more to be careful of.

Quinton: Two companies currently hold federal preliminary permits to study the feasibility of tidal power in the Piscataqua. Philippe Vauthier is president of one of them, the Underwater Electric Kite company based in Annapolis, Maryland. He says his turbine technology won't turn fish into fillets.

Philippe Vauthier: And, uh, we put a screen in front of the turbine to protect the fish to reach that point. Absolutely no problem. Anything bigger than three-quarter of an inch is safe; it will be deflected.

Quinton: Vauthier says smaller fish would be able to glide through unharmed. He predicts his $2.4 million project could produce 40 megawatts, or enough to power about 36,000 New Hampshire homes. The other company that holds a permit— New Hampshire Tidal Energy Company, owned by Oceana Energy—is predicting a much larger power output along three **stretches** of the river. Charles Cooper is a technical advisor for the project.

Charles Cooper: I'd be surprised if it reached, uh, more than 100 megawatts at the most, and that would be very optimistic. And that's not trivial in the sense that it certainly can supply, um, a number of end uses, but it's not going to be the baseload for the region.

Quinton: Cooper says Oceana's prototype looks like a large wheel about the size of a Ferris wheel, with an open **center** that allows large marine animals to swim through. But he adds their technology won't work everywhere.

Cooper: This is not really deep water. We're not dealing with water over 100 feet deep in the Piscataqua. So if Oceana's technology turned out to work best in very large-sized units that might be, oh, I don't know, 60, 80 feet in diameter, they wouldn't be appropriate for the Piscataqua site.

Quinton: In that case, Oceana would likely use another company's technology at its sites. Both companies say there are a lot of challenges and unknowns surrounding tidal energy in the Piscataqua. But the permits give them three years to study the sites. What they learn will also help the state decide if tidal power is worth pursuing. For NHPR News, I'm Amy Quinton.

GRAMMAR Adverb clauses
A. Page 215

1. They applied for a research grant as they wanted to study alternative energy.

2. Since water moves through the turbine when the tide is coming in, hydroelectric power is created.

3. Although fuel from crops like corn can be turned into biofuel, the crops take up a lot of land and use a lot of water.

4. While the wind can indeed create power, the winds are too intermittent, and wind power will not solve our problem.

5. Due to the fact that gas is produced when garbage decays, garbage can in fact be converted into energy.

6. Many scientists support nuclear energy even though there are risks involved.

SPEAKING SKILL Debating opinions
A. Page 218

Moderator: Thank you. I'm sure we'll get back to some of those points later in the discussion. So, on the other side, now, Jack Chen, would you please present the case against nuclear energy?

Chen: I'd be happy to. Although I agree with Emily that we need to reduce our consumption of fossil fuels, many scientists disagree that nuclear energy is the answer. Emily, you mentioned that nuclear energy is cleaner. That's true if we're only talking about the consumption of energy, but we have to look at how the energy is produced and how waste is dealt with.

Regan: You raise an important point, but many scientists disagree with the notion that nuclear energy is somehow dangerous the fact of the matter is that not one single person in North America has been injured at a nuclear power plant or died because of a radiation-related accident. My research confirmed that this is a very well-regulated industry. Right now, nuclear power plants supply 70 percent of the emission-free electricity in the United States. It has a proven safety record.

Chen: While I also found that at the moment, nuclear energy is providing more power than other non-fossil fuel sources, most experts argue that we need to develop our renewable options, energy that can be replaced naturally. Hydroelectric energy, or the energy provided by moving water, provides 25 percent of non-fossil fuel energy at the moment. Environmentalists believe that we should also continue to invest in wind and solar energy.

Moderator: Emily, what did you find out about the benefits of these other sources?

Regan: I'd certainly agree, and scientists and environmentalists confirm, that renewable sources are safe and clean. However, many would argue that we're working at capacity in terms of hydroelectric power. More importantly, according to Dr. David Scott, a professor at the University of Victoria, quote, "We've gotta be very careful about what renewables can provide."

Unit 10 Size and Scale

The Q Classroom Page 225

Teacher: The Unit 10 question is: "Is bigger always better?" Sophy, what do you think?

Sophy: No, not always. I think smaller can often be better.

Teacher: Can you give an example?

Sophy: Sure. Well, I grew up in a small town and I went to small schools where I knew everyone. I'm really comfortable in that kind of place. I feel like my contribution really means something.

Teacher: How about you, Yuna? Do you agree with Sophy?

Yuna: I'm more of a big city kind of person. I like to feel that I'm part of something important, even if I can only be a small part of it. I want to work for a big company when I graduate.

Teacher: How about you, Marcus?

Marcus: I'm with Yuna. I think big cities have a lot of exciting opportunities. And I'm also hoping to work for a large corporation when I graduate.

Teacher: What are some of the benefits of working for a large corporation?

Marcus: Well, there's more security in a big company, and there are more opportunities to move up and expand your career.

Teacher: Sophy, what do you think?

Sophy: I disagree. I think at a smaller company you have the opportunity to take on more responsibility, and you can become very valuable to the company. Your co-workers appreciate you more, and you don't get lost in the crowd.

Teacher: Felix, how about you? Do you think bigger is better?

Felix: In a lot of cases, it can be. For example, I went to a large university with a lot of people, and I really liked it. I had a chance to take some unusual classes and I found a lot of new interests. Even though I didn't know most of the people personally, I think it was a great experience.

Teacher: Great discussion. We'll talk about this question more as we go through the unit.

LISTENING 1 Small Is the New Big
Pages 228–229

Seth Godin: Small is the new big. BIG used to matter. Big meant economies of scale. You never hear about "economies of tiny" do you?

Years ago, people, usually guys, often ex-Marines, wanted to be CEO of a big company. The Fortune 500 is where people went to make a fortune, after all.

Big meant power and profit and growth. Big meant control over supply and control over markets.

There was a good reason for this. Value was added in ways that suited big organizations. Value was added with efficient manufacturing, **widespread** distribution, and very large R&D staffs. Value came from hundreds of operators standing by and from nine-figure TV ad budgets. Value came from a huge sales force.

Of course, it's not just big organizations that added value. Big planes were better than small ones because they were faster and more efficient. Big buildings were better than small ones because they **facilitated** communication and used downtown land quite efficiently. Bigger computers could handle more **simultaneous** users.

"Get Big Fast" was the **motto** for startups, because big companies can go public and find more access to capital and use that capital to get even bigger. Big accounting firms were the place to go to get **audited** if you were a big company, because a big accounting firm could be trusted. Big law firms were the place to find the right lawyer, because big law firms were a one-stop shop.

And then small happened.

Enron (big) got audited by Andersen (big) and failed (big). The World Trade Center was a terrorist target. Network (big) TV advertising is **collapsing** so fast you can hear it. American Airlines (big) is getting creamed by JetBlue (think small). *Boing Boing* (four people) has a readership growing a hundred times faster than *The New Yorker* (with hundreds of people).

Big computers are silly. They use lots of power and are not nearly as efficient as properly networked Dell PCs (at least that's what they use at Yahoo! and Google). Big boom boxes are replaced by tiny iPod shuffles. (Yeah, I know, big-screen TVs are the big thing. An exception that proves the rule.)

I'm writing this on a laptop at a skateboard park that offers free Wi-Fi for parents to surf the Web while they wait for their kids. They offer free Wi-Fi because the owner wanted to. It took them a few minutes and 50 bucks. No big meetings, corporate policies, or **feasibility** studies. They just did it.

Today, little companies often make more money than big companies. Little churches grow faster than worldwide ones. Little jets are way faster (door to door) than big ones.

Today, craigslist (eighteen employees) is the fourth most visited site according to some measures. They are partly owned by eBay (more than four thousand employees), which hopes to stay **in the same league**, traffic-wise. They're certainly not growing nearly as fast.

Small means that the founder is involved in a far greater percentage of customer interactions. Small means the founder is close to the issues that matter and can address them quickly.

Small is the new big because small gives you the **flexibility** to change your business model when your competition changes theirs.

Small means you can tell the truth on your blog. Small means that you can answer email from your customers.

Small means that you will **outsource** the boring, low-impact stuff like manufacturing and shipping and billing and packing to others while you keep all the power because you invent something that's remarkable and tell your story to people who want to hear it.

A small law firm or accounting firm or ad **agency** is succeeding because they're good, not because they're big. So smart, small companies are happy to hire them.

A small restaurant has an owner who greets you by name.

A small venture fund doesn't have to fund big, bad ideas in order to put their capital to work. They can make small **investments** in tiny companies with good ideas.

A small church has a minister with the time to visit you in the hospital when you're sick.

Is it better to be the head of craigslist or the head of UPS?

Small is the new big only when the person running the small thinks big.

Don't wait. Get small. Think big.

LISTENING SKILL Listening for pros and cons
A. Page 232

Speaker: When my father's company started to outsource the work he did to another country, our family had a big decision to make—to stay in our familiar small town or move to a bigger unknown city. My parents' discussions went something like this. My father said that compared to our small town, a city offered more jobs. In contrast to where we were living, a city had public transportation, so he could sell the car. My mother argued that big-city life was more expensive. She conceded that public transportation was cheaper; however, it would be difficult to carry groceries on a bus. The children wanted more space to play and fewer buildings and busy streets. On the one hand, they thought city life might be exciting for a while, but on the other hand, they didn't want to lose the benefits of living in a small community where they knew everyone. After listening to all of these pros and cons, where do you think we ended up living?

LISTENING 2 Sizing Up Colleges: One Size Does Not Fit All
Page 235

Host: As you begin your search for that perfect college, one of the first key decisions you need to make—and one that will help you **narrow** your list—is the size of the school. Luckily, American colleges offer an endless menu of options, from tiny colleges with less than 1,000 students to large state universities with more than 35,000 students. Finding a good match depends heavily on your personality and academic goals.

Do you picture yourself at a Big Ten school that offers everything from televised sporting events to **countless** degree programs? Are you itching to break free of the high school fishbowl and would welcome the opportunity for anonymity that comes with being one of thousands of students? Then a big university is probably a good fit for you.

Beth Finkelstein, University of Michigan, had many reasons for wanting to attend a big university.

Beth Finkelstein: After four years in a small high school with no football team, I was excited about going to a huge university that offers endless opportunities both socially and academically. The whole rah-rah school spirit attitude was something I was looking for.

Host: Another big draw for Beth was the research facilities that a huge school like Michigan has to offer.

Finkelstein: I knew I was interested in social sciences, but not sure exactly what area. At Michigan, I was able to work side by side with graduate students, assisting in their research and getting exposure to a variety of social science fields. It was while working on a research project at a school lab that I discovered my **passion** for education and teaching.

Host: Big universities clearly have many benefits as described above, but there are also a few drawbacks. For example, while you may enroll in a course with a professor that is well-known in his or her field, more often than not the course will mostly be taught by teaching assistants (or TAs). The more **distinguished** professors are often focused on **conducting** research, publishing their work, and overseeing graduate thesis projects. If you're considering a large university, be sure to find out what percentage of classes are taught by TAs and how many are taught by professors.

Another consideration is the red tape often associated with big-school administration. Though large universities offer countless courses, it's not so easy to take anything you want. If you're a psychology major, for example, taking a business course may require half a dozen signatures or more. Again, when visiting the school, be sure to ask what is required in order to take courses outside of your major.

Finally, while huge class sizes may be exciting for some, they can be overwhelming for others. Introductory classes at big colleges sometimes include hundreds of students, making it an **intimidating** environment to ask a question and all too easy to fall asleep, unnoticed, in the back of a lecture hall.

To succeed at a big school, it's best to go in knowing generally the area you're interested in pursuing. Perhaps most importantly, you need to be a go-getter, who's not afraid to speak up and take advantage of the opportunities a big school has to offer.

On the other hand, are you the type that enjoys classes with small-group discussions where active participation and hands-on learning take **priority**? Then a small college may be just what you need.

Jordan Brown, an alumnus of Oberlin College, a liberal arts school in Ohio, decided on a small-school education so that he could pursue a longtime passion—humor.

Jordan Brown: Oberlin turned an interest of mine into a rich, **diversified** experience. Having the opportunity to create my own major and curriculum (An Interdisciplinary **Analysis** of Humor: What's So Funny?) was as much part of the learning experience as the actual courses. It **enabled** me to pursue something that really motivates me and to find ways to connect it to other areas of learning. I could not have easily done this at a big university.

Host: Academics are one of the main reasons to consider a small college. Unlike large universities, small-school courses are usually taught by actual professors, not teaching assistants. In most cases, the professors may even know your name and your areas of interest. Small colleges are more able to meet your unique interests and needs. They are more involved in helping you make the most of your college experience. In contrast to most big universities, smaller schools encourage students to explore areas outside their field of study.

On the other hand, there are a few drawbacks to small colleges. Small schools tend not to have the types of research **facilities** of large universities, nor do they provide opportunities to assist graduate students in their research. If you're considering a small school and are interested in working as a research assistant, you should find out what kind of research work and facilities the school has to offer and if there is a graduate school.

Small schools usually offer less in terms of big sporting events and social opportunities. While small colleges usually provide a strong sense of community, it is also more difficult to move in and out of social groups as you would in a school with thousands of classmates. When you visit a small school, be sure to talk to students to find out what the social life is like and what types of **extracurricular** activities there are.

Small colleges are a perfect match for those who do well in small group environments, are stimulated by a high level of student-teacher interaction, and who are interested in pursuing creative, individual majors focusing in on specific areas of interest.

Whether you're considering a big university, small college, or something in between, you need to carefully look at all perspectives and determine what's most important to you.

GRAMMAR Parallel structure
A. Page 240

1. He is a smart, energetic, and hard-working employee.
2. You can either go to a big university, a small school, or study at a community college.
3. I'm not ready to leave my familiar home, break free of the high school fishbowl, and enjoy the anonymity of being one of thousands of students.
4. Small companies are gaining popularity because their priorities include honesty, limited overtime, and they have health benefits.
5. Godin said big businesses used to be more popular when they had control over supply, control over markets, and control over profits.
6. Students who decide on a small college tend to like a liberal arts curriculum, prefer smaller classes, and avoid intimidating situations.
7. My parents wanted me to go to that Ivy League school because it had distinguished professors, extracurricular activities that were challenging, and an excellent reputation.
8. The salesman said the product was excellent, the price was reasonable, and people could depend on the service.
9. If you want to make more money, you could invest in the stock market, start your own business, or work two jobs at once.
10. Before applying for a study abroad program, students must learn a second language, decide on their major, and they should know what country they want to visit.

SPEAKING SKILL Developing interview skills
A. Page 244

1. **Interviewer:** Why do you feel qualified to work in such a large organization?

   Candidate 1: In a large organization?

   Interviewer: Yes, in a large organization like ours.

   Candidate 1: Oh, yes, I see. I've been trying to get a job for a long time, and at this point I am willing to work in a small or large company. I'm sure I would do a good job.

2. **Interviewer:** Do you think you would be happy working in such a small company?

   Candidate 2: I hope my resume shows that I would be a good fit for your small company. Most of my best jobs have been in small firms such as Office One and Intelligent Investments.

   Interviewer: How would you describe your work characteristics in one sentence?

   Candidate 2: I would say I am ambitious, dependable, and hard-working.

3. **Interviewer:** What about our company interests you the most?

   Candidate 3: Wow. That's a good question. I mean, I guess I just think it's a cool company to work for.

   Interviewer: I see. Can you be more specific?

   Candidate 3: Well, you manufacture a lot of stuff that's really good, and your ads are like, really interesting, so I'd like to be a part of making your products.